PERSPECTIVES IN ISLAMIC LAW

ENCYCLOPAEDIC SURVEY OF ISLAMIC CULTURE SERIES

PERSPECTIVES IN ISLAMIC LAW

Edited by
MOHAMED TAHER

ANMOL PUBLICATIONS PVT. LTD.
NEW DELHI-110 002 (INDIA)

ANMOL PUBLICATIONS PVT. LTD.
4374/4B, Ansari Road, Daryaganj
New Delhi-110 002

Perspectives in Islamic Law

First Edition 1998
ISBN 81-7488-940-X

PRINTED IN INDIA

Published by J.L. Kumar for Anmol Publications Pvt. Ltd., New Delhi-110 002 and Printed at Mehra Offset Press, Delhi.

Contents

Preface

The *Encyclopaedic Survey of Islamic Culture* is a unique reference source. This series seeks to anthologise the most important primary and secondary materials on a wide variety of topics and writers of Islamic culture and civilisation. The scholar, the student and the layman will find in various volumes not only a generous selection of reprinted articles, but original essays, bibliographies, and other materials brought for the first time in a comprehensive and exhaustive fashion.

The need for this collation grew out of our awareness that there is no comprehensive source of information for the study and research of the field. Other published works are too specialised in the topics discussed or neglect the institutional as well the individual role which the Islamic system plays. Few encyclopaedic works do exist, and few anthologies also have appeared. Fewer books, again, have systematically covered such topics as Islam in Africa, Islamic sociology, Islamic polity, Islamic thought, etc. Although these topics have been addressed separately, no attempt has been made to discuss them as part of a united treatment of the literature of the field.

Islam brought a total change in all spheres of life. It revolutionised many societies, both in the east and the west. But this is not always accepted and acknowledged. To quote Major Arthur Leonard from his work: Islam; her moral and spiritual value:

"Never to this day has Europe acknowledged in an honest and whole hearted manner the great and everlasting debt she owes to Islamic culture and civilisation. Only in a lukewarm and perfunctory way has she recognised that when, during the dark ages, her people were sunk in feudalism and ignorance, Muslim civilisation under the Arabs reached a high standard of social and scientific splendour that kept the flickering members of European society from utter decadence.

"Do not we, who now consider ourselves on the top most pinnacle ever reached by culture and civilisation, recognise that, had it not been for the high culture, the civilisation and intellectual, as well as the social splendours of the Arabs and soundness of their school system, Europe would to this day have remained sunk in the darkness of ignorance. Have we forgotten that the Muslim maxim was that, the real learning of a man is of more public importance than any particular religious opinions he may entertain, that Muslim liberality was in striking contrast with the then intolerant state of Europe? Does the magnificent valour of the Arabs, inspired as it was by a theism as lofty as it was pure, not appeal to us? Does not the moderation and comparative toleration shown by them to the conquered, notwithstanding the fierce and burning ardour to regenerate mankind that impelled them onward to conquest, also appeal to us? Does it not all the more appeal to us when we contrast this with the bitterness of the attitude of the Christian sects towards one another? Especially when we consider that in Christendom, as it was then constituted, extortion, tyranny and imperial centralisation, combining with ecclesiastical despotism and persecution, had practically extinguished patriotism, by substitution in its place schismatic and degenerate Church?"

Further the same writer continues to say:

> "Is it possible that Europe is unmindful of, and has the ingratitude to ignore the splendid services of the scientists and philosophers of Arabic? Are the names of Assamh, Abu Othman, Alberuni, Albeithar, Abu Ali Ibn Sina (Avicenna) the great physician and philosopher, Ibn Rushd (Anempace) besides a host of others but dead letters? Is the great work that they have done and the fame they have left behind them in their books to be consigned to the limbo of oblivion, by an ungrateful but antipathetic Europe?

"It cannot be that already we have lost sight of the amazing intellectual activity of the Muslim world during the earlier part of the `Abbaside' period more especially. It cannot be that we have quite forgotten the irrecoverable loss that was inflicted on Arabian literature, and on the world at large, by the wanton destruction of thousands of books that was promoted by Christian bigotry and fanaticism? It cannot be surely said of Christian Europe that for centuries now she has done her best to hide obligations to the Arabs; yet most assuredly, obligations such as these, are far too sacred to lie much linger hidden."

This is one side of the story. The other side is that the West has definitely absorbed much of the Islamic contributions and is "unaware." To quote Marcus Marby and William Underhill "Bold new visions from ancient landscapes" (*Newsweek*, May 29, 1995): Christian and Islamic civilizations have been in conflict for most of their history. But as often as they have clashed, they have enriched each other. In this ninth century, Moors brought advanced architecture, astronomy and medicine to occupied Spain. While Europe lingered in the Dark Ages, courtly poetry from Persia inspired the troubadours, whose verse evolved into the literature of the early French Renaissance. Even whiling away hours over coffee and conversation—the basis for the cafe—came from Arab culture... France's most popular dish today is not escargots but couscous. French slang is peppered with Arab words like kif-kif (50-50) and Insha Allah (God willing). The hottest new music is Arab-inspired rai" (p. 28). The list of Arabic borrowed words in English and Western usages are many more, not mere algebra, alchemy, azimuth, albatross, timbal, zenith, etc.

There is, in short, a lot of misinformation and incorrect representation about Islam. And more so there is a need today to describe and interpret the issues and express in clear terms what this thought actually deals with. Due to social and cultural changes, the salient aspects of the field require examination. The post cold war era has left the world with a unipolar political system. Islam is a system which promises the world that if applied in toto it would solve the multi-dimensional problems of the modern era. But is there any one who wishes to test this module and try it in a space and time to see the truth of the statement?

The primary purpose of this encyclopaedic survey is to serve as a basic handbook on significant topics of Islamic culture. To facilitate an understanding of the field, the series presents a survey and an analysis of the various socio-cultural forces that shape both the structure and functions of the field as well as by the way this society has changed. We also analyse the larger forces outside the community, such as assimilation and acculturation, and forces inside the community, like, role of the leadership, role of the social and cultural groups and the so much alleged 'imbalance' in the theory and practice of the faith.

We are confident that this work will make a permanent and significant contribution to the study of Islam. Its style is simple, and it is presented in a style accessible to a wide audience. Its target audience is faculty, students, and all concerned with the understanding of the faith of the second largest following in the world. While it has scholarly materials, it is nevertheless also of use to those who have no knowledge of the field, as well as to those who are working in related and allied fields. Most important, we hope that this series will be useful in teaching and learning as an educational resource in the academic world.

The series is planned to be both, multi-volume and multi-faceted set, which will run into hundreds of numbers. The compilation of such a huge set is a gigantic task and requires the support and encouragement of all concerned. It requires feed-back and also support from the literary market place and literary circles all over.

A collection of articles, or an anthology, has many benefits, like, it renews our acquaintance with literature which we have neglected, it reveals to us material of which we were ignorant, and it exposes relationships where we did not suppose them to exist. This is the ultimate purpose of our efforts and we wish and pray that this is fulfilled.

A word of acknowledgement is due to the inspiration of the idea of a comprehensive, commulative and compact set of literary works on the Islamic culture. These inspirers are from all walks of life and their efforts must be acknowledged which includes contributors, authors and editors, as well as the publishers who have graciously contributed to this project and we duly acknowledge their cooperation. The well wishers are many more and listing all the concerned by names is impossible here. Each must be duly rewarded for this gesture, and this is our sincere prayer.

—Editor

1

The Structure of the Law

[Abstract: We shall outline the history of the development of these fundamental principles into a juridical structure and briefly describe the history and content of the structure itself. As for the place of the discipline of law as a whole in Islam and the history of that place, which will deal with the most central concept of Islam, the Shri'a.]

PRELIMINARY

According to the medieval Muslim theory of jurisprudence, the structure of Islamic law in built on four foundations, called 'the roots of law.' These are the Qur'an, the Sunna of the Prophet, the Ijma (consensus) and *Qiyas* (analogical reasoning). The mutual relationship of these four principles is highly confusing and it is not at all easy to make it fully clear. Perhaps, as a rough parallel, the famous Aristotelian scheme of analysis will be helpful. Pursuing this analogy, the Qur'an and the Sunna are the material principles (or the 'sources'), the activity of analogical reasoning (*qiyas*) the efficient cause, and the Ijma' the formal principle (or the functional power). To complete the picture of the Aristotelian scheme, the purpose of the structure is to enable man to live under the sovereignty of God and in accordance with His will.

EARLY DEVELOPMENTS

Qur'an and Sunna

At the very root of the Muslim conception of law lies the idea that law is inherently and essentially religious. That is why, from the very beginning of Islamic history, law has been regarded as flowing from or being part of the concept Shari'a (the divinely ordained pattern of human conduct). It must, therefore, have its basis in the Divine Revelation. The Qur'an, the most consummate and final revelation of God to man, must be made the primary and indeed the sole director of human life and the source of law.

Now, the Qur'anic body of statements is both universal and concrete enough to inculcate a definite attitude to life; it enunciates not only eternal spiritual and moral principles, but also guided Muhammad and the early Community through their struggles against the Meccan and Jewish enemies and Hypocrites and in the constructive task of the nascent society and state. These struggles and constructive instructions were of a specific nature. But still the strictly legislative portion of the Qur'an is relatively quite small. Besides the detailed pronouncement on the law of inheritance and lying down punishments for crimes such as theft and adultery, which are not defined legally, there is little in it that is, properly speaking, legislative. As for the specific injunctions about the Muslims struggles against and relationship with the non-Muslims, these varied according to situations and were too specific to be termed 'laws' in the strict sense. These different but also similar responses of the Qur'an to different but also similar situation had to be brought together for a comparative study. But, further, it had to be set out as to which specific command was earlier in time and which later.

The only natural method to be adopted in this comparative and interpretative procedure for a fresh application of the Qur'an to any given new situation was to see it as it had been actually worked in the lifetime of the Prophet, who was its most authoritative factual exponent and to whose conduct belonged a unique religious normativeness. This was the Sunna of the Prophet. As we shall see presently, the doctrine of the sinlessness of the Prophet was formulated considerably later, but it was only the formal outcome of the inner logic of a process which goes back to the starting point of Islamic history. As we have seen in the last chapter, despite the fact that the Prophet consulted his Companions, despite the fact that his decisions were sometimes challenged in some quarters and despite the fact that the Qur'an itself sometimes criticized him, his religious authority was binding. While he was alive, this authority was sufficient for and at any given point of time; the future remained open until it became present and was filled with decisive content by the Prophet bringing his authority to bear upon it. But after his death, that living authority was no longer available and had to be transformed formally into a doctrine of infallibility. This means that whatever decisions or pronouncements of the Prophet were authoritative during his lifetime became *infallible* after his death. This is the specific legal ground of the Prophetic infallibility. There is also a theological ground for a different, more general doctrine of infallibility, embracing all the Prophets, which is based on the consideration that a human who is a recipient of divine revelation cannot be expected to err grossly, especially in moral matters. The theological doctrine, therefore, covers only bigger and serious errors and not small slips of judgment as does the specifically legal theory.

In the early period of Islam (up to about 150/767), there is little trace of the formal doctrine of the Prophet's infallibility although a pragmatic notion of his absolute authority was certainly assumed. This shown clearly by the fact that the first Caliph, Abu Bakr, in his inaugural address after the election, spoke of 'God and (the example of) His Prophet' as deserving obedience and binding upon him. Some modern scholars have raised doubts as to whether the Prophet in his farewell speech on his last pilgrimage included his Sunna, alongside of the Qur'an, as guidance for posterity on the grounds that in somewhat earlier version the words 'my Sunna' do not occur. But this is immaterial and does not gainsay the fact that after his death his authority continued as it had been in his lifetime. Indeed, after his death, and especially immediately after it, there was the added reason that no one person could claim authority except under the Prophet's aegis.

But, as we have seen in the last chapter the Sunna was subsequently materially expanded to include the precedents of the first four Caliphs (the 'patriarchal Caliphs' as they are sometimes called by modern historians) and the agreements of the Companions or of a large number of them. These are known as the Sunna of the 'rightly-guided Caliphs' and that of the Companions respectively. But as we have also seen, these precedents were called 'Sunna' in the derivative sense, i.e., in the sense that the Companions were regarded as the living embodiments of the Prophetic Sunna. The application of the term was not extended to subsequent generations (except in the sense of deducing 'Sunnas' from the Hadith) which rather commandeer the aegis of Ijma or consensus. Indeed, the agreed practice of the Companions is also known as the Ijma of the Companions, and their generation is unique in the sense that with them *the term Sunna ends (including them) and the term Ijma begins (including them) at the same time.* But although no new generation as such was thought capable of engendering new Sunna, the point of liaison between the Companions and the next generation, that of the 'Successors' or followers, produced the bulk of the actual material, by direct deduction and application by individual thinkers, to which the term Sunna and Ijma' both applied. But the term Ijma' gradually gained ascendancy *for the work of this generation* until the advent of the wholesale development of the Hadith transformed much of this material into the Sunna of the Prophet under the aegis of Ijma.

In the early period, the question as to whether the Qur'an was more primary than the Sunna as a source of law was not yet explicity discussed. True, the Qur'an was regarded as the Word of God and the doctrine of the infallibility of the Prophetic Sunna was not yet formulated, but since, with a few exceptions noted above, the Qur'an had only an indirect relationship to law, from the very beginning the Sunna was coupled with the Qur'an as the source of law. Further, the small body of Qur'anic legislation itself had also arisen within the context of the usages and practical norms of the Arab Community. But by the end of the 1st beginning of the 8th century so much massive material had been brought within the field of the Sunna from different sources that to Sunna the further adjective of 'agreed upon' was affixed.

Qiyas

The term *qiyas,* according to the Muslim jurists, means analogical reasoning, i.e., concluding from a given principle embodied in a precedent that a new case falls under this principle or is similar to this precedent on the strength of a common essential feature called the 'reason' (*'illa*). Later on in Muslim philosophy the same term was employed to mean a syllogism or syllogistic reasoning. The common element between the two usages is the movement of thought from the explicitly known to the explicitly unknown. The term, as consciously formulated, most probably shows foreign influence, but the doctrine itself shows unmistakably a consistent internal development.

The earliest predecessor of this conscious analogical reasoning is called 'personal judgment' or 'considered personal opinion' (*ra'y*). This term has a strong subjective note and in the first person singular present means 'I think', 'I opine'. It was so intensively cultivated that many scholarly group were nicknamed 'Do-you-think-ers'. This type of thinking was relatively very free and produced a wealth of conflicting religious and legal opinion. But a rudimentary and almost unconscious analogical method was, of course, always present; when faced with a new or refined and complicated issue, wherever the Qur'an and the Sunna gave no clear and unequivocal decision, a verse of the Qur'an or a general principle or a specific case in the Sunna was taken and a decision was made on its strength with regard to the present issue. But in both the choice of the model and discernment of the point of resemblance almost unbridled liberty was taken and the results varied between sound analogy on the one hand and almost complete arbitrariness on the other.

After several decades, the unregulated products of this pure 'personal opinion' produced a strong and bitter reaction against itself and in the first half of the 2nd/8th century more systematic thought arose both in Medina and Iraq. In Medina, Malik (d. 179/795) continued to use the term *ra'y*, but the procedure had become more systematic, helped no doubt by, and further strengthening, the fact that a more or less uniform doctrine had by this time emerged in Medina, characterized by the concept 'agreed practice' or Ijma'. But in Iraq, Abu Hanifa—the exemplar of logical thought in Islamic law—and his early followers formulated expressions like 'this is in the category of', 'this is similar to'. At the same time the concept *ijtihad* or 'systemic original thinking' which, from its narrower beginnings in the first half of the 2nd/8th century, bloomed into a powerful principle of original thought in the later 2nd 8th and 3rd/9th centuries, swallowing up *qiyas* as its method.

From its beginnings as *ra'y* and other informal expressions, *qiyas* seems to have been established in the second half of the 2nd/8th century. Later on, in the 3rd/9th century, a minority school of jurists called the 'literalists' (*zahiri*) under the leadership of Da'ud (d. 269/882) rejected this principle. But the difference is rather formal because this latter school substituted for *qiyas* the principle of 'evident interpretation' (*mafhum*). Although al-Shafi'i (d. 204/819)—the first jurist to have written on the foundations of the law—is generally credited with having established *qiyas* as a principle, his manner of referring to it clearly shows that it was already accepted. Indeed, as we have already hinted, and as we shall describe presently under Ijma, the development of personal opinion into *qiyas* was a link in that process of securing uniformity and solidification that logically ended in Ijma'. To this we must now turn.

Ijma' Or Consensus

After the period of the first four Caliphs, the multitudinous differences in legal and dogmatic opinion on details began to appear. The secular administration of Umayyad Caliphate left the task of legislation to the recognized religious leaders and jurists of different regions, especially eminent of which was Medina with its lion's share of the legacy of the early Islamic piety. The jurists, in their turn, exercised their minds mainly employing and method of personal opinion on the materials of the Qur'an and the Sunna (both living and verbal traditions). But alongside this free, individual legislative activity, which, as has been said above, produced an uncoordinated body of opinion, went another balancing and complementary movement of coordination and unification. The development of individual opinion into systematic analogical reasoning was a step in this direction. But even before the doctrines of *qiyas* and *ijtihad* ('original thinking'; see further below) were formally adopted, a large measure of 'agreed practice' had been achieved, thus enabling the jurists and traditionists of the 2nd/8th century to project the doctrine of *qiyas* backwards into the earliest generation of Islam. This is clearly brought out in al-Shafi'i's conversation with a group of Medinese jurists:

> *Al-Shafi'i*: 'Shall we say that you, taking, for example, Ibn al-Musayyib to be the authoritative scholar of Medina, 'Ata' to be that of Mecca, Hasan that of Basra and Sha'bi that of Kufa—all

among the "Successors"—regard that as Ijma' what men are agreed upon?'

The opponent: 'Yes.'

Al-Shafi'i: 'But you assert that they have never met together in any assembly you knew of. You, therefore, infer their Ijma' from reports about them, and, indeed, since you have found these men making statements about matters which you do not find dealt with either in the Qur'an or in the Sunna you infer that they have exercised *qiyas* on these matters and you argue that *qiyas* is that established and true body of knowledge on which the scholars have agreed?

The opponent: 'This is what I say.'

Further, in this early period, the interaction between *qiyas* and Ijma' was regarded not as a static principle but as a natural dynamic process of assimilation, interpretation and adaptation. This is brought out in another passage in al-Shafi'i which, although somewhat lengthy, is the most comprehensive on the subject and reveals the true nature and the all-comprehensive character of Ijma':

The opponent: 'Knowledge comes about in several forms. First, what the total community relates from the total community of the previous generations (constitutes knowledge) with a certainty that I can swear upon it by God and His Prophet: this is exemplified by the obligatory religious duties... Secondly, that part of the Qur'an which admits of different interpretations must be accepted in its direct and commonsense meaning: it cannot be given in "inner" or allegorized sense—even though it may admit of such a one—unless it be by a consensus of the people... Thirdly, that knowledge upon which the Muslims agree and have related a previous agreement upon it. Even if this latter may not come from the Qur'an or the Sunna, for me it has the same status as the *agreed upon* Sunna. This is because the agreement of the Muslims cannot be reached merely by "personal opinions" (but only through *qiyas*) for "personal opinion" leads to disagreement... Fourthly, there is the knowledge of the specialists, which does not constitute a conclusive argument unless it is transmitted in a way immune to error. Lastly, the *qiyas*... No disagreement can enter into knowledge in the forms I have described and all things remain rooted in their principles unless the general community agrees to dislodge them from their principles. Ijma' is the final argument on everything for it is immune from error.

Al-Shafi'i: 'As for the first kind of knowledge you have described, viz., the transmission of the general body of the community from the previous generations of the general community, it is granted. But do you know and can you describe the second type with regard to which you assert that the general community is agreed upon it and transmits similar general agreement with regard to it in the previous generations? And what is this general body of the community...? Does it include both scholars and non-scholars..?

The opponent: 'This is the Ijma' of scholars only... for they are the ones who alone can know and agree about it. Thus, when they agree, this becomes authoritative for those who do not know (i.e., for non-scholars); but if they do not agree, their opinions have no authority for anyone and such matters must be referred back to a fresh *qiyas* (analogical reasoning) on the basis of what has been agreed upon... It is immaterial whether their Ijma' is based on a verbal tradition reported by them or without a tradition...; and even when they disargree it is immaterial whether there exists a verbal tradition which agree with what some of them hold or not. For I do not accept any Hadith except those on which there is agreement...'

The first point to be noticed is that not only these passages link *qiyas* or systematic reasoning with Ijma' as being a preparation for it, in the eyes of the early schools of law, but they both distinguish between the Sunna on the one hand and Ijma' on the other, both in the eyes of the early schools and in the eyes of their opponent, al-shafi'i. Sunna, therefore, cannot be identified with Ijma' as such. The former is restricted to the teaching of the Prophet and is extended to the Companions inasmuch as they are the source for its transmission; the latter begins with the Companions and is extended to subsequent generations.

But further, and far more important, the principle of Ijma' is given an overriding and absolute authority, is made 'the final and conclusive argument on everything', by the representative of the early schools of law. This certainly does not mean that no differences were allowed; indeed where it was felt that relatively minor differences had come to stay, they were all incorporated into the Ijma'. But Ijma' was regarded as absolutely authoritative not only for discerning the right at present and in the future, but also for establishing the past: it was Ijma' that determined what the Sunna of the Prophet had been and indeed what the right interpretation of the qur'an was. In the final analysis, therefore, both the Qur'an and the Sunna were authenticated through Ijma'.

The common denominator between these two different operations—on the past on the one hand and on the discovery of the right for the present on the other—expresses the essence of Ijma. This is the idea of authority or 'working security' from error. One must distinguish between authority and infallibility in this context. Many modern writers on the subject and pre-eminently Snouck Hurgronje have sought to draw sustained parallels between Ijam and the *ex cathedra* declarations of the Catholic Church. What is regarded as infallible by the early Muslim scholars, an infallibility more assumed than expressed, is the Ijma *as method and principle* rather than its contents which are regarded as authoritative, not infallible. The Muslim doctrine of Ijma' has a strong practical bent and there is no talk of absolute truth-value of its content, but only of a practical rectitude-value. But rectitude-values change. And certainly this is the only view compatible with the practice and theory of the early schools according to which Ijma' was an on-going process, thanks to the fact that the activity of 'original thinking' (*ijtihad*), carried on through systematic reasoning, intervened between the Sunna and the Ijma'. It is true that these schools, against attacks by al-Shafi'i on their Ijma', projected the contents of this Ijma' back to the early generations, thus giving the impression that they thought of Ijma' as tradition, but this was, in part, only a device to defend themselves against attacks.

Because of its very nature, Ijma' is the most potent factor in expressing and shaping the complex of belief and practice of the

Muslims, and at the same time the most elusive one in terms of its formation. It is an organic process. Like an organism it both functions and grows: at any given moment it has supreme functional validity and power and in that sense is 'final' but at the same moment it creates, assimilates, modifies and rejects. That is why its formation could not be vested in any institution. The body of scholars and lawyers that grew rapidly in the 1st/7th and 2nd/8th centuries and thence onwards could discuss and formulate the results of their thinking which were very influential, especially when they agreed (or rather concurred—this is known as the Ijma' of Scholars), but the formation of Ijma' could not be achieved in the school room. It was more akin to an enlightened public opinion in whose creation the formulation of schools was the most potent factor but which, as we shall see, gradually vetoed many schools of law and theology even out of existence and discredited or modified or expanded the validity of other.

Al-Shafi'i and After

In the development of the foundations of Muslim law portrayed so far, the Qur'an had its own identity, but the other three 'roots' or principles—Sunna, *qiyas* and Ijma' stand in a very intimate relationship to one another. Sunna and Ijam' especially, although distinct, pass into one another. The bridge, the inalienable link, is the *qiyas.* This principle of systematic reasoning, which not only interpreted the Prophetic sunna into law but also integrated the new social and administrative institutions and practices with the Sunna into 'living tradition', had by virtue of its activity, embedded itself in the Sunna. On the other hand, the result of *qiyas* activity, by conflict, compromise and adjustment, gradually crystallized into Ijma' which had the ultimately decisive authority.

By the middle of the 2nd/8th century, however, a large body of Hadith, claiming to emanate from the Prophet, had appeared on the scene. Al-shafi'i, who is credited with being the first jurist to have propounded the foundations of the law in the latter half of the 2nd/8th century, attacked the existing methodology and made a vigorous plea for the acceptance in law of the Hadith materials on a mass scale. His programme, though he did not perhaps see it quite in those terms, was to attack the doctrine of Ijam' of the law schools and to restrict it to essential religious obligations and practices. Thereby he would do away with 'living Sunna'; and the Ijma' having been made quite innocuous, i.e. reduced to the essential and broad religious duties embodied in the verbal Sunna of the Hadith as well, he would fill the whole vacuum with the Hadith. In other words, Hadith and Hadith alone would represent the Sunna, not the living tradition or the Ijma.' One all-important result of this world be to dislodge *qiyas* or the reasoning element from its intermediary position between the Qur'an and the Sunna on the one hand and Ijma' on the other.

That the large body of 'isolated' Hadith (i.e. traditions transmitted verbally and later on it writing in the 2nd/8th and 3rd/9th centuries, through only one or two channels) opposed Ijma' is the one outstanding lesson taught by al-Shafi'i's controversies. Against these Hadiths, the law schools upheld their Ijma' or 'agreed practice'. Al Shafi'i argues against them that, in fact, outside the main religious duties, there had been no Ijma', that the Ijma' which the schools attribute to the early authorities and scholars is not a real consensus but at best a concurrence and that on several details there was still conflict. But his chief argument is to point out that if there were an Ijma' on a question, it could only be transmitted through certain channels of narration, a fact which the schools disallowed as basis for the Hadith. Al-Shafi'i comes back tirelessly to this argument whereby he seeks to turn the tables on the old schools. But his conception of Ijma' was that of a neat and precise 'event' if not of an institution, whereas the schools' conception of it was that of the elusive but potent process of gradual crystallization and stabilization of opinions. In their zeal to defend themselves, however, they projected Ijma' back to earlier generations in many matters.

Largely because of al-Shafi'i's efforts, the verbal tradition or Hadith presently supplanted 'living tradition' as the vehicle of the Prophetic Sunna. Some such solution was inevitable because 'living tradition' could not go on indefinitely and had in some way to be standardized. According to al-Shafi'i's proposal, the four foundational principles of law were to be reached in this order: first, the Qur'an, then the Sunna of the Prophet as Communicated in the Hadith, next the

Ijma' of the Community, and last the effort at original thought (*ijtihad*) of scholars to be exercised through *qiyas*. It is quite clear that *ijtihad* or *qiyas* instead of being at the service of Ijma' and preparatory to it, as we the case in the old schools, is put outside it. Indeed, al-Shafi'i contends insistently that disagreement not Ijma' or agreement, would be the necessary result of *ijtihad* and that the claims of his opponents to reach Ijam' through original thinking were vain pretensions. But, on the other hand, not much scope for *ijtihad* and disagreement would be left, thanks to the wholesale development of the Hadith.

Ijma' however, finally accepted Hadith but on its own terms and without losing any ground whatever. This result also, despite al-Shafi'i's efforts to the contrary, was inevitable. For, what other authority besides Ijma' could there be to discriminate between the Hadith representing the true Sunna from that bearing the false? Or, who could finally decide what the teaching of the Hadith is? (We have pointed out in the preceding chapter that the criticism of the transmissional chains to establish the genuineness of a Hadith was more a formal criticism than a real one). Thus, even in order to establish Hadith, Ijma' was needed. In the middleof the 3rd/9th century when the Hadith had virtually conqurred the field, even a crusading defender of the Hadith such as IbnQutayba gives priority to Ijam' over it: 'We hold that Ijma' is a surer vehical of truth (or the right) than the Hadith for the latter is subject to forgetfulness, neglect, doubts, interpretations and abrogation. But Ijma' is free from all these contingencies.

But in the subsequent development, *ijtihad* or *qiyas* fared differently. Although the Hadith materials were once more reinterpreted to obtain new legal norms through *qiyas*, this largely remained a scholastic activity. Shorn of its function as leading to Ijma', it gradually lost vitality until, when at the end of the 3rd/9th and beginning of the 4th/10th centuries, both the dogma and the law had taken a definite shape, the Ijma' arrived at by that time was declared final and the door of *ijtihad* was closed. It other words, once Hadith had been established by Ijma', it ousted Ijma' by its very logic. Islamic law and dogma have developed but little since. One of the most creative and brilliant epochs of all intellectual history came to a sudden close. Why did this happen? Many answers may be adduced to solve this important question of the religious and cultural history of Islam. A partial answer is that Islam had passed, during the preceding three centuries, through a period of great conflict of opinions and doctrines and had finally attained stability, through the emergence of an orthodoxy, only towards the end of the 3rd/beginning of the 10th century. When that point was reached and a difficult and stormy formative period had ended, the results were give permanence. But, as we have just noticed above, the mechanism of development was disturbed just before this point of fruition was reached. The body of Hadith, sanctioned by Ijma', relegated *ijtihad* to a subsidiary place cut off from Ijma'; in its turn, Ijma', which was originally a function of the 'living tradition' dislodged from fresh thought or *ijtihad*, could not continue it function for the organism needed both for its growth. A stabilizing principle without a principle of expansion necessarily becomes a static tool of oppression. Now a theory of the infallibility of the Ijma' was developed whereby the early concept of a *pragmatic authority* of the Community's consensus was changed into a theoretical absoluteness of the Community in terms of truth-values. A Hadith was circulated according to which the Prophet said: 'My Community shall never agree on an error'. Thus, Ijma' became a theoretically founded mechanism of traditional authoritarianism.

Actually, Ijma' did continue to function in some form or another even after the 3rd/9th century, which was also inevitable in face of the ever changing circumstances of the religious attitudes and the fortunes of the Community. A striking example is the acceptance into orthodox Islam of Sufism after a series of Muslim orthodox Sufis (Muslim mystics), culminating in the great al-Ghazali (d. 505/1111) who won for it recognition among the 'Ulama'. Again, the gradual change in the constitutional theory of Islam supplies a no less striking instance. Early in Islam, because of internecine wars, the Ijma' adopted the principle that fanaticism and war in the Community was unlawful, and that the ruler, despite his failings and even positive injustice ought to be obeyed. Al-Mawardi (d. 450/1058) quotes a Hadith that a sinful ruler should be obeyed provided he does not give a sinful command. Indeed, later the idea had fully gained ground that even an unjust ruler may not be rebelled against. And subsequently the ruler was described as the 'shadow of God'. For the 'Ulama' this meant a point of cohesion against chaos and lawlessness, but in the popular belief, influenced by the old Iranian ideas of kingship, this phrase assumed literal truth. But in all these cases Ijma' followed rather than led: instead of being a moulding principle acting formatively on circumstances—through *ijtihad*—it became a passive follower, a mere recognizer of the brute force of circumstance.

The qualifications for *ijtihad* were made so immaculate and rigorous and were set so high that they were humanly impossible of fulfilment. The pictures of the early religious leaders of the Community during the formative period were accordingly idealized more and more and fiction mixed with facts. The power of 'absolute *ijtihad*' was completely abolished; a 'relative *ijtihad*' was allowed. This meant either that one was allowed to reinterpret law *within one's own school of law* or, and this was the highest point of the original legislation, one could carry on an eclectic and comparative study of law of different schools and thus find some scope for limited expansion in details. Some rare, bright and bold spirits such as Ibn Taymiya (d. 728) claimed the right of absolute *ijtihad* of themselves, but their recognition in this matter remained limited during the medieval period. We shall see subsequently in the present work how the question has been reopened in modern Islam with vehemence by modernist thinkers. But throughout the medieval centuries the law, definite and defined, was cast like a shell over the Community.

The Law and the State

During the period of the first four Caliphs (up to about 40/660), the Muslim state and government was headed by the Caliph but was indistinguishable from the public body thanks to the large number of Companions in Medina, especially the senior members who advised on, controlled and participated in both legislative and executive functions. Indeed, at that stage, law can hardly be separated or even distinguished from administration. Legislation in this period can, therefore, mainly by courtesy be attributed to the contemporary Calipsh, for it was the joint work of the Community or its senior members. With the Umayyads, however, the government became vested in the ruling autocracy which became distinguished from the public. The Umayyad rulers carried on their administration from Damascus, largely guided by the Qur'an and the Sunna, but these were interpreted by their advisers and officers on the principle of expediency and in the light of local practices in different provinces. In face of this lay authority, the leaders of the religious community centred in Medina began to construct the body of Islamic law. The local practice of the Hijaz was indubitably a factor in their body of laws. Soon the religious legislative activity also arose in Iraq, in Basra and Kufa. The Umayyad state was influenced by this legislative activity and the Caliph 'Abd al-Malik (d. 86/705) was himself educated in Medina. But the first Umayyad Caliph to take the application of the Shari'a law seriously and systematically was 'Umar ibn 'Abd al-'Aziz around the close of the 1st/early 8th century and tradition credits him with sending out emissaries to all the outlying provinces to teach people the Shari'a law and to record traditions from the Prophet.

The state was thus the executive institution which applied in different provinces the Shari'a law as it had been formulated by local legal authorities. But this body of law (*fiqh*), although uniform in its essentials, differed largely in details both because of the different local practices and because of variations arising out of *ijtihads* of several scholars. The scholars even of a single town differed in detailed legal opinion. After the Umayyads were ousted, Ibnh al-Muqaffa' (d. 140/757), a Persian convert to Islam, an eminent man of letters and a Secretary of State, wrote a treatise advising the Caliph that he should systematize the law and exercise his own *ijtihad* on the Qur'an and the Sunna. Ibn al-Muqaffa' was probably the first man in Islam to advocate state legislation, advice (apparently not followed) which was probably motivated both by the chaotic differences in legal practice at the time and the Persian background of his ideas of rulership

The 'Abbasid Caliphs gave full recognition and validity to the Shari'a law and perfected the machinery for it application. But several new developments took place. Not only did the Caliphs (or later when the Caliphal power became weak and titular, the powerful sultans owing only nominal allegiance to the Caliphs) begin to enact special laws of their own from time to time to cope with exigencies, a new, although small, body of law emerged devised by the lay authorities to supplement the Shari'a law. The later Muslim lawyers (*fuqaha'*) attempted gradually to integrate this new body of laws into the Shari'a law, but the fact that it had originally arisen outside the Shari's was a significant development.

But large scale lay legislation by the state was effected by the Ottomans who assumed the title of the Caliphs in the 10th/16th century. This lay body of law was called the *qanun* (canon) and Professor Sir Hamilton Gibb has remarked with perfect justice that canon law in Islam means the exact opposite of what it means in Christianity. Among the Ottomans, however, the two functions of Sultanate and Caliphate were separately invested in the same ruler, and Caliphate never returned to its original state. The function of *ijtihad* which all the later constitutional theorists had been attributing to the Caliphal office was never used, and the Ottomans, in so far as they functioned in the field of positive law, functioned only as Sultans. The *qunun*-law was a product of the Sultanate, not of the Caliphate. We shall see later on in this work, when we discuss modern Islam, how the challenge of the modernization of law is being met by Muslims in modern times.

The administration of the law was carried on in the courts by the *qadis* appointed by the state. These were drawn from the ranks of the 'Ulama.' Thus appointed by the state, the *qadis* could be used as instruments of the ruler's will and in every age, beginning with the early Umayyad times, we read recurring condemnations of the *qadis* by pious 'Ulama' and jurists (but later on above all by Sufis), many of whom refused to accept governmental office holding that their integrity was thereby in danger of being compromised. Besides these law courts, the Caliphal held special courts called the *mazalim* courts (and similarly various sultans had their *diwan* courts) for the redress of personal wrongs. Very often these functioned like courts of higher appeal against the decisions of lower courts and officials of the administration. Here the head of state personally decided cases and dispensed justice according to his Judgment. Between these two, a third moral-judicial department of 'moral practice' was instituted called *ihtisab*. Its function was to keep an eye on public morality and to decide 'obvious' cases on the spot such as defective scales, counterfeit money or adulterated commodities, etc.

The task of specific interpretation of law and its application to individual cases was vested in the *muftis* who could be either official or private. The verdict given by a *mufti* on a specific case or point of law is called *fatwa*. In course of time, a large body of case-law was built up comprising the collections of *fatwas* of authoritative 'Ulama'. These were in turn used by *qadis* in deciding cases that came before the courts. The *mufti* was thus a jurisconsult, a *qadi* a judge. The *fatwa*-collections provide for us the best source for the knowledge of the development of Islamic law throughout the Middle Ages and in the different regions, and reveal to us that long process whereby local customary laws were gradually Islamized and integrated into Islamic law.

Formation of the Legal Schools

It is an evidence of the characteristic freedom of legal thought in early Islam that during the 1st/7th and 2nd/8th centuries a host of accumulations of legal opinion grew up in different centres in Iraq, the Hijaz, Syria and Egypt. These were centred on or attached themselves to an eminent legal personality. The differences in these bodies of legal thought were largely due to the various ways in which the Qur'an was interpreted, in the light of local customary law, i.e. in the different ways in which *qiyas* and *ra'y* were applied to the Sunna. The body of law that resulted from such application of rational activity in different regions was also called Sunna. Hence, the local Sunnas differed in detail in the different provinces.

But slowly, with the development of the concept of Ijma', these particular centres merged into one another by mental interaction and the accumulations of legal opinion gradually crystallized into schools in the 2nd/8th and 3rd/9th centuries during which the schools themselves came closer to one another, thanks to the wide measure of agreement not only on principles but even on major details. In Iraq, the school associated with the name of Abu Hanifa (d. 150/767) called the

Hanafi school, developed and was systemized by his two disciples Abu Yusuf (d. 181/797) and Muhammad al-Shaybani (d. 189/805) and ousted that of Sufyan al-Thawri (d. 161/778) and others. This school, favoured by the 'Abbasids whose capital was in Baghdad, was most characterized by the exercise of free opinion and became the favourite object of the bitter invectives of the Ahl al-Hadith in the 2nd 8th and 3rd/9th centuries, since these latter strenuously rejected free opinion.

The Syrian school of al-Awza'i (d. 157/774), whose reliance on the 'living tradition' was greater than on legal Hadith, in contrast of Sufyan al-Thawri, was overcome by that founded by Malik ibn Anas (d. 179/795) in Medina. Malik himself resembled al-Awza'i in that at bottom he placed his reliance on the 'living tradition' (*Sunna*) of Medina, but was equally anxious to support of vindicate this tradition through Hadith. He collected a body of legal traditions and, testing them in the light of the living practice of Medina, constructed a system of juridical opinions into a famous work called *al-Muwatta'*—'the levelled path'. The Maliki school, the second surviving one after the Hanafi, takes its name from him.

The third major surviving school is called the Shafi'i school, after Muhammad ibn Idris al-Shafi'i (d. 204/819), references to whom have figured prominently in the present and the preceding chapter of this book. A pupil of Malik, he formulated the principles of Islamic jurisprudence in the form that these have retained ever since, wherein, as we have described before, the verbal tradition was regarded as the sole vehicle of the Prophetic Sunna and *ijtihad* was thrown outside Ijma'. The influence of al-Shafi'i has been incalculable on the development of Islam.

In the 3rd/9th century arose two new schools and at least one attempt at a school. The first and only successful one of these continued at push the logic of al-Shafi'i's insistence on the Hadith in law to its extremes. The founder of this school, called the Hanbali school, was the famous doctor and arch-traditionalist Ahmad ibn Hanbal (d. 241/855) whom we shall meet again in the next chapter as the orthodox opponent of the rationalist school. Ibn Hanbal's teaching was systematized after him by his disciples but after a widespread following was commanded by this school up to 8th/14th century, the numbers suffered a continuous diminution although a series of brilliant and sensational representatives of the school appeared across the centuries. In the 12th/18th century the Wahhabis—the puritanical movement in the Arabian Peninsula—derived their doctrine and inspiration from Hanbalism as it had been expressed by the celebrated doctor and theologian Ibn Taymiya (d. 728/1328).

Da'ud Khalaf (d. 269/882), called at-Zahiri—'the literalist' - established the literalist school in the 3rd/9th century. It sought to reject *qiyas* altogether and even restricted the Ijma' to the consensus of the Companions only. Acceptance of the literal interpretation of the Qur'an and the Hadith was the keynote of their doctrine. But on closer analysis, they were not as literalist as they claimed to be because the rejection of the reasoning element in jurisprudence freed them to extend the acceptance of the Word to include what the Word 'assumes' or 'implies' (*mafhum, fatwa*). But the restriction of the mechanism of interpretation that they advocated found little support among the large body of Muslim although their point of view has from time to time to time found eminent champions. Al-Tabari (d. 310/922), whose voluminous and monumental works on the exegesis of the Qur'an and history are full of information about early Islam, attempted to found a new school of law, but not only was this attempt unsuccessful, even the work in which he laid down its principles does not seem to have survived.

By Ijma' the four schools, or *Madhahib* (pl. of *Madhhab*), as they are called, were accepted, and accepted one another as equally orthodox A detailed history of their mutual interaction still needs to be written. But there is not only no fundamental difference of jurisprudence between them, even the difference in detail has been largely turned into a remarkable unity thanks to the limited *ijtihad* that continued to be allowed and exercised by the scholars. At present the Hanafi school is predominant in Western Asia, lower Egypt, Pakistan and among the Muslims of India. The Maliki rite holds sway in North and West Africa and in Upper Egypt, the Shafi'i in Indonesia, and the Hanbalite in Northern and Central Arabia.

Conclusion

As indicated at the beginning of this chapter, the place of law in Islam, and consequently it nature, where we shall attempt both an analysis of the concept of Shari'a and a history of it, but a general characterization of it may be in place here. It will have become clear by now that the real basis on which rests this whole structure is religious, the idea of God as the sovereign and 'the Ordainer Whose Will is Law'. Man must discover, formulate and execute that Will of which the final index is the Qur'an and Muhammad the most perfect commentator. Accordingly, Islamic law, in its first intention, is a system of 'ought' and 'ought-nots' rather than a specific legal code. That is why every book of Islamic law starts with a discourse on religious duties. That is also why actions are ethically classified into five categories: (1) obligatory, (2) recommended, (3) permissible or indifferent, (4) reprehensible and (5) forbidden. Indeed, the trans-legal religious and moral state of the agent's heart (faith, intention and will) is demanded by this system to be present in all behaviour. Nothing illustrates this traith better than the fact that most actions classified in the above categories and especially (2), (3) and (4) are made subject to a general rule known as the law of 'resoluteness and relaxation ('*azima* and *rukhsa*)'. These categories which primarily apply to the agent's will, whereby he should regard, under special circumstances, the permissive actions to be unpermitted and vice versa (because of moral consideration), are erected into a quasi-legal enactment. This trait of the *fiqh* system is further evidenced by the fact that frequently religious penalties (known as *kaffara*) run concurrently with strictly legal sanctions. A further example of this translation of the spiritual into legal terms is the verbalization, in many cases, of the act of intention by uttering 'I intend..' such considerations should warn us against applying the term 'law' in its ordinary denotation to a system which, in its primary intention, is trans-legal but which can undoubtedly constitute the raw materials for a properly legal system.

2

The Importance of Hadith as a Source of Islamic Law

M. ZUBAYR SIDDIQI

The importance of Hadith as an important source of Islamic law has been laid down in the Qur'an, emphasised by the Prophet, recognized by him immediate successors and other companions, and accepted by all the important orthodox Muslim jurists.

The Qur'an says: "Whatever the Prophet gives accept it, and whatever he forbids you abstain from it." It also says: "He does not speak out of his desire. It is nought but the revelation revealed (to him)." The Prophet also very often emphasised the importance of his own *sunna* as a guide for his followers. He was happy at the reply of Mu'adh b. Jabal who said to him when he was appointed as an official in Yeman that the would follow his (Prophet's) *sunna* if he failed to find guidance in the Qur'an. He also instructed his followers many a time, to hold fast to his practice. Once he said to them: "So long as you hold fast to two things which I have left among you, you will not go astray; God's Book, and his messenger's *sunna.*"

After the death of the Prophet, Abu Bakr followed the practice of the Prophet if he could not find guidance in the Qur'an and it was available in his *sunna*. If he did not know of any decision of the Prophet on the subject, he made enquiries from the companions about it and if any of them informed him of any Hadith on the subject he decided the case accordingly. And if they also showed their ignorance of it, he called together the leaders of the people, discussed the matter with them and ordered according to their agreed opinion. After Abu

Bakr's death, 'Umar I also followed the same procedure, and followed the tradition of the Prophet in the absence of the injunction of the Qur'an, provided he was convinced of its reliability as well as of its applicability to the case in question. But if he had doubts about the reliability of the tradition or of its applicability to the case before him, he did not take the tradition into account. Thus in fixing the number of *takbir* in Jinaza-prayer, in the imposition of poll-tax on the Zoroastrians, in the use of *tayammum* in case of night-pollution and in many other cases he laid down laws according to the practice of the Prophet, which he found out after keen enquiry. Many other cases in which 'Umar accepted the practices of the Prophet and decided according to them have been mentioned by al-Shafi'i in his *al-Risala* and other works.

But 'Umar examined critically the reliability of the traditions and their applicability to the cases which were brought to him, before he accepted them. A well-known case in which he did not accept the traditions is that related by Fatima, the daughter of Qais, who related to him that she was not granted by the Prophet the right of residence with her husband and maintenance by him after she was completely divorced by him. On hearing her, 'Umar said that he could not rely upon the report of a women who might have forgotten what the Prophet had said. He, therefore, could not disregard on account of her the text of the Qur'an which says: "Lodge them (the divorced women) where you lodge according to your means." Many other cases of this type are found in the works on traditions and law in general and those of Imam Shafi'i in particular.

Almost all the companions, however, decided the cases with which they had to deal, on the basis of traditions of the Prophet, if they failed to find any guidance in the Qur'an, and followed their opinions only when they could not find any tradition on the subject, but as soon as they came to know of it, they changed their decisions if necessary and followed the traditions. Many of them refused to express their opinions about those legal cases on which no tradition was known to them. As a matter of fact, some companions like Abu'l-Darda' and Abu Sa'id al-Khudari migrated away from their places of residence when they found there some people who preferred their own opinions to the traditions which were related to them.

As a matter of fact, all the important orthodox Muslim jurists are unanimously of the opinion that every tradition of the Prophet which is of religious character and which is proved to be reliable according to the canons laid down by them is of great legal importance next only to that of the Qur'an. In this there is no difference of opinion between the traditionists and those who are known as Ashab al-Ra'i (the people of the opinion). The practice followed by the companions of the Prophet after his death were also generally accepted by the jurists of the next generation because they reasonable presumed that the companions must have followed the traditions and practices of the Prophet after due consideration. This was the basis of the principle followed by Imam Malik in accepting the decisions and practices of the companions as an important legal authority.

Whereas almost all the companions and all the orthodox Muslim jurists are unanimous in accepting the religious and reliable traditions as an important legal authority next to the Qur'an only, they differ from one another in accepting certain classes of them as an unimpeachable authority because of their doubtful religious character or questionable reliability.

In the connexion it must be borne in mind that all the deeds and words of the Prophet do not serve as basis of law for his followers. Many of his practices were confined to his individual self as a Prophet and were not meant for his *Ummat*. As, for instance, he very often fasted for several days continuously. But when some of his companions wanted to emulate his example, he told them that this was his special privilege as a Prophet and they should not follow his example in this matter.

By being a Prophet, however, he did not cease to be a human being. The idea of Prophethood in Islam is very different from that in Christianity and some other religions, as it has been explained in the Qur'an at many places. In Islam the Prophet is neither an angel nor God nor a demi-god. He is a human being like other human beings, having the same needs and requirements as they have. The only difference between a Prophet and other human beings is that he is gifted with a special capacity to enter into communion with God and of receiving inspiration from Him, and possesses great self-control, self-denial, self-confidence and great capacity for influencing the thoughts and activities of people at large, and leading them to the right path. The inspirations which a Prophet receives from God have been classified by Muslim doctors into two classes: (i) those which are included in the revealed book, and (ii) those which are not included in it. The latter forms a part of the traditions. But among the traditions are included also such of the sayings and doings are the based on his own individual observations and experience without any inspiration from God. Such of the tradition as are based only on the personal observation and experience of the Prophet have no religious legal authority for the Muslim community. The Prophet himself has said: "I am a human being. When I order you about matters concerning your religion follow it, and when I ask you to do anything on the basis of my personal opinion them (know) that I am also a human being." A well-known tradition of the Prophet relates that when he found the Muslims of Medina grafting the date-trees, he advised them to stop this practice. His advice was followed. But as a result of it, in the next season the crop was very poor. People naturally complained to the Prophet. He replied, "It was my personal opinion. You may not follow me in my personal opinion. But when I tell you anything from God then follow it, for I never say anything wrong from God." To this class of non-religious personal opinion belong the traditions which constitute what is known as *Tibbun-Nabi* and many other sayings of the Prophet which are based on his own personal observations or experience, as well as such of his deeds as were done by him on account of peculiar political or military situations in what he had to act. None of them are obligatory for the whole community or for all time.

Such of the practices and traditions of the Prophet also as are of religious character and are based either on the Qur'an or non-Qur'anic inspiration are, at times, open to different interpretations as can be realised by every thinking educated man. About the interpretation of some of them, the Muslim jurists differed among themselves since the death of the Prophet. An interesting and important example of it is the problem of the share of the relatives of the Prophet in the one-fifth of war-booty. It has been thoroughly discussed by Shibli in his *al-Faruq*. I summarize his discussions below.

The Qur'an says: "And known that whatever you acquire in war, a fifth of it is for Allah and for the Prophet and for the near of kins and the orphans and the needy and the wayfarer..."

Following the principle the Prophet used to spend one fifth of the booty (i) on his own personal requirements, (ii) in helping his relatives, (iii) on the orphans, (iv) on the poor, and (v) on the wayfarers. But he neither spent the money on these five items in equal proportions not did he help all his relatives out of this fund.

He gave help to only some of relatives, i.e., the descendants of Hashim and Muttalib and did not give anything to other relatives in spite of their demands. And even such of them as he helped he did not do so equally not in one and the same way, but according to his own discretion, and in the way he liked and according to their real requirements, e.g., the payment of the debts, supplying the needs of the poor and getting married the unmarried among them.

After the death of the Prophet during the Caliphate of 'Umar when large booty was received at Medina, there arose the problem of the share of the relatives of the Prophet, in the one-fifth of the booty. 'Abdullah b. Abbas and many other relatives of the Prophet claimed, as one of the five beneficiaries of the fund, that they had legal right to the whole of the one-fifth of the one-fifth of the booty. This view was accepted by Imam al-Shafi'i also at a later period. But 'Umar I held that neither the Qur'an not the practice of the Prophet justified it. For the Qur'an did not say that each one of the five beneficiaries should get equal share, to did the prophet distribute the one-fifth of the booty among the five beneficiaries equally. He was strongly of the opinion that the share of the Prophet and of his relatives lapsed after his death and that his privilege to distribute it among the beneficiaries according to their requirements and his own discretion, as the head of the state, had devolved upon his successor. 'Umar, therefore, had offered the relatives of the Prophet to take from this fund the money necessary for the remarriage of their widows and for the payment of the debt of the poor among them, according to the practice of the Prophet during the lifetime. The view of 'Umar I was shared by Imam Abu Hanifa at a later period.

The attitude of the two parties of the companions and other jurists, to this and other problems on which they held different views, towards the traditions and practices of the Prophet shows that they did not deny not did they minimise their legal authority, but only interpreted them differently.

All the important orthodox Muslim jurists since the death of the Prophet, however, recognized the *Mutawatir* and the *Mustafid* classes of the tradition as the second important source of Muslim law. But they differed from one another about the Ahad class of them, i.e., those traditions which are handed down by one narrator only at any stage of its transmission.

Imam Abu Hanifa and Imam Malik held that the traditions belonging to this category were not necessarily superior to the *qiyas* or opinion based on reason. Imam Malik was of opinion that the *qiyas* was superior to all such Ahad traditions as were not backed by the practices of the companions and the *followers*. Imam Abu Hanifa like 'Umar I differentiated between the individual Ahad traditions. He accepted the superiority of them to the *qiyas* if they dealt with ordinary matters of life, provided their narrators possessed acute legal acumen and critical faculty. But he preferred the *qiyas* to such *Ahad* traditions as dealt with intricate legal problems, unless they were supported by circumstantial evidence and basic Islamic principles. This is in keeping with the common practice of all thinking people. Ordinarily we act on the report of a single individual in every-day affairs of the life. But when important matters and intricate problems are concerned, we are as critical of the reports and the reporters as the importance of the matters concerned may demand.

Imam Shafi'i, however, attached great importance to all the Ahad traditions also. He held that all of them were not only superior to the *qiyas* but they might also narrow down the general injunctions laid down in Qur'an, as well as cancel them. He has tried to prove it in most of his works by quoting a large number of cases in which the Prophet and after him many of his companions, including 'Umar I, accepted and acted upon the report of single individuals. But he overlooked the cases in which the Prophet as well as his companions rejected the reports of single individuals. Numerous such cases are mentioned in the work on *Hadith*.

This brief account of the recognition of the traditions of the prophet of Islam by the Qur'an and by the Prophet himself, and of the acceptance of such of them as may be of religious character and are proved to be reliable, by almost all the companions and all the important jurists as an important legal authority, shows that its recognition as such did not originate with Imam Shafi'i, as Dr. Joseph Schacht holds. As a matter of fact, the recognition of the traditions as a second important source of Islamic Law has been an accepted principle with all the important Muslim jurists, since the death of the Prophet. What Imam Shafi'i did was to give recognition and to attach great importance to the Ahad category of traditions in general without trying to test strictly their reliability and without making any distinction between the traditions of religious character and those of non-religious character.

Prof. J. Robson in his introduction to the English translation of the *Mishkat al-Masabih*, Part I of which has been just published by Muhammad Ashfar of Lahore, having accepted the conclusion arrived at by Dr. Jospeh Schacht, remarks: "There were different schools of thoughts in early Islam, one of which was the party, which upheld the importance of tradition traced back to the Prophet, and it was only after a period of contention and dispute that the traditionists won the day. The one who deserves most credit for establishing traditions as a basis of Islam was Shafi`i, (150-204 A.H.), the great exponent of jurisprudence."

This remark, as may be seen from what has been discussed in this article, is not based on facts.

3

The Mughal System of Escheat and the Islamic Law of Inheritance

ZAFARUL ISLAM

The problem of succession to the property in Mughal India has been a matter of great controversy among medieval as well as modern scholars. The statements of contemporary European travellers leave the impression that there was no concept of private property in those days and that the king was the sole heir of the property of his subjects. They were led to this conclusion, at least in case of state officials, on the basis of the system of escheat that was in operation in Mughal India. It appears that they passed their judgement without going deeply into the cases of escheat and examining them closely. Here, an effort would be made to study the relevant rules and regulations as well as the actual cases of escheat in the light of the Islamic law of inheritance. Such an analytical study would, of course, help us to arrive at some definite conclusion about the nature and purpose of the escheat and to understand the actual working of the system under the Mughals.

As regards the origin of the escheat it is difficult to trace it in the history of Muslim countries. In the Islamic law of inheritance there is no provision for such a practice, but the general rules are that (a) the property of a deceased person would not be distributed among his heirs unless his debt has been paid and (b) the heir-less property would be deposited with the *Bayt al-Mal.* In the annals of Islamic history we come across plenty of cases of heirless property (left by state officials or people in general) going to public treasury, but nowhere is any reference made to the confiscation of property of officials by the state claiming its ownership. We are, however, informed by some Arabic sources that during the Abbasid rules it was an established some Arabic sources that during the Abbasid rule it was an established practice to confiscate property of the fallen vizirs and that of state officials dismissed from service for embezzlement or other serious offence. The practice known as *musadarah* (confiscation) formed a part of punishment in case of defaulting officials. Commenting on this practice, Adam Mez comes to the conclusion that originating as a punishment in the beginning of the 10th century, it was later resorted to very frequently with regard to state officials at the slightest pretext. He has also given some cases showing the confiscation of the property of the deceased officials. But it appears from a close scrutiny of the cases that the property of the deceased official was seized by the Abbasid state to recover their ill-gotten wealth and that it was never done as a legitimate process of the state's claim to their property as its owner. It is also assumed by some modern scholars that the Abbasid caliphs chose to recruit their officers from among slaves mainly to have 'a legal pretext' for claiming their property after their death, but no evidence if given from contemporary sources to substantiate the point.

There is also no evidence to suggest that the practice was borrowed from the Mongols. We are informed by *Ta'rikh-i Jahankusha'i* that one of the rules formulated by Chingiz Khan was that the property of the deceased officials and other persons in the state would not be taken into state custody, and if anyone of them died heir-less his property would be entrusted to his disciple of slave. It was clearly stated that in any case the property of the deceased person should not be deposited with the state-treasury. We get nearly the same information about pre-Islamic Iran. It is reported that in the reign of Nushirwan (A.D. 531-579), the revenue-collectors collected about three thousand *dirhams* as heir-less property from Ispahan and brought them to the king to be deposited with the state-treasury. The king returned the amount to the officers of the said province and ordered investigations to find the heirs of the deceased person. In case no heir could be traced, the property was to be distributed among the needy and poor people and it was not to be kept in the state-treasury. However, the author of *Siyar al-Muta'akhkhirin* has asserted that not only under all the Mughal emperors of India but also among all the Timurid races it was standard practice to confiscate the estate and wealth of their deceased ministers and servants and to exclude the natural heirs from inheritance. Whatever had been the origin of the escheat in India it cannot be denied that it was practised throughout the Mughal empire.

As far as the rules for the property of the deceased are concerned, we find that from time to time the Mughal emperors issued instructions to the concerned officers to take care of the property of the deceased persons and to hand it over to the legal heirs, but if no legal heirs were found, to deposit it with the *Bayt al-Mal* after deducting the state-dues. Akbar is reported to have appointed some special officials to supervise the property of the deceased and absconding persons and to trace and hand it over to their legal heirs, provided the deceased had no state-dues. One of the twelve edicts issued in the first year of Jahangir's reign reads that the property of the deceased persons, whether Muslims or non-Muslims, was to devolve of their heirs without any interference. In case the deceased was heir-less, it was, then, to be taken in the state's custody.

For the reign of Shahjahan we get no direct reference to any new rule which would have been formulated regarding the escheat. Manucci, however, gives a different version. Referring to the restoration of the property of Sa'adat Khan (an imperial slave, in-charge of betels consumed by the emperor) by Shahjahan to the widow, Manucci points out that the emperor violated the rule made by Akbar regarding the confiscation of the property of the deceased officials. However, the cases of escheat as recorded by the contemporary sources from his reign do not mark any departure from existing practice in the state polity with regard to the escheat. Awrangzib not only retained the practice of escheat, he also laid down certain definite rules and amended the existing ones to bring more efficiency in its working.

It appears from a letter of Awrangzib to Shahjahan that the escheat was an old practice, followed strictly in the pre-Awrangzib period, and that it was denounced by Awrangzib who called it unjust and cruel. On the other hand, we see that in reference to the escheat of

Amir Khan's property Awrangzib justified the practice on the ground that such kind of property belonged rightfully to the common people (*'ibad*), because a ruler might have violated the *Shari'ah's* rules in conferring financial grant on an official and so encroached upon the rights of the Muslims in general. The emperor explained that in the lifetime of the official he endured the burden of that sin only as a mark of his favour towards him. But after his death why should he not take back what he had given to him? Since it is not clear in the case of Amir Khan on what ground his property was escheated it cannot be said definitely that Awrangzib's justification for the escheat was general or only in case of heirless or indebted deceased. But his justification for the property of heirless deceased becomes quite clear from his view expressed in relation to the escheat of Mahabat Khan's property, Here, he not only ordered the confiscation of his property but instructed that full care be taken in collecting it as it was one of the proceeds of the *Bayt al-Mal*, which belonged to the common people.

From the rules and regulations formulated from time to time in his reign it is quite clear that the confiscation of the property of a deceased person was not permissible except when he died heirless or owed state-debt. In the case of the property of heirless persons, the state officilas were instructed to deduct the amount due from him and deposit the rest in the *Bayt al-Mal*, otherwise, it was to be distributed to the lawful heirs. But if the property left by the deceased was less in value than the state-debt the whole property was to be escheated. In 1691 it was ordered by Awrangzib that the property of those officials whose heirs were also state employees would not be confiscated. This was obviously a new development in the working of the escheat system.

From the existent rules and regulations regarding the confiscation of the property of the deceased officials during the period it is evident that the Mughal emperors did not claim, at least in theory, to be the owner of the property of their officers. They permitted only temporary escheat of the property to adjust the state-dues, and permanent confiscation was allowed only in case the deceased left on heir. How far these regulations were acted upon may be judged only by an analysis of the actual cases of escheat. But as the chronicles do not always specify the actual reasons for escheat, the problem of analysis is a difficult one. However, an attempt would be made to scrutinize them and draw some conclusion.

The origin of the practice of escheat in India is generally traced back to the Delhi Sultanate, and the case of 'Imad al-Mulk Bashir is cited from Firuz Shah's reign in support of the assumption. But it may be clarified here that it was a case of the escheat of an official's property for state-dues. The sultan is reported to have taken away nine crores out of twelve crores left by 'Imad al-Mulk Bashir, minister of war and *muqta*' of Rapri, and left the remaining three cores to be distributed among his heirs. There is no clear information about the exact amount standing against him as arrears of the state but it is confirmed that he had paid no state-dues for several years and had accumulated enormous wealth. When it was brought to the notice of the sultan, he remarked: "What difference does it make, whether it is my property or the property of Bashir?" The latter is also reported to have misappropriated the salaries of the soldiers.

Out of fifth cases of escheat from the Mughal period taken up for study by us, in five cases the property of the deceased official was escheated as they had died heirless. Mun'im Khan Khan-i Khanan, the governor of Bengal, died in 1575 and his entire property was confiscated at the royal order for he had left behind no heir. In 1602, Shah Quli Khan Mahram, the Governor of Punjab, died heirless. His property was escheated to the state.

Rani Jaduni, the wife of Raja Rai Singh, died in 1673. Her property was seized and deposited with the *Bayt al-Mal*. There were three surviving sons of Rai Singh, but as they were from another wife they could not inherit the property of their step-mother, Rani Jaduni. Firdaws, as domestic servant of Raja Jaswant Singh, died in 1679 leaving seven hundred and eighty-four rupees. The entire amount was seized. A hundred rupees were spent on his burial and the rest of the money deposited with the *Bayt al-Mal*. Though no clear reason for the escheat has been given, yet the fact that after meeting the burial expenses, the remaining amount was deposited with the *Bayt al-Mal* confirms the assumption that he died heirless. Mahabat Khan

Haydarabadi, the Governor of Berar, passed away at Lahore in 1698. His entire property was escheated the deposited with the *Bayt al-Mal.*

There are seventeen cases in which the property of the deceased was escheated to the state, because there were some kind of state of private dues. Of these, in five cases the escheat was total and no part of the property was given back to the heirs. Their details are as follows:

On the death of Raja Jaswant Singh, the Governor of Gujarat, in 1679, his entire property was confiscated at the imperial order. It is confirmed in his case that he had huge amount of the state-dues against him. Najib Khan, a *mansabdar*, had borrowed twenty-eight thousand rupees from his servants to purchase horses and meet other requirements. After his death in 1681, his property valued at four thousand rupees was escheated and given to the creditors in proportion to their amount due to them. Furqat-Allah, a *mansabdar,* passed away in August, 1681, and at the royal order Mirza Fakhr, the *fawjdar* of Saharanpur, took twelve elephants of the deceased in his custody and sent them to the royal court. His liability to the state is not definite, but it is confirmed that he had not paid the salaries of the soldiers and that they were harassing his relatives for it. It cannot be ruled out that the elephants of the deceased were seized to adjust the arrears of the soldiers. The property of Diler Khan, an interim governor of the Deccan, who died in 1683, was ordered to be seized and deposited with the state-treasury. He had left behind two sons, but the confiscation was made to clear the state-dues. Sha'istah Khan, the Governor of Agra, died in 1694. The emperor ordered the escheat of his entire property, because he owed money to the state.

There are none cases which show that the property of the deceased official was confiscated to adjust the state-debt. The property which was left after deducting the debt was restored to the heirs of the deceased. A brief account of these cases will clear the point.

Shaykh Ibrahim Chisti, the Governor of Fatahpur, died in 1591. The property left by him included twenty-five crore rupees in case, elephants, horses and some other valuables. The cash was escheated to the state-treasury and the rest of the property was given to his sons and agents. Asaf Khan, the Governor of Punjab, died in 1641. Apart from two and half crore rupees which he left in cash, his house of Lahore had an estimated value of twenty lakh rupees. Out of the case, twenty lakh were distributed among his three sons and four daughters. The hose of Lahore was exclusively given to Dara Shikuh. In both the cases there is not clear indication to the any liability to the state. But is appears that the partial escheat was effected to clear state-dues standing against them.

Islam Khan, the Governor of the Deccan, died in 1647 leaving five sons. At the imperial order his property was temporarily escheated and after the state-debt was deducted the remainder was distributed among the heirs. 'Ali Mardan Khan, the Governor of Kashmir, died in 1657. His property was valued at one crore rupees. Out of it, fifty lakh rupees were taken by the state as he owed that amount to the state and the rest was left to be distributed among his heirs. In 1662, 'Ali Yar Beg a government officer, died during an expedition to Tilangana. His property was seized and information was sent to the royal court. The emperor ordered that after deduction of the state-debt, the rest of the property should be distributed among his heirs. The property of Rahmat 'Ali, the *divan-i buyutat*, who died in 1665, was confiscated by the state officials on the ground that he died in state debt. On representation of his son-in-law to the royal court, the emperor ordered that after deducting the debt and the salary arrears of the soldiers the remaining property he handed over to his sons. Pahar singh, a Rajput *zamindar* and *mansabdar* who died in 1670, left behind nine *muhars*, one hundred rupees and two elephants. The emperor ordered the confiscation of one elephant to the value of nine thousand rupees to adjust the state-debt and the return of the rest to his son. Lutf-Allah Khan, the Governor of Berar, had a state-debt of one lakh and seventy thousand rupees. After his death in 1702, the heirs were permitted to inherit his entire property. But when the *na'ib-i mir saman* made known his liability to the state, the property was taken back; the heirs were allowed to keep only houses and elephants. In 1707 'Abd al-Baqi, a *qil'ahdar*, died leaving some property valued at one lakh rupees. Some part of his property, particularly the cash, was embezzled by the local news reporter and state officials. On complaint of the widow, it was ordered that after deducting state-dues his property by given to his widow.

There are three cases in which the property of deceased officials was escheated on the ground that they owed money to the state. But the entire property was restored to their heirs on their promise to clear the state-dues as it is evident from the following cases: Islam Khan, the Governor of Malwa, passed away in 1676 leaving three lakh rupees, twenty thousand *ashrafis* in cash and some other property. As he had some state-dues, his property was to be escheated. But when his sons promised to clear the state-dues the entire property was restored to them without any deduction. After the death of Shaykh Muhyi al-Din, the *sadr* and *amin* of *jizyah* of Gujarat in 1687, his son assured the authorities that he would pay the state-debt of his father. On this assurancc he was allowed to inherit the property of his father. Rashid Khan, the *divan-i khalisah*, died in 1701. The whole property of the deceased was given to his son on condition of paying the state-debt of his father.

There are seven cases (out of the remaining twenty-eight cases) in which the property of the deceased officials was entirely returned to their heirs at the imperial order. But it appears that the property of the deceased was temporarily confiscated to ascertain their liability to the state. After they were declared to be free from any dues, their property was given to the heirs as may be shown from the detailed study of the cases. Khan-i Dawran Shah Beg Khan, the Governor of Thatta, passed away in 1620, leaving the property of the value of four lakh rupees. At the imperial order his entire property was entrusted to his four sons. I'timad al-Dawlah, the grand vizir of Jahangir, died in 1621. The property left by the deceased was handed over at the instance of the emperor to his daughter Nurjahan Begam in spite of the fact that he had also left several sons. Sa'adat Khan, an imperial slave and incharge of the betel consumed by the emperor, was put to death in 1644 for violating the imperial order that the betel should not be given to anyone else at the court. The emperor gave his entire property to his Christian wife, the only surviving heir. Raja Bithaldas, the *fawjdar* of Ajmer, passed away in 1651 leaving ten lakh rupees. At the imperial order this amount was given to his four sons. Shaykh 'Abd al-Wahjhab, *qadi al-qudat*, who died in 1675, left behind two lakh *ashrafis*, five lakh rupees and certain other property. The government did not interfere with his property and permitted its distribution among his sons. Muhammad Sami', a soldier, died in 1680 leaving one horse and some other valuables. By the order of the emperor his entire property was handed over to his heirs. Shuja'at Khan, the Governor of Ahmadabad, died in 1701, and his heirs were allowed to divide the property among themselves. The houses, elephants and other animals were, however, sent to the royal court. There is only one case from the reign of Awrangzib wherein the restoration of the property of the deceased took place on the basis of the rule formulated by Awrangzib that the property of those deceased officials whose heirs were in government service would not be escheated. Sayyid Idris Khan, the *fawjdar* of Naryad (Gujarat), died in 1691. The provincial *divan* sent his officials to escheat the property of the deceased. On being informed, Awrangzib issued instruction to the *divan* that the property of those officials whose heirs were in the government service should be given to the heirs of the deceased.

In the remaining twenty cases we come across references to the escheat of property but no apparent reason for it has been given. The liability of those officials to the state is also no mentioned. Only in a few cases it is clear that the heirs of the deceased were alive. However, on account of lack of information about the circumstances in which the property was escheated, no definite conclusion can be drawn regarding these cases. Most probably the escheat could have been made on either of the two well-known grounds (i.e., dying heirless or in state-debt).

In the light of the analysis of the above cases of escheat we can say that the Mughal Government usually confiscated the property of its officials after their demise in the application of this rule no distinction was made on religious grounds. It appears that there was no hard and fast rule for the working of the system. The property of the deceased officials was escheated generally for two reason—leaving no heir or having any dues to the state. If one died heir-less or one's heir were untraceable, one's property was taken by the government permanently.

But in case the state had any claims to settle with him then his property was temporarily escheated to settle the accounts. In such cases of the escheat, either the entire property of the deceased was restored to his heirs, or after deducting the state-debt the remaining property was restored to the heirs. The conclusion that the most important reason for the confiscation was the liability of the deceased to the state is substantiated by the fact that the property of the deceased was not touched by the state if his heirs took surety for payment of the state-debt or they happened to be government employees in accordance with the rule laid down in Awrangzib's time. Moreover, the view that the Mughal emperors did not claim ownership of the property of the state officials or nobles is further supported by the fact that the sources not only refer to the restoration of the deceased's property to his heirs but in relation to a number of the deceased officials they have also given details of its division among the heirs.

As regards the division of property of the deceased officials among their heirs there was found no uniform rule. In some cases the Islamic law of inheritance was adhered to while in other it was overlooked. Examples of both kinds are available in the contemporary sources. After debiting the state-dues from Islam Khan's property, Shahjahan ordered that the rest should be distributed among his heirs strictly in accordance with the *Shari'ah*. Mahabat Khan died in 1698 leaving only one grandson whose father had died earlier and there was no other surviving heir of the deceased. Awrangzib ordered the property of Mahabat Khan to be deposited with the *Bayt al-Mal* in which people in general had a share. The possessions of 'Ali Mardan Khan were ordered to be distributed among his heirs but here the Islamic law was disregarded in the division of the inheritance. He left behind four sons and ten daughters. Out of one crore rupees left by him, fifty lakh were paid to clear his debt. From the remaining fifty lakh, thirty lakh were given to Ibrahim Khan, the eldest son, and twenty lakh were distributed among his three sons and ten daughters. The unequal division of the property was obviously in violation of the Islamic law of inheritance. After the death of I'timad al-Dawlah his entire assets were handed over to his daughter. Nurjahan Begam, by the imperial order and the sons of the deceased were not given the legal share. The property of Shuja'at Khan was ordered to be distributed among his heirs. Those who inherited his property included one adopted son and one daughter. The former according to the *Shari'ah* was not entitled to inherit any share of the deceased's possessions, for in Islam an adopted son is not to be treated as a real son.

The property left by Raja Bithaldas amounting to ten lakh rupees was distributed at the imperial order among his four sons. It is sometimes maintained that the procedure of distribution was not in accordance with the Hindu law of inheritance. Here, it may be stated that as a matter of principle the Hindu law of inheritance, as explained by Manu, requires the equal distribution of property of a deceased father among his sons. But it appears from the detailed clauses of the same source of law that there was no rigidity in maintaining the equal distribution among sons and that he eldest son was entitled to get a bigger share in view of his seniority and responsibilities.

The entire property of Sa'adat Khan was entrusted by the order of Shahjahan to his widow who was a Christian. It is not clear that the deceased had left any other heir or not. Out of thc two and a half crore rupees left by Asaf Khan in cash, two crore and thirty lakh rupees were escheated to the state and the remaining twenty lakh were given to his three sons and four daughters, but the details of distribution are not available.

In view of the aforementioned cases of inheritance it may be concluded that the distribution of the property of the deceased officials was not always done by the Mughals in accordance with the Islamic law. Sometimes the emperor's opinion prevailed in contravention of the *Shari'ah* rulings. Irrespective of the fact that in the disposing of the deceased's property *Shari'ah* rules were followed or not, the cases of inheritance positively prove that the state official himself, and not the emperor, was the sole owner of his property. The above discussion further shows the hollowness of the opinion of foreign travellers that the state officials (nobles) during the Mughal empire were denied the right of private ownership.

4

Sunna's Role in Expounding Islamic Rulings and Refutation of Suspicions Cast on its Authenticity

SHEIKH ALY EL-KHAFIF

Meaning of 'Sunna'

Linguistically the word 'Sunna' means tradition, good it may be or bad. This generalisation is borne out by the Prophet's saying as reported by Muslim in his *Sahih* to the effect that he who institutes a good tradition 'sunna', in Islam, will get his own reward for it and the reward of those pursuing that tradition after him will be the same, without the latter's reward being reduced in the least. Conversely, he who institutes in Islam a bad tradition, its burden will be on him as well as the burden of those who act according to it without anything being subtracted from their burden. 'Sunna' is also meant to apply to God's verdicts as in the Almighty's words:

> 'That was Allah's way with those who passed away of old—-and the commandment of Allah is certain destiny.'

In the language of scholars of the Muslim canon law, the term 'Sunna' is used in the following contexts:

> As conceived by the expounders of the Prophet's traditions, and particularly those who wrote biographies, the term refers to all that is reported of the Prophet's sayings, doing, statements, behaviour, conduct, attributes, news, or moral qualities regardless of whether these have established legal rulings or otherwise, and

whether they occurred before or after the Prophet's mission.

In the language of Usulists, Ashabul Usul, or jurists, the word is attributed to the Prophet's sayings, acts, and statements denoting legal rulings. It is often used by jurisconsults in this sense, and applied by them also to all well-known acts of the Prophet which were neither an obligation nor a duty, such as acts done but not repeated by the Prophet. In this sense it corresponds to obligation. Through such generalisation it was said that performing two raka'as 'kneelings' in worship before the morning prayers is Sunna, like the two that follow the midday prayers. The term could also have been used by them to mean innovation such as in their saying 'divorce, according to Sunna, is such, and as such in innovation.' It is the Usulist's conception of Sunna that we shall adopt in the following study.

The word 'Hadith,' tradition or news might well be used for Sunna, but such usage should call for a clarification and an indication of any difference between them, for both Hadith and Tradition correspond to the general meaning given to them by contemporary interpreters, according to a majority of scholars. In the view of some contemporaries Hadith is more comprehensive than Sunna. To their mind Hadith comprises all that is reported of the Prophet's acts regardless of whether they constituted a mode of action or otherwise, while Sunna is used only to denote acts which entailed established rules of behaviour in the early years of the Prophet's mission.

Certain sayings therefore may be described as running counter to the Sunna is force, a situation which would call for their conciliation or judging one to be more likely than another. This difference between the two names could be seen in the words of Abdul Rahman Ben Mahdi. When asked about Sufian al-Thawri, Al-Auza'i and Malek, he said that Sufian Al-Thawri was a scholar of Hadith and not of Sunna and Malek was a scholar of both. As for news, it is used by contemporaries to denote what is reported of saying by the Prophet, his companions and his followers. It is regarded by the majority of scholars as synonymous with reports.

Generally speaking, such names were not so used as to determine their meanings and distinguish them from each other. Their usage by contemporaries and scholars alike was occasionally based on their common meaning and significance, their synonymity, as judged by some such scholars or as a result of the general or particular meanings common to them.

By explaining here the role of the Sunna in expounding Islamic rules and refuting the doubts cast on its authenticity and transmission, we mean only what is quoted of the Prophet's sayings, doings, or rulings in the sphere of legislation and reported by those who are apparently loyal to the Prophet's message. In this sense Sunna means those situations in the Prophet's life and conduct where he had the choice between two or more alternatives, and chose what he thought was proper. This is distinct from such acts of ordinary life as the prophet, by his very nature as a human being, performed without choice of distinction from other people, such as eating, drinking, sleeping, wearing, etc. The former acts and the means, ways and procedures connected therewith, thus constitute traditions of the Prophet, and come under the name of Sunna in the sense we have in mind, for he had a choice in them which entailed preference of one situation to another, the acts preferred and performed being acts which were deemed more beneficial to humanity and which could therefore be a source of guidance. wisdom and legislation. In other words, this would constitute legislative tradition. But such acts could have been performed through actions, tendency, or temporary inclination under certain circumstances, and thus represented what is known as individual standpoints or private discretion, 'Ijtihad,' as distinct from guidance, wisdom or legislative tradition. By Sunna, therefore, we mean only those acts and saying of the Prophet which provided guidance and legislation for the people; in other words, we have in mind only what was conveyed to the Prophet by revelation, other than the Qur'an, and that which the Prophet arrived at through contemplation and deduction which God duly approved. The sum-up of these acts in the Prophet's pronouncements in explanation of a creed, as instructions for prayers, guidance to a godly act, improvement of conduct or treatment, admonition to avoid vice or corruption or as warning against evil. All the Prophet's acts in these spheres represent Sunna and legislation which people are required to follow. All other irrelevant acts are not binding on people, even though they are regarded as part and parcel of Sunna. This is because such acts were performed by the Prophet as ordinary sayings or lawful doings to satisfy human needs, carnal instincts or habits. Accordingly, if the Prophet should demonstrate land cultivation and means of agricultural investment, to point out what is lawful in such acts, the rights attached to them,a nd their consequences, these shall constitute compulsory canon law. If such demonstration, on the other hand, be intended to show methods of cultivation, irrigation and the care of land produce as can be known by experience, such acts will constitute experimental guidance and a viewpoint derived from local conditions which could turn out to be right or wrong as is the case with ordinary people, and thus constitute no compulsory code. In such acts the Prophet could possibly err without being reminded of his error by revelation. A report by Muslim Bin Rafa' Bin Khadig bears this out. He said that the Prophet once arrived in Medina to find people engaged in pollinating palm trees. He advised them against the process, but when they acted upon his counsel, the fruit dropped. Told of the fact, the Prophet answered: "I am just a human being; if I command you concerning your religion, follow my command but orders based on my personal views are the orders of a human being." The point here is that what the Prophet tells of God is the religion which should be followed in obedience to God. Conversely, the Prophet's performance in worldly affairs is just his own thoughts and views inspired by intuition or gained through observation and deduction. Here he could be right or wrong like all other men. Other people might well have more experience and expert knowledge, and even see more clearly into things.

If the Prophet should make a military plan or place his army where he decides it to be stationed to the best advantage, such views of the Prophet shall be obeyable in the same measure as orders of other military leaders and commanders who give them after proper deliberation, which may prove correct or mistaken. Such orders of the Prophet do not represent divine revelation.

This is best illustrated by the attitude of the Prophet when he followed the advice of Al Hubab B. Al Mundhir who suggested their going to the well nearest the post of the enemy, instead of the well nearest Badr. Al Hubab said, "O Apostle of Allah, is this a place appointed for you by Allah, so that we may neither go forward nor backward, or is it simply a matter of opinion or military tactics and stratagem?" The Apostle answered, "Indeed, it is simply a matter of opinion and tactics and stratagem." So Al Hubab said "O Apostle of Allah, this is no place for you. Go up with the people till you come to the well nearest the post of the enemy, for I know the abudance and the extent of its water. Let us descent there and dry up all the other wells. Then we will build upon it a reservoir which we will fill with water to drink while they do not have anything to drink." Said the Apostle of Allah: "Verily, you have hit the mark."

The Prophet's commercial dealings should likewise not be regarded as revelation. An incident between the Prophet and Jabir Bin 'Abdullah provides an example in point. The Prophet offered that Jabir might sell him his camel, but the latter declined, saying that the camel was his sole property. The prophet did not deem Jabir's behaviour as blameable disobedience, showing thereby that his offer to Jabir was not of the nature of legislation inspired by revelation but only a wish which he expressed in the same way as other people did.

The same applies to the Prophet's directives for the remedy of certain ailments which were also not the outcome of revelation, but rather of knowledge and experience acquired from local conditions. Abu Daud quoted Osama Bin Shoraik as saying that he had seen the Prophet with his companions around him, all in a mood of deep contemplation, "I greeted him and sat down when Arabs converged on the place from all parts asking the Prophet if there was any remedy for their ailments. The Prophet answered in the affirmative, saying that God had prescribed a remedy for all ills except one, death."

Muslim and Abu Daud, upon the authority of Jabir, related that the Prophet once sent to Obey Bin Ka'ab, a physician, who cut off a vein in his body. 'Amr Bin Dinar also reported the Prophet to have visited a sick man, and advised his people to send for a physician, saying that there existed no disease for which God had not prescribed a remedy. Had medicine been law or legislation revealed to the Prophet, he would not have sent a physician to Obey, nor ordered another to examine the sick man, and would have asked the Arabs to approach him for treatment. If directives of medical nature had been revealed, they would have constituted guidance to means of remedy, but not the only means to this end: neither would they have impeded resort to other remedies. The same applies to the Prophet's food and attire, for such matters were influenced by local custom and tradition. Had the Prophet lived in another atmosphere, or had been a citizen of a country other than Arabia, both his attire and food would have been different. An incident serves as an illustration here. The Prophet was once offered a dabb (lizard) meat but he declined to eat it. Asked whether it was unlawful, the Prophet answered in the negative, but said that it did not exist in the land of his people and he therefore found it distasteful.

These and similar other acts such as the way the Prophet sat, slept, ate, and walked, were performed by the Prophet as a human being who lived and behaved as other people did in the daily routine of life, in satisfaction of their physical desires. In the daily routine of life the Prophet was no legislator: nor did his relevant acts of sayings constitute a canon law which people are required to follow. If such sayings were sometimes given as orders, this was only by way of guidance to the preservation of national tradition and the customs in practice which would have their appeal and charm in local environment but not in other localities with different customs and tradition. However, it any of the Prophet's acts in these matters were intended to preserve good or virtuous conduct, or to avert harm or corruption, they would constitute binding rules which the Prophet must have given through revelation and not as a result of established custom.

The above explanation would determine what is considered obeyable law (Sunna) whose role in expounding legal rulings is now engaging our attention.

Sunna's Role in Expounding Islamic Rulings

God's book and the Sunna of His Prophet are the main sources for the establishment and clarification of Islamic rulings, to which and other sources are subsidiaries. The Holy Book, however, is the first source and the structure on which the Sunna is based, and which is does not deviate from. It therefore provides the origin of all legislation as in God's words, "Verily, We reveal unto thee the Scripture with the truth, that thou mayst judge between mankind by that which Allah showeth thee" (Chapter 'Women'). "And We reveal the Scripture unto thee as an exposition of all things, and a guidance and a mercy and good tidings for those who have surrendered to Allah" (Chapter "The Bee"). "And this Qur'an hath been inspired in me, that I may warn therewith you and whomsoever it may reach" (Chapter `Cattle'). "Falsehood cannot come at it from before it or behind it. (It is) a revelation from the Wise, the Owner of Praise").

These are but some of the numerous relevant verses in the Holy Book. The Sunna served to interpret and explain the Qur'an as in the case of prayers, Zakat and the Pilgrimage which the Qur'an dealt with only in general terms and which had to be set out in detail through the Prophet's tradition, both verbal and practical. Of prayers the Prophet specified appointed times as well as the manner and all other matters related to worship. In the case of Zakat, he defined the forms of wealth on which it is due, and the amounts payable as Zakat. As regards Pilgrimage, he explained relevant acts, rites and behaviour. In such verses of the Qur'an "as after bequeathed legacy or debt" where God's rulings were given in absolute terms, the Sunna restricted bequests to persons other than heirs: in the Prophet's words, "No will for an heir." Other Qur'anic verses, being of a general nature, were specified by the Sunna as in God's words: "Lawful unto you are all beyond those mentioned, so that ye seek them with your wealth in honest wedlock, not debauchery" this occurred in its Qur'anic context after a reference to forbidden women. The generalisation here was made specific in the Sunna by excluding from it marriage to a woman in addition to her mother's or father's sister. Also excluded were those whose marriage is prohibited because of suckling, who were not mentioned in the verse just quoted; the Prophet said, "Shall be prohibited through suckling what is forbidden through blood relation."

The Sunna also detailed several acts forbidden to Muslims in such Qur'anic verses as God's words in the Chapter "The Heights": "Say: My lord forbiddeth only indecencies, such of them as are apparent and such as are within, and sin and wrongful oppression, and that ye associate with Allah that for which no warrant hath been revealed, and that ye tell concerning Allah that which ye know not.

But all such additions to Qur'an were made in perfect conformity with its general principles and basic rules. They revolved within the orbit of the Holy Qur'an, keeping to its limits, and thus became subservient to its provisions. Among the additions so made by the Sunna was the prohibition of having a woman as a wife together with her father's o mother's sister. Eating the flesh of wild asses was also forbidden, along with that of every beast with teeth, or bird of prey with claws, and such other creatures as came under the generalized principles of the Qur'an. He will make lawful for them all good things and prohibit for them only the foul. This is in substantiation of God's words in chapter 'The Bee'. 'And we have revealed the Scripture unto thee only that thou mayst explain unto them that wherein they differ, and (as) a guidance and a mercy for a people who believe," and in Chapter 'Abraham,' "And We never sent a messenger save with the language of his folk, that he might make (the message) clear from them," and also in Chapter 'The Bee': "And We have revealed unto thee the Remembrance that thou mayst explain to mankind that which hath been revealed for them and that haply they may reflect."

That the Book is given precedence over the Sunna is due to the certainty of its contents both as a whole and in detail, which is not the case with the Sunna. The latter could be deemed certain only if viewed as a whole and not in detail, for while the Prophet's sayings, acts and rulings on Muslim affairs are sure to have emanated from him, and constituted what is known as Sunna, no particular one of them could be taken for granted unless it has been commonly reported, which is rare. The Qur'an, therefore, should have an upper hand over the Sunna, being definitely certain and not supposed.

The Holy Book having thus precedence over the Sunna as a basis of the religion and a source of its basic principles, general rules and objectives, the Sunna becomes subservient to it and an interpretation of Qur'anic rulings without departure from its limits. It is reported that whenever a case was referred for advice to the companions of the Prophet, they used to consult the Holy Book in the first place and then the Sunna in the absence of a relevant Qur'anic ruling; and that they formed an opinion of their own if they failed to find the answer in the Sunna.

This procedure had received the Prophet's approbation, for upon sending Ma'az Bin Jabal as a judge to Yemen, the Prophet asked, "Upon what will you administer justice in Yemen?" Ma'az said, "On the strength of God's Book." The Prophet again asked "And if you fail to find a relevant ruling in the Qur'an?" Ma'az replied "I will judge by the Sunna of God's Emissary." "And if you again find no ruling there?" "I will then form an opinion," Ma'az replied. Whereupon the Prophet approvingly said, "Thanks be to God for having guided the messenger of God's Emissary to God's path." (Related by Ahmad Al-Tirmizi Al-Darimi, and Al-Bayhaqi in the *Madkhal*, Ibn Sa'ad in *Al-Tabakat*, and Ibn `Abdul-Barr).

This approach by the companions of the Prophet does not mean that their consultation of the Holy Book in search of relevant rulings excluded reference to the Sunna, for such consultation entailed by necessity a relevant reference to such rulings as might have been given by the Prophet concerning the case at issue. This, no doubt, was the intention of Ma'az when he said, "I will judge upon the strength of God's Book," for his judgment could not have been in line with God's Book unless it was given in conformity with the meaning and intention of the Book as often clarified in the Sunna. If the latter were abandoned, no such judgment could be said to have been given in accordance with God's revealed world but rather in contradiction thereto.

This should be out understanding of the attitude of the Prophet's companions in seeking some ruling on a certain situation. They looked such a ruling up in the Holy Book while not overlooking the provision of the Sunna as an indispensable interpretation of such rules. The Sunna, furthermore, served to clear up the meaning where the context is open to more than one interpretation. Absolute stipulations were sometimes restricted by the Sunna and general ones made specific. Examples in point include Sunna's clarification of the meaning underlying the word 'hand' in the verse on theft, the persons for whom bequests may validly be made, and the extent of such bequests in the verse on

Wills and those who should suffer punishment for adultery, etc.

It will be seen from the foregoing remarks that the Sunna was designed to interpret the Qur'an, and was therefore subservient to it, revolving in its orbit, and strictly adhering to its principles: Being thus in keeping with the Book, the Sunna could not be said to have annulled the Qur'an. About this view advocated by a school of thought headed by Al-Shafei, contradictory statements have been made by a majority of scholars to the effect that the Book in some of its rulings had been annulled by the Sunna. In support of their argument they refer to God's words on bequest. "It is prescribed for you, when one of you approacheth death, if he leave wealth, that he bequeath unto parents and near relatives in kindness. (This is) a duty for all those who ward off (evil). And whosoever changeth (the will) after he hath heard it, the sin thereof is only upon those who change it. Verily, Allah is Hearer, Knower," and say that this was annulled by the Prophet's saying "No bequest for a Heir," and the Qur'anic verse on adulterers' flogging: "The adulterer and the adulteress, scourge ye each one of them (with) a hundred stripes; And let not pity for the twain withhold you from obedience to Allah, if you believe in Allah and the Last Day," was abrogated by the Prophet's sayings on lashing as reported in *Al-Mohassan*. Opposers of the opinion see no evidence in such verses that the Qur'an could be abrogated by the Sunna, nor that such abrogation had actually taken place. This was held by several scholars, including Al-Shafei, most of his companions, and many Usulists. It is also the doctrine of the rationalist school of thought, and was reported by Ahmed. It could possibly be also the opinion of most of those who had held the view on the abrogability of the Qur'an by the Sunna in an intellectual, as distinct from actual, sense. For even the scholars who defended the view made it a condition that the annulling provisions of the sunna should have been commonly reported; instead, they are rare, highly doubtful and controversial. There could thus be no provision in the Sunna which would validly abrogate the Qur'an, and any investigation into this matter would be of little utility, as al-Shafei had said.

As for scholars who treated the type of Hadith called Mashhoor (famous) of the Sunna as equivalent to commonly reported Hadith concerning the abrogability of the Qur'an—a view attributed to the

Hanafite—they were grossly mistaken as it would be confirmed by reference to the Principles of Sunna (Usul-e-Hadith).

This goes to confirm the soundness of our assertion that the Sunna is but a subordinate and an interpreter of the Book, and that it has enacted no new legislation, a fact which was indicated by the Book in general terms, as in God's words; "We have neglected nothing in the Book (of our Decrees) (Chapter 'Cattle' No. 38). And we have revealed the Scripture unto thee only that thou mayst explain unto them that wherein they differ, and (as) a guidance, and mercy for people who believe" 'Bee' No. 64.

It follows that in this matter of such rulings as may be given in contradiction to the Qur'an, its principles, and provisions validly neglected as held by Traditionists the Qur'an should be given precedence over them. This being the case, God has ordained the obedience of His Messenger, His orders in this regard having been given in such manner, fashion and tone as confirmed His injunction to this effect. These orders were explicitly passed in many a Qur'anic verse such as:

"Obey Allah, and Obey the Messenger."

Chapter 'Women' No. 59.

"O ye who believe! Obey Allah and His messenger,"

Chapter 'Spoils of War' No. 26.

"Obey the messenger, that haply ye may find mercy",

Chapter 'Light' No. 56.

"And whatsoever the messenger giveth you, take it. And whatsoever he forbiddeth, abstain (from it),"

Chapter 'Exile' No. 7.

"Whoso obeyeth Allah and the messenger, they are with those unto whom Allah has shown favour, of the Prophets and the saints and the martyrs and the righteous. The best of company are they."

Chapter 'Women' No. 69.

"Whoso obeyeth the messenger obeyeth Allah,"

Chapter 'Women' No. 80.

Of the Prophet, God also said,

"He will enjoin on them that which is right and forbid them that which is wrong. He will make lawful for them all good things and prohibit for them only the foul; and he will relieve them of their burden and the fetters that they used to wear."

Chapter 'The Heights' No. 157.

The order was also given in conjunction with caution for prospective offenders as in the divine verse:

"And let those who conspire to evade orders beware lest grief or painful punishment befall them.

Chapter 'Light' No. 63.

"And it becometh not a believing man or a believing woman, when Allah and His messenger have decided an affair (for them), that they should (after that) claim any say in their affair, and whose is rebellious to Allah and His messenger, he verily goeth astray in error manifest.

Chapter 'The Clans' No. 36.

God the Almighty has even made it a pre-requisite of true faith that those who visit the Prophet on some business should not leave without permission. He said, "They only are the true believers who believe in Allah and His messenger and, when they are with him on some common errand, go not away until they have asked leave of him."

Chapter 'Light' No. 62.

Several other verses may be quoted to this effect, which go to prove that the Sunna provided the second source of both the Usul Fiqh (Jurisprudence), and of the Muslim Canon Law, in the days of the Prophet and after his death. It has remained as such up to the present day, and will continue to be so until the Day of Recokoning.

Sunna is Binding

Now that the Sunna has been shown as a principle of the Religion (Jurisprudence) and the second source of Muslim legislation, it is incumbent on Muslims to act upon it in demonstration of their obedience to God and His messenger. Its abandonment, on the other hand, would be a refutation of God's Book, and a rejection of God's ordinance as set out in the verses we have just quoted. This represents the unanimous attitude and practice of Muslims at the time of the Prophet and in subsequent eras, and should undoubtedly be out stand in relation to the Sunna in general, and to such of its individual elements as are commonly reported. For the former, could safely be attributed to the Prophet, while individual reports could not be judged as having actually emanated from him unless they are commonly confirmed, otherwise they cannot be ascertained, but the probability of their authenticity or otherwise may be presumed through study and the consideration of available evidence in the light of controls prescribed by the scholars of the Hadith, and established by news reporting and verification rules.

A researcher who ultimately deems a report to have most probably emanated from the Prophet, and over whose judgment this conclusion prevails together with the likehood that the report had not been annulled, should act upon it. If a different conclusion be reached, the report will not be binding upon him. This is because a ruling derives its compulsion from presumption and not from its certainty. Many scholars did not act upon reports they themselves had related, because they suspected their authenticity or thought that the reports had probably been annulled. Other scholars would act upon them, nevertheless. Abu Bakr Al-Abhari found over seventy sayings attributed to the Prophet in Malik's records, which Malik himself had not acted upon, though he had conveyed them.

Consequently, our intention here is to answer suspicious cast on the Sunna and its authenticity in general, and not in relation to a certain Hadith on which are doubts cast on or arguments made against a particular news, proof, of source constituting partial issues. The arguments thus involved cannot be deemed as directed against Sunna as a binding principle of the Muslim canon law. Answers to them were the subject of independent books and papers of varying lengths, and could not be accommodated in research such as ours. The purpose here, therefore, is to refute the suspicions being cast on Sunna as a basis and an authoritative source of the religion and to its transmission as a proper means of conveying it to us as produced by the Prophet.

The following is a review of doubts and suspicions cast on the Sunna in contemporary times. Some of them will be found to bear on the way Sunna was related, while others stress the necessity of applying it in a permanent manner to that which does not change with the change of time or people.

Arguments against Transmission of Sunna

Reference has already been made to the fact that Hadith is binding once it is found to have been correctly attributed to the Prophet, whether this conclusion is arrived at through conviction or supposition.

Scholars of the Hadith paid such attention to verifying the authenticity or otherwise of reports so attributed that the biased people and the critics failed to detect the slightest gap through which they would direct their criticism at the bases and rules laid for the testing of sources and their reporters, and subsequently at the ruling based thereon which helped in testing the power and weakness of the different Hadiths, and the identification of those genuine among them. Such rules and bases were the outcome of constant research into the status and condition of reporters, their life history, sources, contemporaries, accuracy, truth, or otherwise, and other attributes. No people has excelled the Arabs in accurate investigation into such matters, or in formulation of rules and bases for the judgment of news and reports. It follows that all criticism by orientalists and critics, prejudiced they be or otherwise their followers and those deluded by their thoughts, was mostly directed to the text. Critics alleged that the scholars of the Hadith did not pay as much attention to the text as to the sources, and that the rules they laid down for the appraisal of texts were deficient and thus failed to distinguish the genuine from the ungenuine, due to the confidence placed in reporters. In substantiation of their views they quote specimens of the Hadith as reported in the Sihah, which they deemed unacceptable to their minds, or contradictory to the facts and cases they had accepted as genuine. A report they quoted in this context was the one conveyed by Bukhari upon the authority of 'Amer ben Sa'ad who quoted his father as saying. "The Prophet on whom be God's Peace and Blessings," said He who eats several pressed dates every morning could not be harmed by poison or magic in that day till night. In another version the number of dates is given at seven, which Muslim, quoting Sa'is Ben Abi El-'As, confirmed.

Muslim, upon the authority of Anas Ben Malik, also reported a man to have asked the Prophet when the day of judgment would come. The Prophet kept silent for a while and then, looking at a boy standing beside the questioner, said, "This boy will not have reached old age when the hour will struck." Anas, commenting, said the boy was the same age as he. (Anas died in Hegira year 93).

This criticism was grossly unjust, however. It underestimated the efforts made by Sunna scholars in judging Hadith from the angle of the text, though their efforts to test detailed material were inferior to those exerted to judge sources or Isnad (witness-chain). But this was not due to deficiency or negligence in considering the text, but rather to the fact that texts are not so varied and diversified as the sources. This led to multiple studies and research on sources without, however, overlooking the study of texts, the elements they should fulfil as proof of authenticity, and what signs and other evidence they should be clear of, lest they should be identified as not genuine. Among such signs are:

1. Prosaic or Proof Meaning

In this context, Al-Hafez Bin Hajar said a prosaic meaning of a Hadith indicates its status even though such prosaic meaning does not coincide with prosaic style, for the Religion is all beauties and shorn of weaknesses.

2. Absurd Meaning

Such as in cases where a Hadith conflicts with sound judgment and does not lend itself to interpretation, also where it clashes with obvious facts or admitted general rules of judgment of ethics, and where it calls for the satisfaction of lust or vicious instincts or runs counter to feelings, perceptions, established facts of history or the universe, the obvious facts of medicine, or the attributes of God or His Emissaries, or where it contains absurdities no sensible man would accept. In this Ibn Al-Jawzi said, "If you come across some Hadith which conflicts with common sense or principles, know that it is not genuine. In *Mahsul* he said, "Every report is not true which conveys vice, does not lend itself to interpretation or is lacking in that which removes such vicious impressions."

3. Contradiction with the Book or the Sunna, Commonly or Unanimously Reported

Ibn Qayyem Al Jawzieh here said, "Of means whereby some Hadith could be ascertained as ungenuine, is its contradiction with the explicit meaning of the Holy Qur'an." An example of this is the Hadith giving the duration of the universe as 7000 years which, he said, clashed with God's words.

'Say: Knowledge thereof (of the hour) is with my Lord only' 7:/ 86 'With Him is knowledge of the Hour, (6/186),

4. Contradiction with Established Historical Facts

Such as those reported by Muslim, quoting Abu-Wail; he said Ibn Mas'ud turned up at Saffeen, and on seeing him, Abu Naim asked if he had come back to life, Ibn Mas'ud had died earlier.

A similar report is about the Prophet having waived the tribute payable by the people of Khaybar, and relieved them of conscription as certified by Sa'ad Ibn Ma'az and written by Mu'awyieh Ibn Abi-Sufian. This is despite the fact that tribute was not in force at the time Khaybar was conquered. The verse on tribute was revealed after Tabbuk; Sa'ad also had died beforehand in the battle of Al-Khandaq, 'the Ditch,' and Mu'awyieh embraced Islam in the year of the conquest of Mecca.

5. Cases where a Hadith is related by a reporter of the type of an extremist or a fanatic in support of his doctrine such as those emanating from the followers of theological doctrines in favour their beliefs or the belief of their leader, for example:

"He who raises his hands in prayers, will render his prayers null and void," and "Gargling and inhaling three times for the dead are an ordinance of God," and "He who says the Qur'an is created commits idolatry."

6. Promise of handsome reward for slight deeds, or threat of severe punishment for insignificant acts stated by story-tellers for a reward for certain actions and punishments for certain offences and crimes.

7. A Hadith whose transmission would have given some advantage to the transmitter would have been reported only by one transmitter. On this basis, the Sunnites do not believe in the Hadith of the pool of Khumm declaring 'Aly's succession to the Caliphate.

These, no doubt, are sound and perfect bases for distinguishing genuine Hadith from the ungenuine, which no fair-minded person would challenge as inadequate or insufficient. Nevertheless, scholars of the Hadith are not contented with them in their criticism of texts, for they based their judgments also on the existence or otherwise of any weakness, abnormality, poor structure or irregularities which the scholars of the Hadith committed in their works.

We have already seen that the rules and measures laid down to detect any soundness or weakness in the Hadith were not designed to provide conclusive proofs that the sayings at issue had actually emanated from the Prophet, but rather to establish their genuineness to be more likely. Hence the conception that individually-reported Hadiths, proven as genuine, might turn out to be not so. This, however, is a poor probability which should not impede action as set out before. Advocates of this view say it was imperative to base the criticism of the texts on other principles to which the scholars of Hadith paid no attention, namely:

1. Consistency of the sayings attributed to the Prophet with the circumstance in which they emanated, and their conformity with established historical facts.
2. The absence from the Hadith of philosophical interpretations

contrary to what is familiar of the Prophet's sayings and also the absence of theological statements on conditions and essentials of worship such as were not known at the time of the Prophet.

3. Conformity with facts and the absence of any political or psychological motives for the transmission of the Hadith.

These are the points raised in the criticism levelled against the rules laid down to test the genuineness of the reported Hadith.

Critics, through careful scrutiny, should have noticed that all the points they raise had already been covered by such rules. Scholars refuted, for instance, the Hadith on the Prophet's entry into a bath on the strength of the fact that no such incident had taken place, for baths were not known in the Hedjaz at the time of the Prophet. Other reports were also repudiated for their non-conformity with facts such as: "There will be no birth after one hundred (years) for which God has any need," and "Egg plants are a remedy for all pains."

Reports by extremist Sheites on Caliph 'Aly's merit, and by fanatical Bakrites on the merits of Caliphs Abu Bakr, were similarly repudiated because of the political motive involved. They regarded in the same light a Hadith quoting the Prophet as saying, "I developed ophthalmia and on complaining to Gabriel he advised that I should constantly look into the Book." The repudiation here was due to inconsistency with conditions under which the Hadith is claimed to have been uttered for there were no bound copies of the Qur'an at the time of the Prophet.

Other sayings were likewise rejected for the psychological motives behind them, or the occurrence in them of judicial terms and expressions which were not used in the Prophet's days.

However, certain remarks may be made in connection with the rules or principles for the scrutiny of Hadith.

a. Many of these rules are based on personel appreciation, judgment and understanding, and with the difference in approach, talents and reasoning between one person and another, it was only natural that different rulings should be given. Thus the application of such principles to the various sayings should give different results in line with the different standpoints of those who apply them.

The application of such measures and principles is contingent upon the fact that the interpretation of a Hadith within the scope of its possible shades of meanings or in a metaphorical sense should not be such as to exclude it from the sphere of the application of such rules. Therefore, if a Hadith stands an interpretation which excludes it from the sphere of that application, the rules should not be applied to it; like-wise, if the metaphorical significance given to it should isolate it from those principles, they too should not be deemed applicable. The interpretation of a Hadith and its application to it in a metaphorical sense, are subjects where people hold different views. They may be accepted by some and get rejected by others. Therefore, judgments on a Hadith should differ according to persons and their divergent views.

The application of the rules is based on understanding a Hadith in such a way as would bring it within the reach of such rules. People would hold different views also in this context, for while one would regard a Hadith as reasonable, of sound meaning and in line with the accepted principles, another might hold a different opinion about it.

A Hadith of sound Isnad, and reported by people of authority, is likely to have emanated from the Prophet. The fact that the prophet is not like other people in his knowledge, wisdom, and relation with God, entails that the measures of criticism applied to his traditions should be different from those applicable to other people. For the Prophet received revelation from God, and was given access to many secrets of the Unknown which He had kept from other people. This means that the Prophet's judgment is superior to that of other man; so are his sayings and rulings which could possibly have been given a level beyond people's understanding in any age but whose secrets may be unravelled at a later time. Hence common people with their inferior faculties should not assume the authority of judging the soundness of the Prophet's pronouncements which they might be mentally incapable of understanding. Neither should their failure to understand, through inferior intellect or deficient knowledge, be taken as evidence of the invention of a certain Hadith. Therefore, if some Hadith should mention characteristics of a certain plant, for instance, or news of a future happening, as yet unknown to mankind, this should not be treated as evidence of ungenuineness.

For all these reasons, scholars applied the said rules within narrow limits, and only where such application was deemed expedient and where an interpretation was considered impossible without it.

Their procedure here was also governed by their own judgments with due regard to the soundness of relevant Isnad, and the absence of all doubts about their inferior intellect or poor knowledge. Nevertheless, they often differed because of divergent viewpoints and, subsequently, of their judgments on certain Hadiths. What some of them held to be genuine was not so considered by others, with the result that the inclusion of certain traditions in the reliable books of traditions was criticised on the above-mentioned lines.

It is noteworthy that such criticism did not go beyond certain sayings which were found to have no support in the principles or fundamental rules of the religion; nor could their non-observance be deemed as contradictory to the obligation of abiding by the Prophet's traditions. For such obligations are incumbent only where the traditions are genuine. What the scholars have laid down in the way of rules and measures to judge texts and sources is apt, when properly applied, to distinguish, the genuine from the ungenuine, and once a Hadith was judged as likely to be genuine, it had be followed. The criticism here could not be deemed to have been levelled against Tradition or the obligation to observe it where the texts and Isnad are judged as sound and proper, for the mere thought of a text as likely to be genuine would render it applicable.

5

The Shari'a

[Abstract: Traces development of the conceptual framework refornistic efforts and the applications.]

Preliminary

The most important and comprehensive concept for describing Islam *as* a *function* is the concept of the Shari'a or 'Shar'. This word originally means 'the path or the road leading to the water', i.e., a way to very source of life. The verb *shara'a* means literally 'to chalk out or mark out a clear road to water.' In its religious usage, from the earliest period, it has meant 'the highway of good life', i.e. religious values, expressed functionally and in concrete terms, to direct man's life. It differs from the term 'Sunna' in that the subject of the Sunna 'leads the way' by actual example and, therefore, his action as such is of the same kind as those who follow him in accepting the example, whereas the subject of Shar' shows or ordains the way and is, therefore, none else than God, the source of religious values.

The correlate of Shari'a is Din, which literally means 'submission', 'following'. Whereas Shari's is the ordaining of the Way and its proper subject is God, Din is the following of that Way and its subject is man. It is in this correlative sense that the Qur'an says: God 'hath ordained for you a Way-to-be-followed, and again 'Do they, then, have any partners of God who have ordained for them the path-to-be-followed?' But if we abstract from the Divine and the human points of reference, Shari's and Din would be identical as far as the 'Way' and its content are concerned. One may, therefore, so far as the Qur'anic idiom goes, speak of Shari's and Din interchangeably so far as the content of religion is concerned. But since the basic mood of the is moral exhortation to man, i.e. to follow, submit and seek, assuming that the 'Way' for a genuine seeker 'is there', the terms Din the its almost equivalent Islam are used far more frequently in it than the term Shari'a. For the Muslim Community, however, which had so submitted, the primary task was to explain the Shari's—the 'Way' or the 'Command of God'.

From the very beginning, a definite practical intent was part of the concept of the Shari'a: it is The Way, ordained by God, wherein man it to conduct his life in order to realize the Divine Will. It is a practical concept having to do with conduct as such. But it includes all behaviour—spiritual, mental and physical. Thus it comprehends both faith and practice: assent to or belief in one God is part of the Shari'a just as are the religious duties of prayer and fasting, etc. Further, all legal and social transactions as well as all personal behaviour, is subsumed under the Shari'a as the comprehensive principle of the *total way of life*. But the problem is: how is the Shari's *to be known*?

In the earliest period after the Prophet, two sources or methods were recognized for the explanation of the Shari'a. On the one hand was the traditional source, the authoritative 'given' - i.e. the Qur'an and the Sunna of the Prophet which must serve as the base. But since the 'given' could obviously not suffice for the developing needs of succeeding generations, the second principle of human intelligence and understanding was recognized almost from the outset. The first principle was called 'learning' (Arabic: *ilm*, not 'knowledge' as it has been sometimes rendered); the second was called 'understanding' or 'comprehension' (Arabic *fiqh*).

Texts are not infrequent from this period drawing this contrasted but complementary distinction between 'learning' and 'understanding' and one often meets with such passages as 'so-and-so is good in '*ilm* but not so good in *fiqh*', or 'so-and-so excels both in '*ilm*—i.e. in his learning in traditions and the Qur'an—and in *fiqh*—i.e. in his capacity to understand the traditional "given" and draw further deductions from it'. Now *fiqh* in this period is nothing other than the *ra'y* or the 'personal considered opinion.' This brings out the contrast between the *'ilm* and the *fiqh* in another form. For whereas *'ilm* is something unshakably given and objective, *fiqh* is something subjective, since it represents the personal understanding of a scholar. This give us one further point of contrast: whereas *'ilm* is both a process of learning and refers to an objective, organized and disciplined body of data, *fiqh,* at this stage, is not the name of a particular discipline or objective system, but only the name of a *process* or activity of understanding and deducing.

But although *fiqh* and *'ilm* are thus distinguished as ways or avenues of knowledge, they are not distinct as regards their subject-matter which is identical. They are indeed applied universally to entire range of knowledge. Thus, there is an *'ilm* of the Arabic language (i.e., learning of the traditional philological material) as well as an *'ilm* of religion; and equally, there is a *fiqh* or appreciation of this *'ilm* as well as a *fiqh* or religious matters. Gradually, however, as the study of religious matters became preponderant, *fiqh* came to be restricted to the religious field. But still the whole range of religious thought was *fiqh*—belief as well as practice, dogma as well as law. Thus, a book attributed to the founder of the Hanafi school, Abu Hanifa (d. 150/767), entitled *The Greater Fiqh*, is devoted entirely to dogmatic and theological questions.

In this early phase, which roughly extended to the middle of the 2nd/8th century, the *ensemble* of traditional learning and the exercise of free, individual reasoning upon it produced religious knowledge. But it is both interesting and important, to note that the term Shari'a was seldom, if ever, applied to the result of this activity which was most usually called Din and the sum of knowledge in which it was established, 'knowledge of the Din'. And this is the case not only with reference to the dogma but also with regard to the law. The term Shari'a (used in this period especially in the plural) is very rare and then it is used concerning certain specific injunctions of the Qur'an. This contrasts strikingly with the overwhelming preponderance of the term Shari'a in later Islam. This could, of course, be a pure accident and in so far as the concrete content of both Din and Shari'a, as we have indicated above, is identical, may even seem unimportant. But there are two significant considerations which probably furnish the answer, one religious and the other, allied to the former, historical.

As for the religious factor, we have noted at the outset that the Qur'an, anxious to regulate the attitude of the believer, speaks much more of Din, Imam (faith) and Islam than of Shari'a. So long as the impulse of the Qur'an was fresh and lively, the Muslim was more likely to stress his effort to submit to and follow God's guidance. Under this attitude, whatever the Muslim 'understood' of God's Shari'a, he would naturally regard as his attempt at Din rather than claim it as Shari'a from God. For it is up to God to know whether it is really Shari'a, i.e. His Will, or not. Secondly, as a historical fact, as we have reiterated, *fiqh* or 'understanding' was a process rather than a consolidated body of knowledge and it was personal, free and somewhat subjective rather than an objective discipline. It would be impossible for any single person to claim that the result of *his* thought was the unique content of the Shari'a. The task of spelling out the Shari'a should rather devolve upon the Community as a whole, through the guidance of the 'Ulama'.

In the next phase, which may be taken to begin around the middle of the 2nd/8th century, this is precisely what happened. The rise and development of that mechanism which constitutes the methodology of Islam. We have pointed out that in this mechanism for 'understanding' the Word of God and the exposition of that Word in the Sunna, the place of over-riding paramountcy is occupied by the institution of Ijma' or the consensus of the Community. Our present argument gives the rationale of the historical fact of this development and shows that this development occurred by the necessity of an inner logic of the religious history of Islam. This does not deny the influence of foreign elements and especially the influence of certain precepts of Roman Law, much discussed by scholars, but insists that essentially the genesis and the structural character of Islamic methodology are to be explained on internal Islamic grounds rather than on the basis of foreign influences.

With the establishment of Islamic methodology (i.e. interrelationship of Sunna, *ijtihad* and Ijma') a radical change took place in the nature of *fiqh* which passed from being a personal activity to mean a structured discipline and its resultant body of knowledge. This body of knowledge was thus standardized and established as an objective system. *Fiqh became an 'ilm.* Whereas in the first state one used to say 'one should *exercise fiqh* ("understanding")', the proper thing to say now was 'one should "learn" or "study" *fiqh*. But what was the content of this *Fiqh* (which, as a discipline or science, we write here with a capital 'F')?

At the same time when the system of Islamic methodology was fully developed, it seems to have become restricted to law and jurisprudence. *Fiqh* became identified with the science of law. It does not seem to the present writer that the explanation sometimes advanced—viz. That the term *fiqh* was adopted to correspond to the *jurisprudentia* of the Roman Law—explains this change adequately. The change, indeed, was so far-reaching and affected the future development of religion so profoundly that a purely philological explanation such as the one suggested seems utterly trivial. Let us, therefore, seek an answer in the events that occurred in Islam itself.

We have noticed earlier in this chapter that in the first stage *fiqh* and *'ilm* both applied to the whole of the religious field and that dogma, morals, law were all embraced by these two terms. From the very beginning, however, there is to be seen a preoccupation with law rather than way theology. It may be said that this was because curiosity in theological and purely moral issues was not yet fully aroused as it became in the 2nd/8th century. But there is also the fact that the actual state of affairs required legal thinking as an immediate desideratum. And although this legal thought has, from the outset, a school-room character, there is little doubt that the material on which it operated was the concretely given situation of legal practice in a real administrative and judicial environment.

But besides these factors, perhaps the most crucial was the native tendency amounting almost to reticence towards purely theological issues. An unconscious type of reasoning lies behind the attitude which looks upon discussions about the nature of God as being at best foolhardy adventures. It is to be noted that the Qur'an itself contains only a modicum of theological doctrine, the minimal essential for religion. It is certain that those traditions which positively discourage theological speculation such as 'Do not cogitate on God but on the creation of God' or 'Earlier communities perished because they plunged into discussions of *qadar* (Divine Will)' express the most ancient attitudes of Muslims, even if they do not verbally go back to the Prophet. It is almost sinful to exercise human reason on God. This attitude, as we have seen in the previous chapter, was kept intact by the Ahl al-Hadith throughout the ages. But when the throbs of moral and theological speculation were generated with full energy within the body of Islam, *fiqh* and Shari'a were isolated from rationalism as such, which came to be denoted by the term *'aql.*

In the pre-speculative and pre-controversy period, reason (*fiqh*) and tradition (*'ilm*) were regarded as complementary and there is no doubt that in the ancient Muslim attitude reason and revelation or reason and Shari'a were not distinct. But in the later 2nd/8th and 3rd/9th centuries, the Mu'tazila rationalists introduced an opposition between '*aql* (reason) and *sam* (tradition or authority) or Shari'a. By this time law had been fixed by Ijma' and the methodology of legislation had been established. It had, thereby, become a part of authority or tradition, bringing about a change in the concept *figh*, as we have seen. The Mu'tazila, in general, accepted this legal structure, together with such moral precepts and maxims as it contained as part and parcel of the established authority (*sam'* or *shar'*). But they declared both theology and basic moral principles to be fit objects for the human reason to investigate; Good and bad, they held, was not *shar'i* or ordained by Divine law but *'aqli* or rational (cf. the Stoic distinction between that which is 'by nature' and that which is 'ordained' God has forbidden killing because it is bad; it is not bad because God has forbidden it.

The Mu'tazila did not, then, question the binding and divinely ordained character of the law but restricted the concept of the Shari'a to it and in a real sense isolated it from the basic moral principles of right and wrong and from theological metaphysics wherein they advocated almost untrammelled freedom for human reason. The right wing of the orthodoxy opposed this. They exerted themselves to keep ethics and theology as well as law within the concept of the Shari's. As for reason, they accentuated the Power and Will and God as opposed to the Mu'tazilite idea of Divine justice, as outlined in the last chapter. They did not defend the thesis that God's actions are irrational or non-rational but that what God ought to do cannot be dictated by human reason and that from a religious point of view it is wisest to attribute God's actions to His Will. The Mu'tazilite offensive forced the extreme wing of orthodoxy, therefore, to change the pre-controversial attitude of ancient Islam and explicity to reject human reason.

In the synthesis of the orthodox Ash'arite *kalam* which emerged in the 4th/10th century, a compromise was undoubtedly attempted from this point of view. All the *practical* issues, including law and ethics, that impinge on actual, concrete life were given to the authority of the Shari'a or the Divine Commandment, but all purely theological and metaphysical issues were given to *'aql* (reason). One very fundamental result of this development was the isolation of theology from law and morality. This produced a sharp distinction between Shari'a and Din which in the beginning were identical, as we have argued early on in this chapter. Theology was installed as 'Principles of Religion' (*Usul al-Din*), moral and legal precepts as the Shari'a. This is clearly brought out by the following passage from al-Ash'ari:

> (The early generations) have discussed and disputed about such matters as arose at that time concerning Din from for side of the Shari'a (i.e. law)... like the legal duties... such as punishments and divorce which are too numerous to mention here...

.....Now, these are legal matters which pertain to details of life and which they (i.e. the early generations) brought under the Shari'a which concerns itself with the detailed conduct of life (*furu*) and hence can never be comprehended except on the authority that comes from the Prophets. But as for the matters that arise in the field of the principles for the determination of questions (of Faith) every intelligent Muslim must refer these to the general and agreed principles founded upon reason, sense-experience and immediate knowledge, etc. Thus the questions of details of the Shari's (i.e. law), which are based on traditional authority, must be referred to the principles of the Shari'a whose source is traditional authority, whereas questions arising out of reason and experience must be referred to their own bases, and authority and reason must never be mixed up.

The re-inclusion of morality under Shari'a, against the Mu'tazila, was based on an attempt to show that reason, in fact, yielded no universal moral principles. The state of natural rationality, in a contention not unlike Hobbes, led to a state of *bellum omnium contra omnes* wherein each individual regards that as 'good' which is in conformity with his own desires and the opposite of this as bad. Even the so-called universal proposition of rational ethics, e.g. 'Telling lies is bad' was said to derive its pseudo-universality from the fact that this dictum is applicable in *most*, not all cases. The Mu'tazila strongly protested against this denial of universality of rationalistic ethics:

> Your discourse comes to this: that (rational) 'good' and 'bad' are reducible to being conducive to and thwarting desires. But we see that a rational being regards as good that wherein he does not (necessarily) see any benefit and (sometimes) regards as bad that wherein he may find benefit .. If someone sees a man or an animal on the verge of perishing, he regards it as good to save him.. Although not believing in the Shari'a and even when he does not expect any benefit from this in this world, and even though this may occur in a place where there is nobody to see him and praise him for doing so. We may indeed suppose the absence of every (selfish) motive... It is clear then that 'good' and 'bad' have a meaning other than what you have described.

In his reply, al-Ghazali vigorously defends his utilitarian account of rationalist ethich by undertaking a psychological analysis of motivation. The rescuer, he insists, is primarily led to save a living being in danger, because if he does not do so this would hurt his own natural strong feelings of compassion: he is thus satisfying himself by rescuing the person in danger. Further, he thinks that if he himself were in danger and a person capable of rescuing him did not do so, he would not like this. And so on. But if pure reason in its natural state is inducing capable of yielding moral principles, still less is it capable of producing positive obligations (*wajibat*). Both must flow from the Shari'a or the divinely ordained Path and al-Ghazali concludes decisively, 'No obligations flow from reason but from the Shari'a.

Thus, morality and law constitute Shari'a. But what about theology? Here, as described in the previous chapter, al-Ghazali, following an earlier development of orthodox Sufism, struck a synthesis. Dissatisfied with the logical formalism of the *kalam*, he sought to integrate the Sufi method with the formulations of thc *kalam* and strongly advocated the 'living through' or 'interiorization' of purely rationals beliefs which he regarded as being unworthy of a living faith. Further, this synthesis, worked out into a programme of inner, spiritual purification culminating in the single minded love of God, he declared to be the true meaning of the Shari'a. This inwardness of the faith he called Din. The Din is then the essence of the Shari'a, its inner life. The Shari'a without the Din is an empty shell and the Din without the Shari'a obviously cannot exist.

But although al-Ghazali established a necessary and intimate connection between the two the Din and the Shari'a still retained a certain duality and the pristine and original identity of the two was not restored. Indeed, it is significant that he entitled his *magnum opus* on religion *Revivification of the Sciences of the Din* rather than of the Shari'a. After him, a new type of religious literature grew up, viz. 'the science of the inner meanings of the Faith (*'ilm asrar al-Din*)' which undoubtedly performed a great service in grounding the Shari'a on enduring spiritual bases or, as al-Ghazali himself put it, on 'the subtle and difficult middle course between the utter free-lancing (of the pure rationalists) and the stolidity of the Hanbalites. But the dualism of the inner and the outer was not exorcised and the precarious balance was disrupted by subsequent developments characterized by a conflict between Sufism and the Shari'a.

Henceforth, theology itself split into two distinct types: the dogmatic and formally rational theology of the *kalam* and the speculative theology of Sufism. As for the latter, it developed on lines completely its own under the auspices of its sharply formulated cleavage between the Shari'a and thc mystic 'truth' as we shall study subsequently. The dogmatic theology, whose course and content we have described in the previous chapter, continued to defend the cradle structure of the Shari'a with rational weapons re-invigorated by the new philosophical material. But as soon as this happened, thc scope of the science of theology came under question. Some advocated a separation of theology and metaphysics, the former restricting itself to the defence of the creed, the latter investigating the ultimate problems of philosophy *proper*. But the majority of theologians feared that this would set up a branch of knowledge beyond and above the Shari'a and rejected this view. Thus although they adopted a good deal from the doctrines of the pure philosophers, including the philosophical doctrine of the natural development of the (Prophetic) intellect, they insisted that he task of theology is merely to *defend* by rational arguments the *tenets* of the creed and not to *investigate* and *interpret* by rational methods. The result was that whereas the religious dogma remained the same in form as well as in content, without any substantial re-interpretation, the complicated and sophisticated formulas and arguments borrowed from philosophy became inaccessible to the common man.

Theology thus monopolized the whole field of metaphysics and would not allow pure *thought* any claim to investigate rationally the nature of the universe and the nature of man. It thus claimed for itself the title of the 'highest science of the Shari'a' as the formulator of the 'Principles of the Faith' (*usul al-Din*). The Shari'a thus became once more identical with Din. But in the meantime the law had developed apart from theology and although the legists had recognized all along the validity of the *kalam*-theology as defender of the Faith, the authorities of the law now dictated to theology what problems it should deal with and what its scope should be.

The jurist al-Shatibi (d. 790/1388), who belongs to the generation immediately succeeding that of the theologian-philosopher al-Iji, wrote a work entitled *Kitab al-Muwafaqat* on the philosophy of law and jurisprudence. He not only advocated the separation of strict matters of Faith from the science of law but condemned outright theoretical and purely intellectual discussions as being anti-Shari'a and thus outside the scope of theology:

> Every problem in jurisprudence on which law many be based but controversy over which does not lead to difference in actual legislation, it is entirely superfluous to defend or refute any definite view concerning it.... Thus... the controversy (between

> the orthodox and the Mu'tazila) is a credal one based on a principle established in theology, although it finds *expression* in juristic terms also, viz. Are obligatoriness and prohibition... referable to qualities of things themselves (i.e. are they discoverable by natural reason?), or do they originate in the Shari'a commandments?

And, again, pronouncing not on law but on the Shari's as such:

'Investigation into any question which is not a basis for an action is not recommended by any proof from the Shari'a. By acts I mean both mental and physical acts' (Vol. I, p. 46). 'The philosophers assert that the essence of philosophy is to investigate the existents in general... These are, then, the proofs for an absolute recommendation of all knowledge in general. The answer is... that this general recommendation is really specific' (p. 52). 'And so is the case with every branch of learning that claims a relationship with the Shari'a, but does not (directly) benefit action, nor was it known to the Arabs' (p. 54).

Al-Shatibi goes on to contend that it is useless and 'outside the pale of the Shari'a' to search for scientific definitions which ought to be as direct and practical as possible—not only for law but in general. It is much better to define a star as 'that (shining object) which we see at night' rather than as 'a simple circular body whose natural place is the heaven,' etc.

The points made so far are (1) that in the beginning although the term Shari'a or Shar' was relatively little used, its use is commensurate with that of the term Din according as whether the point of departure is God or man; (2) that the crucial point at which the word Shari'a becomes common is characterized by the controversy as to whether it is reason or the Shari's that yields moral principles and practical norms; (3) that, therefore, Shari'a began to be applied rather to law than to theology, which, making use of rational arguments, was termed Din rather than Shari's; (4) that in its later development, theology came once again within the scope of the Shari'a and indeed claimed to be the highest and ultimate science of the Shari'a, but, finally, (5) the law in fact had developed independently of theology and not only was it difficult to forge a real, living link between the two but that the legists in fact claimed the law was the manifestation of the Shari'a *par excellence* and even positively discouraged theological and other allied and auxiliary studies and sciences.

The Traditionalist Reform: Ibn Taymiya

The four major currents characterizing religious life in Islam and, to an ever increasing extent, dividing it among themselves from the 4the/10th century onward, viz., rationalism, Sufism, theology and law, could only be synthesized and integrated under some comprehensive *religious* concept like that of the Shari'a. This concept, however, as our foregoing historical account has shown, was, from the very moment that it came into common use, used by the rationalist in opposition to reason and identified with the law. Next, it was used by the Sufis in opposition to the mystic 'truth' (*haqiqa*) and applied to the law. The theologians themselves, as we have just seen, at first used it to distinguish law from theology although gradually it came to be applied to the latter as well. The discord between Shari'a *thus used* and reason, and between Shari'a and the mystic truth, as used by the rationalists and the Sufi adepts respectively, is obvious. But, within orthodox circles, the discord between the *kalam* theology and the bases of law is not less deep, although it may not be so obvious because it was claimed that this theology had been expressly evolved to defend the law.

In his orthodox synthesis of the Mu'tazila doctrine of human freewill and the traditionists' stands in favour of the Omnipotence of God, as we have seen in the last chapter, al-Ash'ari had accentuated the Will of God and His creation of the human act, although he had sought to retain human responsibility. Al-Ash'ari, on close examination, cannot be called a theistic determinist because he expressely distinguished between the voluntary and involuntary actions of man. Indeed, al-Ash'ari's doctrine of God's creation, through His Will, of all human actions (and, indeed, any event whatsoever) has nothing to do with the question of determinism and free-will. His assertion is simply that nothing whatever occurs without the Will and Power of God. Nevertheless, both al-Ash'ari and his successors, when pressed to explain their doctrine of the 'acquisition' by man of his acts (created by God), treated the problem as though man and God were rival powers in the production of acts, capable of being substitutes for one another: and thus they came to deny the efficacy of the human will in favour of God's and defined the production of acts as being simply 'occasioned by' or being 'conjoined with' human volition. As we have also seen, this doctrine, corroborated both by the philosophical doctrine of natural necessity and the Sufi doctrine of God as the Sole Existent, developed, during the next two centuries, into a veritable doctrine of rigorous fatalism. This was made worse by two other Ash'arite doctrines. First, in order to raise God above the human categories of 'purpose' and 'justice' which were central themes of the Mu'tazila, the Ash'arises rejected the attribution of either to God. Secondly, in their doctrine of atomism, the Ash'arites denied causation and along with it the idea of potentialities or capacities latent in things.

But no law worthy of the name can be based on these concepts. Law requires than the human being be both free and efficacious. It requires that man be possessed of objective powers and capacities. Further, the concept of Divine Law, which the Shari'a is, requires that both purpose and justice be attributed to God or else the whole idea of Divine Command and Prohibition falls to the ground. And, indeed, the collaboration of *kalam* and Sufism (and philosophy) in *substituting* the Will and Efficacy of God for His Shari'a or Command, constitutes the greater parts of the religious history of medieval Islam.

We have briefly described above al-Ghazali's attempt at the synthesis which constitutes the first landmark of the religious integrative capacity of Islam. But al-Ghazali's impulse being essentially of personal purity and piety, his synthesis has a decisively personal character. His reform of theology and law consists fundamentally in giving them a personal meaningfulness and depth. Without his work, it is no exaggeration to say, Sufism and philosophic a rationalism might well have made a clean sweep of the Islamic ethos. Against the philosophers' First Cause and the Prime Mover, al-Ghazali brought to the fore the 'Command' or the Qur'an. Against the formulas of the theologians and the pantheism of the Sufis, he resuscitated the living God who demands and fulfils, who inspires genuine hope and fear.

Al-Ghazali's work may be described as a bilateral synthesis between theology and Sufism on the one hand and law and Sufism on the other. Sufism stands in the centre, which is in perfect consonance with the personal character of al-Ghazali's reform. But al-Ghazali did not reform the content of orthodox theology. Nor did he bring theology into a genuine contact with the law, again because of his preoccupation with personal piety. Indeed, he does not seem to have taken the law seriously. For, the Shari's cannot remain personal, even though it must be grounded in a personal understanding and acceptance, Indeed, law is essentially a non-personal phenomenon. And we may recall the fact with a fresh realization of its force that al-Ghazali's *magnum opus* is devoted not to the Shari's but to Din. On the balance of the religious forces as they existed in the 7th/13th century, the traditionists (Ahl al-Hadith) were the only group who were not in any of the currents we have described but who stood observing and waiting. And, just as they had appeared at an early religious point in Islam in the form of these forces which were behind al-Ash'ari, now from their ranks emerged the dynamic personality of Taqi al-Din ibn Taymiya (661-728/1263-1328).

It is, indeed, a curious and striking fact about the religious history of Islam that at each critical point of its career the force that comes to the forefront and takes over the situation is not the then formalized established 'orthodoxy' but rather something that present itself at every juncture as the 'raw material' of the orthodoxy subsequently to be formed. In itself this force is something non-descript and for want of a better designation is called by such terms as 'Ahl al-Hadith' or 'Ahl al-Sunna' by the Muslims themselves and identified as 'conservative' or 'orthodox' by modern Western scholars. But the Ahl al-Hadith or the Ahl al-Sunna is not the name of any particular group, sect or party; and if there is an 'orthodoxy' or a 'conservatism', this is surely the one that is an 'orthodoxy' or a 'conservatism', this surely the one that is in ascendancy at the point of time concerned. To some extent, of course, this happens with all developing religions. But whereas in Christianity, or even in as little 'reified' a religion as Hinduism, there is something that runs through it like a wave with the new elements riding on its crest, Islamic orthodox seems to develop in recreated formations of quanta that issue from time to time from the very heart of Islam. It is characterized by an indistinguishable blend of reinvigorated fundamentalism and progressivism: it develops not by self-propulsion, so to say, but by watching, adjusting and absorbing within itself that which moves within it. It is a synthetic activity and this very character it is that signifies 'orthodoxy.'

Ibn Taymiya's programme fundamentally consists of a restatement of the Shri'a and a vindication of religious values. Shari'a is a comprehensive concept and includes the spiritual truth of the Sufi (*haqiqa*), the rational truth (*'aql*) of the philosopher and the theologian, and the law. This 'inclusiveness' is not formal and 'aggregative' but points to a religious quality which is the source of these three. 'Traditional authority' and 'reason' may, indeed, be distinguished and even opposed, but Shari'a and 'reason' cannot be meaningfully opposed: 'The fact that a proof is rational or is based on authority is not in itself an object of condemnation or appreciation, or itself a guarantee of truth or falsity. "Authority" and "reason" are only avenues of knowledge although "traditional authority" can never be divorced from "reason". But the fact that something is a Shari'a-value cannot be validly opposed to something being rational...'

Similarly, the concept of the Shari'a as being a collection of purely external legal precepts and decisions, divorced from their inner bases, must be rejected. This dichotomy was rendered popular by the Sufi movement. On the contrary, the Shari'a is that which makes law possible and just and which integrates the legal and the spiritual into one living religious whole. Commenting on different opinions concerning the execution of the Sufi al-Hallaj, Ibn Taymiya has an important and interesting passage which clearly shows that contrary to the opinion generally held, he was not only not inimical to Sufism as such, but considered it as necessary, a part of religion as law:

> These people (who regard at-Hallaj as having been unjustly slain) are two parties. One party ways that he was unjustly killed.. And they regard the Shari'a and its protagonists as their enemies.. Some are against all lawyers and scholars believing that they have killed al-Hallaj. These are the kind of people who

say, 'We have a law (Shari'a) and we have a "truth" (*haqiqa*) which contradicts that law'. People who talk in this way do not understand clearly the distinction in the meanings of the word Shari'a as employed in the Speech of God and His Apostle (on the one hand) and by common people on the other... Indeed, some of them think that Shari'a is the name given to the judge's decision; many of them even do not make a distinction between a learned judge, an ignorant judge and an unjust judge. Worse still, people tend to regard any decrees of a ruler as Shari'a, while sometimes undoubtedly the truth (*haqiqa*) is actually contrary to the decree of the ruler.

The Prophet himself said: 'You people bring disputes to me; but it may be that some of you are able to put their case better than others. But I have to decide on evidence that if before me. If I happen to expropriate the right of anyone in favour of his brother let the letter not take it, for in that case I have given him a piece of hell-fire'. Thus, the judge decided on the strength of depositions and evidence that are before him while the party decided against may well have proofs that have not been put forward. In such cases, the Shariia' in reality in just the opposite of the external law, although the decision of the judge has to be enforced. In many cases, the inner truth is contrary to what appears to some people... In this case if it is said that the inner truth in the opposite of the externals, this will be true, but to call the inner 'the Truth' and the externals 'the Shari'a' is a semantic question.

But there are people according to whom 'the Truth' is the 'inner' absolutely and the Shari'a concerns only the externals. This just as 'Islam' when it is juxtaposed to 'faith', means external acts, whereas by 'faith' is meant that which is in the heart... Thus, by a juxtaposition, one speaks of the 'Shari'a (laws) of Islam' and the 'truths of faith', which distinction may be (technically) valid. But when each is used by itself alone, a person possessing only the law, without the inner truth, cannot be called truly a man of faith, and, similarly, a person possessed of a bare 'truth' which is in disagreement with the Shari'a... cannot be even a Muslim, let alone being a pious saint of God.

Sometimes by 'Shari'a' is meant that which the lawyers of the Shari'a say on the basis of their own effort of thought, and by the 'truth' is intended what the Sufis find by direct experience. Undoubtedly, but these groups are seekers of truth; sometimes they are right and sometimes wrong while neither of them wish to contravene the Prophet. If the findings of both agree well and good, otherwise neither of them has an exclusive claim to be followed, except by a clear proof from the Shari'a.

Having formulated the concept of the Shari'a in this comprehensive spirit, it is necessary to establish a real and living contact between theology and law lest the former become arid formulas and the latter an empty, rigid and lifeless shell. But in order to do this it is necessary to reformulate theology. Ibn Taymiya does not even use the term *kalam* for his theology which he more usually calls 'science of the Unity of God'. A radical re-orientation of theology is, indeed, needed, for the doctrine of the Divine Will (*qadar*), accepted and one-sidedly developed by the 'official' theology, undermines the religious moral life. A sharp distinction is required between the omnipotent Will of God and God's function as the Commander. If the former is needed by religious *belief*, the latter is the pivot of religious *action:* 'The Divine Power and Will is not an argument for anyone over against God and His Creation... Thus, the *qadar* is an object of faith, but cannot be the premise of an argument, he who does not believe in *qadar* is like the Magians (i.e. the Dualists), but he who argues from it (in the sphere of action) is like the polytheists (who argued against Muhammad that if God had willed they would not have been polytheists).

Especially guilty of the furtherance of moral laxity is the Sufi doctrine which states that 'he who witnesses the Will of God feels no longer bound by the Command of God'. It is an infidelity which the Jews and the Christians also reject and which is impossible both rationally and religiously. But the conceptual groundwork for this negative philosophy has been provided by the 'official' theology itself which, having regarded God and man as rivals, so to say, gave the entire field to God. Thereby theologians shut themselves off from the Divine imperatives which are the spring of religious life. Ibn Taymiya praises in this connection the Mu'tazila who at least kept and idea of good and evil, of Divine Commands and Prohibitions as a live religious force. This is characteristic of Ibn Taymiya, who, contrary to the general belief about him, shows an extraordinary lack of prejudice and an open-mindedness to all opinions and constantly makes such pronouncement as 'the truth does not belong to one party exclusively but is divided among all group.'

Accordingly, Ibn Taymiya reinstates into Muslim theology the doctrine of the purposiveness of the Divine behaviour, a doctrine so strenuously denied by Ash'arism, Maturidism and Zahirism as compromising the omnipotence of God's will and His dissimilarity to His creation. This purposiveness is God's involvement in the destiny of man and from this he directly deduces the idea of God as the Commander or the Shari'a Giver. He next strives to distinguish the planes at which the Will and Wisdom of God are respectively meaningful. The Will and Power of God are the efficient cause, but His Command or the Shari'a is the final cause of His activity. The omnipotence of God must not be denied for whatever comes to be, is through His Power, but to explain events in this way, to affirm the efficient cause is to look backwards 'towards the beginning'. But the Shari'a, the Wisdom and the Command of God, is forward looking, 'towards the end and the purpose.

Ibn Taymiya bluntly points out the discord that exists at bottom between the Sunni orthodox theological formulas and the presuppositions of the law: 'You will find many jurists involved in self-contradiction. Thus, when they think along with the theologians who affirm the sole Power of God by saying that the (human) power and efficacy (does not precede) the act (but it created by God) together with the act, they agree with this. But when they think in terms of law, they have to affirm a preceding (and free) human power which is the foundation of the Command and the Prohibition'. The human power and the Divinc Power are not, indeed, mutually exclusive rivals to determine and produce the human act. The Shari'a, in order to be possible at all, requires free human agency. If what is possible is co-extensive with the actual, then the Qur'anic saying, 'Fear God as much as is possible for you' must be translated as 'Fear God as much as you do fear', the the Prophet's dictum, 'When I command you something, act upon it to the best of your ability' should be rephrased as 'When I command you something, do what you do', a senseless proposition, indeed. Certainly, what is possible cannot be coextensive with what is humanly possible but it would be absurd to conclude from this that nothing, in fact, is humanity possible.

The influence of Ibn Taymiya remained restricted to his immediate disciples and did not issue forth into a movement. In the long run, however, it seeped gradually through the religious intelligentsia and the 12th/18th century Wahhabi movement was only one, if the most organized and spectacular, of its manifestations. While dealing with Sufism, how similar movements subsequently grew within Sufism, which brought Sufi though and practice closer to orthodox Islam. There is visible, in fact, a widespread trend, of which Ibn Taymiya's is the most forceful example, which ultimately resulted in those reform movements of various shades that characterized Islam immediately before the impingement upon it of modern Western influences. This explains why many modern Western scholars have observed on more than one point that the influence of Ibn Taymiya is a major signpost for the accumulation of forces that we shall describe in the chapter on the pre-modernist Reform Movement.

The Shari'a and the Law

The religious developments that took place from al-Ghazali to Ibn Taymiya visibly affected legal science. The legal theory whose history was exclusively devoted to the task of establishing and elaborating the mechanism for creating laws and deducing particular legal enactments from the Qur'an and the Sunna. The 'Principles of Law' (*Usul al-fiqh*) were just this mechanism. But now a philosophy of law developed which discussed and elaborated the moral-religious based of the law - 'the objectives of law' (*maqasid al-Shar'*) or 'the intentions of the Shari'a obligations' (*asrar al-taklif*). A series of brilliant scholars and thinkers from the 8th/14th to the 12th/18th centuries sought to work out the rational, moral and spiritual foundations of the legal system of Islam. Thus, Abu Ishaq al-Shatibi speaks of his philosophy of law as infusing spirit into the dead body and real substance into the external shell (of the law)'. As we have seen in the case of Ibn Taymiya, a central problem also of all these philosophies of law is to prove how moral obligation is related to Divine Omnipotence and Will and how the former in fact necessarily flows from the latter.

The Shari'a itself is defined as comprising both 'the acts of the heart as well as *overt* acts'. It is indeed the assembly of Divine imperatives to man, imperatives which are frankly admitted to be primarily of a moral character. The Shari'a is thus not an actual formal code of particular and specific enactments but is coterminous with the 'good'. But, surprisingly, little attempt was made to *rethink* and reformulate the actual body of the *fiqh*—the earlier attempts at actual legislation by the representatives of the four schools of law. For this the main reason seems to be that this law was looked upon as flowing necessarily from the principles of the Qur'an and the Sunna and was further *consecrated* by Ijma'. The Ijma', was considered final, the 'gate of *ijtihad*' (original thinking) was closed and, therefore, no thinker however bold, dared to tough it.

The *motivation* behind to acceptance of the Ijma' as final in the 4th/10th century was to ensure permanence and stability to this legal system since it had passed through great conflicts and controversies through its formative period. But in course of time it became rigid, its rigidity being softened only by casuistries which, however, further tended to make it ineffective. It was mainly also because of this hardening process that in the Middle Ages the secular authorities produced the body of secular law known as the *qanun* which at times supplemented and at others supplanted the Shari'a law. Once the *concept* of the Divine Law was thus restricted, a grievous blow was dealt to it and to the prestige of the Shari'a legists themselves.

The fact that no real and effective boundaries were drawn between the moral and the strictly legal in Islamic law must have also contributed to the fact that law was regarded as immutable. But this argument can be pushed too far and would not hold good for the early, creative phase of Islamic law. Indeed, the Muslim law books are full of moralizing themes and discuss at length, for example, the concept 'intention' not merely from a legal point of view but from from the deeply religious ethical angle. But this has, in general, kept the moral fiber alive with a keen sensitivity to right and wrong. And a living moral sense is in any age better for humanity than an expediently clever and effective law. Indeed, it will become clear from our treatment of Modern Islam that the real charge of the practitioners of the Shari'a against modernist reformers is not so much that the latter contravene the law of the Qur'an and Sunna, but that the secularist has no ethic beyond the expedient and the utilitarian (even though much of the time neither side correctly understands the other).

6

Divorce in the Islamic Context

JAMSHID MOMENI

Relation of Marriage to Divorce

The incident of divorce in a society is greatly associated with the nature of marriage in that society. Thus, in considering divorce, one must also consider the nature of marriage.

Marriage may be defined "as an institutionalized type of personal relations." This short definition reveals that marriage has two aspects: the *institutional* and the *human relations* aspects. At the human relations level, marriage involves a host of personal adjustments which always entails sex, values, norms, beliefs, temperaments, personality traits, economic arrangements, religious beliefs and the like. These adjustments often may involve not just the married pair, but their relatives as well. From the institutional point of view, marriage "is, at any time, the group sanction of the existing sex *mores*." The group's interest, which is external to the interpersonal relations within a marriage, is to regulate and maintain the marital status. It is from this point of view that family has been regarded as one of the most important social units in all human social orders.

Divorce statistics provide an index of the relative failure (or success) of marriage (or the family) as an institution. But, neither for its origin nor for its continuation the human relations aspect of marriage is dependent on sanctions by any external group. As Lichtenberger so forcefully argues, the human relations aspect of marriage is not the creature of law; it has existed from the very first day the human animal was created, which was long before the enactment of the varied existing laws on the subject. Theoretically speaking, and from the biological point of view, human relationship has a "natural origin" embedded in the human biological drive, like all other animals, to mate and perpetuate the species. Thus, the continuation of the human relations aspect is independent of any external sanctions; it solely depends on the *mutual* attachments of the married couple.

However, historically speaking, this potentially voluntary character of the biologically determined relation between men and women has been dramatized by variable degree of coercion such as capture, sale or purchase, parental arrangements for mates, or some other forms of coercive arrangements, some of it for the purpose of regulating and maintaining marriage as an institution, irrespective of the free choice of the parties directly involved in the interpersonal relations. The coercive forces of religions, laws, and socio-cultural customs and traditions are used to their fullest potential to maintain the marriage as an institution. On the contrary, and specially in the Islamic societies, very little attention is paid to the necessary ingredients essential to the health of the human relations aspect of the marriage.

In today's marriages, what is not taken into account is that the modern family has lost most of its original (traditional) functions which made it an important social unit. The loss of functions has been due to the social structural differentiation which has made the family to lose most of its economic, educational, political, religious, and even child-rearing functions. These functions have been transferred to the factories, schools, political parties, the church, and the nurseries, respectively. Consequently, the survival or the stability of marriage today, and in the future, must primarily rest on its human relations or its internal rather than its institutional aspect.

As master trends such as urbanism, industrialism and modernism proceed unimpeded by the wishes of any interest group who may attempt to preserve the traditional from of the family, the mere survival of marriage will more and more depend on its internal aspect. The social welfare and the individual's happiness in a democratic and just society are of paramount importance. The real cause of divorce, or the source of unhappiness must be sought within the range of human relations in a marriage. Divorce is the end result of either an unhappy marriage, which perhaps has been going on for a number of years, or the maladjustment of the institution of marriage in meeting the basic needs of the married couples.

Among all social groups—religious, political, reformist, social scientist, educational, etc.—there is a general consensus regarding the social, psychological (especially in the case of children of divorce), and the economic menace resulting from divorce. But when it comes to the remedy of the problem, there are a host of divergent views as to what is the best path to follow. Some demagogues suggest that coercion and force be used to hold marriages together. Others, more appropriately, suggest that the real causes of divorce must be examined before any action can be taken. This divergence in views is primarily due to the fact that interest groups most directly involved either cannot or do not wish to distinguish the *cause* from the *effect*. Divorce is the effect or the symptom of the social abnormality or the disease. The real germs causing it are the incompatibility of the characters of the marrying couples, lack of mutual understanding and affection, improper channels of communication, generational gap between the much younger wife and the older husband (as is very common in the Islamic world), physical and mental immaturity of either or both spouses (as many marriages in the Islamic societies are child marriages), adultery, desertion, drunkenness, addiction, poverty and the like.

Indeed, divorce takes place after all but the last marriage ties have *de facto* been several. A couple asking the court (or the religious magistrate as is still the case in some Islamic societies) to grant them divorce, is merely having the courage to break-up their long-held secret, and against the tremendous external social coercion announce to their relatives and friends (the public) that in reality no marriage existed. What they want at this time is imply to severe that last artificial religio-legal bond and once again assume their status as singles.

As pointed out by Murdock, in virtually every known human society some from of institutionalized marriage exists. Berelson and Steiner point out that in all these societies divorce in deplored. But divorce being what it is—the severence of religio-legal artificial bond after the proof that marriage ties *de facto* has dissolved—it should not be the divorce per se that should be condemned and deplored. The real causes or the interest groups instrumental in the perpetuation of the factors that destroy marriages must be the proper target of condemnation.

Many researchers have dicovered that when the conditions for a real and sound marriage are lacking—such as proper age at marriage, physical and mental competency of the couple, mutual and voluntary choice of mate and affection—the marriage will not last long. This translates into saying that to concentrate on the institutional or the external form of the marriage is to avoid to treat the real causes of divorce. That is, to legislate against divorce, poverty, or a disease is no more than a mere exercise in futility. What needs to be done is to employ creative legislative actions and constructive measures to eradicate the causes of divorce, or the social disease. It is only then that a positive step towards improving the couple's welfare and the individual's happiness is taken.

It is the light of the foregoing points of views that we define the main *objective* of this study which is to examine some of the major socio-demographic correlates of divorce in the Islamic context—more specifically in a Shi'ite Islamic society.

Legal Aspects of Divorce in Islam

As stated by Ling "sociologists are in general less interested in divorce laws than in patterns of divorce and distribution of divorces among the various social groups." This is not to deny the fact that laws, especially the Islamic laws, generally influence divorce rates and a large portion of divorce differentials by community can be attributed to differences in laws and established procedures. For instance, the relatively large number of divorces in the U.S. is partly due to more liberal marriage nd divorce laws. Or, the very low divorce rate in the first three years of marriage in Singapore (only 2.6%) is "due to the fact that divorce laws in Singapore do not allow anyone to apply for divorce before the end of three years of marriage." Similarly, the Islamic principles related to divorce play a role in determining the rate and the distribution of divorce.

Prior to the advent of Islam in Arabia women virtually had no legal status. The women was sold into the marriage by her guardian, and the husband terminated the marriage at will; the women had very little, if any, property and succession rights. The holy Qur'an, also the major source of domestic laws in the Islamic societies, represents a great degree of improvement in the status of women over the pre-Islamic laws. For example, the Qur'an gives a woman the right to buy and maintain personal property, including her dower; the Qur'an also curtails the unlimited right of man to repudiate his wife at will, by the introduction of the concept of *'iddah* (the waiting period of three menstrual cycles before a *talaq* (repudiation) could take effect). No doubt for its time (over 1,300 years ago) the advent of Islamic laws represented a considerable upgrading in the status of women. Demanded by the changing times, almost all Islamic societies have enacted Civil Codes regulating marriage and divorce and the related topics. Despite many minor local difference, in these Codes, a considerable unity and similarity throughout the Islamic world exists, for they are all derived from the same basic Qur'anic laws. The current divorce laws in the Islamic countries are primarily based on the following Qur'anic injunctions:

Surah "al-Baqarah" (Chapter II)

Verse 226: Those who swear that they will not go into their wives should wait four months; so if they go back, then Allah is surely Forgiving, Merciful.

Verse 227: If they have resolved on a divorce, then Allah is surely Hearing, Knowing.

Verse 228 : And the divorced women should keep themselves in waiting for three courses; and it is not lawful for them that they should conceal what Allah has created in their wombs, if they believe in Allah and the last day; and their husbands have a better right to take them back in the meanwhile if they wish for reconciliation; and they have rights similar to those against them in a just manner, and the men are a degree above them, and Allah is Mighty, Wise.

Verse 229: Divorce may be (pronounced) twice; then keep (them) in good fellowship or let (them) go with kindness, and it is not lawful for you to take any part of what you have given them, unless both fear that they cannot keep within the limits of Allah; then if you fear that they cannot keep within the limits of Allah, there is no blame on them for what she gives up to become free thereby....

Verse 230: So if he divorces her she shall not be lawful to him afterwards until she marries another husband; then if he divorces her there is no blame on them if they return to each other (by marriage)..

Verse 231: And when you divorce women and they reach their prescribed time; then either retain them in good fellowship or set them free with liberality...

Verse 232: And when you have divorced women and they have ended their term (of waiting), then do not prevent them from marrying their husbands when they agree among themselves in a lawful manner....

Verse 233: And the mothers should suckle their children for two while years for him who desires to make complete the time of suckling; and their maintenance and their clothing must be borne by the father according to usage; no soul shall have imposed upon it a duty but to the extent of its capacity; neither shall a mother be made to suffer harm on account of her child, nor a father on account of his child, and a similar duty (devolves) on the father's heir, but if both desire weaning by mutual consent and counsel, there is no blame on them, and if you wish to engage a wetnurse nurse for your children, there is no blame on you so long as you pay what you promised for according to usage...

Verse 234: And (as for) those of you who die and leave wives behind, they should keep themselves in waiting for four months and ten days; then when they have fully attained their term, there is no blame on you for what they do for themselves in a lawful manner....

Verse 236: There is no blame on you if you divorce women when you have not touched them or appointed for them a portion, and make provision for them, the wealthy according to his means and the straitened in circumstances according to his means, a provision according to usage; (this is) a duty on the doers of good (to others).

Verse 237: And if you divorce them before you have touched them and you have appointed for them a portion, then (pay to them) half of what you have appointed, unless they relinquish or he should relinquish in whose hand is the marriage tie.

Surah "al-Nisa" (Chapter IV)

Verse 35: And if you fear a breach between the two, then appoint a judge from his people and a judge from her people; if they both desire agreement, Allah will effect harmony between them.

Verse 128: And if a woman fears ill usage or desertion on the part of her husband, there is no blame on them, if they effect a reconciliation between them, and reconciliation is better...

Surah "al-Ahzab" (Chapter XXXIII)

Verse 49: O you who believe! when you marry the believing women, then divorce them before you touch them, you have in their case no term which you should reckon; so make some provision for them and send them forth a goodly sending forth.

Surah "al-Talaq" (Chapter LXV)

Verse 1: O Prophet! when you divorce women, divorce them for their prescribed time, and calculate the number of days prescribed, and be careful of (your duty to) Allah, your Lord. Do not drive them out of their houses, nor should they themselves go forth, unless they commit an open indecency...

Verse 2: So when they have reached their prescribed time, then retain them with kindness or separate them with kindness, and call to witness men of justice from among you, and give upright testimony for Allah...

Verse 4: And (as for) those of your women who have despaired of menstruation, if you have a doubt, their prescribed time shall be three months, and of those too who have not had their courses; and (as for) the pregnant women, their prescribed time is that they lay down their burden...

Verse 6: Lodge them where you lodge according to you means, and do not injure them in order that you may straiten them; and if they are pregnant, spend on them until they lay down their burden; then if they suckle for you, give them their recompense, and enjoin one another among you to do good; and if enjoin one another among you to do good; and if you disagree, another (woman) shall suckle for him.

In brief, these Qur'anic injunctions on divorce: (1) define the *'iddah*, or the waiting period, as a check; somewhat limit the husband's right to divorce at will, as reconciliation may be possible during the the waiting period; (2) specify that *talaq* may be revoked twice, but after the third time it becomes irrevocable unless the women legally marries another man and she is divorced by him before she could remarry her first husband; (3) emphasize that liberty has to be exercised when divorcing woman; (4) make it clear that remarriage either with the first husband or with another man, immediately after the prescribed waiting period is over, is possible; (5) recommend the appointment of judges as preliminary to divorce to attempt at reconciliation; and, (6) define the wife as the care-taker of children for suckling purposes till weaning time, and grants the father custody and guardianship from the very first day of divorce.

MATERIAL AND METHODS

Background

Special methods have been used to collect the data utilized in this study. Contrary to the registration of birth and death, which remains highly incomplete, the registrations of divorces (and of marriages) are quite complete in Iran. This is primarily due to the fact that divorce entails legal and economic implications which necessitates its accurate recording. This registration of divorce takes place in special bureaus called *Mahdars*, which are generally headed by some religious figure—a *Mulla, Agha,* or a *Shaykh*. Once registered, the information remain burried in the well-guarded books at the *Mahdars*. Hardly anyone has tried, before this study, to analyze the wealth of information contained in these books maintained at the *Mahdars*. The exact terms of divorce decree (those important to the *Mahdars*, the Court, and the couples themselves) are written in these books, which include the names of the divorcing couple, their birth date, date of marriage (not always), date of divorce, type of divorce, amount of dower, number of children alimony (if any), place of residence, and rarely some information relative to the occupation of the divorcing couples. These documents invariably contain any specific agreement made between the couple. These decrees seldom provide information on income and the reason for divorce. But, their files at the Family Protection Court do contain information on occupation and the reason for divorce. Although not adequate for a detailed analysis of the socio-economic or demographic correlates of divorce, these documents provide the best and most reliable date anyone can get relative to the incidence of divorce, age at marriage of the divorcing couples, age at the time of divorce, marriage duration, number of children of divorce, then amount of dower and how it is paid, alimony, child support, and husband-wife age differentials. For information on occupation and reasons for divorce the best source is the files at the Family Protection Court.

Data

This study utilizes two main sets of date. The major sources of data consists of reading all divorce decrees registered at all the *Mahdars* in shiraz during the years 1335, 1345 and 1352 (approximately, 1956,

1966 and 1973) and extracting all the relevant socio-demographic information. The years 1956 and 1966 were chosen because these were the years when the first and the second nation-wide censuses of iran were taken, which provided us with various socio-demographic characteristics of the population of shiraz. The year 1973 was chosen because at the time of this study it was the last completed year of registered divorces. A total of 2,071 decrees were examined: 699 decrees in 1335/1956, 694 in 1345/1966, and 678 in 1352/1973.

Prior to the 1979 revolution in Iran there were two main stages in the granting of a divorce: First, an application had to be made to the Family Protection Court requesting for a Certificate of Irreconcilability be granted. The second stage began after the Court had entertained the application; if the Court's attempt at reconciliation failed and it was judged that the marriage *de facto* had dissolved, then a Certificate of Irreconcilability was issued. The couple had three month to bring this Certificate to the *Mahdar* where divorce was registered and marriage was officially dissolved. The second set of data utilized in this study consists of reading the file of 104 couples who were granted by the Court the Certificate of Irreconcilability, during the first two months of 1978. The primary reason for examining these files was to obtain information (such as the age and sex of the children of divorce, occupation, reason for divorce, custody, or who initiated divorce, etc.) which could not be found in the divorce decrees registered at the *Mahdars.*

RESULTS

Rate of Divorce

One of the first questions asked is that how frequently divorce take, place and what is the extent of its variation in different Islamic countries? There are many methods of computing the rate of divorce, but none is really totally satisfactory. The ratio of divorces to the marriages in a given year is one of the better measures, however. Table I shows the ratio of divorces to the marriages in a given year for Iran, the city of Shiraz, and a number of selected Islamic and non-Islamic societies.

Islam encourages marriage and discourages divorce. This is expressed in several Qur'anic injunctions as well as the following *hadiths* (the saying of Prophet Muhammad): "The beat of you are those who are best to their wives,"; "The evil-doers of my nation are the bachelors in it"; "Get married and do not divorce, for when a family breaks asunder, the very throne of God is jolted"; "He who renounces marriage for fear of exigence has a poor opinion of God"; and , "the thing which is lawful, but most disliked by Allah is divorce." Despite this religious emphasis on discouraging divorce, the divorce rates in many Islamic countries are higher than the divorce rates in several non-Muslim nations. In fact, the highest divorce rate in the world is observed in an Islamic society. Weekes states: "The Maldive divorce rate is the highest among countries in the United Nations. In 1974, for each 100 marriages there were 85 divorces (87 in Male)... The man can repudiate his wife according to Islamic law and report it to the *qadi*. Based on the figures reported in the United Nations Demographic Yearbook, as shown in Table 6.1, in 1976 there were 5,033 marriages and 3,662 divorces in Maldive. That is, for every 1,000 marriages there were 728 divorces. Or, Mernissi states: "Morocco has one of the world's highest divorce rates, compared to either developed countries (four times the divorce rate of the United States for married women aged between 20 and 24) or developing ones (eight times the rate of India for similar age groups)."

As it may be noted from Table 6.1: (1) The divorce rates in the Islamic countries are generally higher than the rates for some non-Islamic nations; and, (2) there is a great deal of variation in divorce rates within the between the Islamic societies. The national divorce statistics reported may not quite reflect all the divorces registered in these countries. Generally speaking, the reported statistics under estimate the number of divorces registered. This is primarily due to the fact that divorce in an index of social disorganization; it may also reflect economic problems at the family level. In view of the fact that all Muslim countries are among the developing nations, and that they generally have unstable governments, the authorities tend to downplay the incidence of divorce, for it may be interpreted as a sign of weakness of the regime or the socio-economic problem in the country. This is best illustrated in the case of Iran. As shown in Table 6.1, if we compare the divorce rate for Iran with that of the city of Shiraz (the data for which I collected after overcoming many hurdles to get the governmental permission to do so, and I know that the data are reliable) the under-reporting of divorce statistics in Iran easily surface out. For example, in 1973 the ratio of divorces per 1,000 marriages for the nation as a whole was reported to be 94, while the ratio for Shiraz was found to be 236. Of course, part of the difference is due to the fact that Shiraz is a large urban centre, and the figure for Iran relates to both the urban and rural areas combined. But, part of the difference is due to the fact that the authorities do not want all of the "bad news" out.

TABLE 6.1

Number of Marriages, Divorces, and the Ratio of Divorces to Marriages in Some Selected Muslim and Non-Muslim Countries

Country	*Number of Year*	*Number of Marriages*	*No. of Divorces/ Divorces*	*1,000 Marriages*
1	2	3	4	5
Iran	1956	137,826	24,868	180
	1966	152,467	24,451	160
	1973	209,34	19,773	94
Shiraz[a]	1956	2,644	699	264
	1966	2,524	694	274
	1973	2,866	678	236
Egypt	1956	222,011	57,187	258
	1966	294,630	63,257	186
	1973	339,105	75,883	224
Iraq	1956	17,170	2,065	120
Jordan	1956	12,780	1,615	126
	1966	15,870	2,124	133
	1973	11,158	1,919	171
Kuwait	1966	1,820	834	458
	1973	6,051	1,186	196

1	2	3	4	5
Maldive Islands	1976	5,033	3,662	728
Syria	1956	26,600	2,222	84
	1966	35,653	3,203	90
	1973	67,812	3,859	57
Turkey	1956	53,393	11,205	210
	1973	79,488	11,130	140
Denmark	1966	41,424	6,627	162
England and Wales	1956	352,944	25,718	73
	1966	384,497	38,352	100
	1973	400,435	105,199	262
Israel	1956 [b]	15,098	2,070	137
	1966	20,662	2,237	108
	1973	29,347	2,672	91
Northern Ireland	1956	9,359	111	12
	1966	10,735	150	14
	1973	11,212	393	35

(a) Shiraz is a city in Iran; (b) Statistics included the Arab population, For 1966 and 1973, the statistics are only for the Jewish population of Israel.

Source: Except for the city of Shiraz, all other data are from the *United Nations Demographic Yearbook.*

From among other Islamic countries, Kuwait, Egypt and Turkey also have high divorce rates. Among the non-Muslim societies, Northern Ireland has one of the lowest divorce rates in the world. As it may be noted from Table 6.1, the divorce rates in the Islamic countries are many times higher than those for Northern Ireland.

Another way of studying the relative magnitude of divorce in a country is to examine the number of divorced population per 1,000 married population at a given time. Census data can be used for this purpose. This method is specially useful when vital registration data are either incomplete or do not exist. For example, based on the 1966 and 1976 census of Iran, we obtained the data presented in Table 6.2.

TABLE 6.2

Number of Divorces Per 1,000 Married Population Based on the 1966 and 1976 Censuses of Iran

Residence	*Married*	*Divorced*	*+of Divorces 1,00 Married*	*Married*	*Divorced*	*+of Divorces 1000 Married*
Iran						
Both sexes	9,707,486	116,060	12.0	13,023,794	111,408	8.6
Male	4,830,316	40,418	8.4	6,468,416	36,735	5.7
Female	4,877,170	75,642	15.5	6,555,378	74,673	11.4
Urban Areas						
Both Sexes	3,657,217	64,792	17.7	6,081,983	71,966	11.8
Male	1,838,882	19,623	10.7	3,046,521	21,916	7.2
Female	1,818,335	45,169	24.8	3,035,462	50,050	16.5
Rural Areas						
Both Sexes	6,050,269	51,268	8.5	6,941,811	39,442	5.7
Male	2,991,434	20,795	7.0	3,421,895	14,819	4.3
Female	3,058,835	30,473	10.0	3,519,916	24,623	7.0

The number of divorced persons per 1,000 married population, age 10 and over, presented in Table 6.2 are not to be compared with those in Table 6.1, for the figures in Table 6.2 represent the cumulative number of divorced individuals minus those who had either died or had remarried during the years prior to the time of census. However, the figures in Table 8.1 represent divorces registered and reported in a given year even if some of the divorcees had either died or had remarried during the same year. Assuming that mortality and remarriage schedules in the Islamic countries are roughly the same, the ratio derived from the census data has the advantage that it overcomes the problem of under-reporting of divorce statistics. Thus, it would be a better measure for comparative purposes. Also the ratios derived from the census data provide us with some measures regarding the differentials in remarriage rate by sex and urban-rural residence. For instance, in 1976 for every 1,000 married men, age 10 and above, in Iran there were 5.7 divorced men; but, for every 1,000 married women there were 11.4 divorced women. What does this tell us? In view of the fact that every divorce produces one divorced man and one divorced woman, if the rate of mortality and remarriage were the same for both sexes, there should be the same number of divorced men as there are divorced women per 1,000 married couples. But figures derived from the 1976 census of Iran show a significantly lower ratio for men indicating that in Iran the man's chance for remarriage after divorce is much higher than that for women. This conclusion is, of course, on the assumption that neither the incidence of polygon nor the male-female mortality differentials are large enough to account for the large differences in the ratios of divorced persons to the married population.

The differential is even higher in the urban areas. For every one divorced man there are about 2.3 divorced women in the urban areas of Iran; the corresponding ratio for the rural areas is only 1.6. Based on the above hypothesis, this means that the chances for remarriage in the urban areas for women in lower than their chances in the rural areas. Female rural-urban migration differential by martial status may play a minor role in accounting for the rural-urban differentials in the ratios, but certainly will not be able to explain all of the variation. This is because the Islamic customs even do not permit the women to travel on their own, let alone living by themselves. A divorced women invariable returns to her parents or brother's home. In fact, a married women has a higher chance to follow her husband to the city than a divorced woman, Thus, the higher ratio of divorced women in the cities is primarily due to their lower chances for remarriage in the urban areas.

Age at Marriage of Divorced Couples

Many researchers have concluded that age at marriage is inversely related to divorce rate. Glick and Landau, in their study of 'Age As a Factor in Marriage," concluded that women who marry at an extremely young age are more likely to have their martial relations dissolved by divorce than those who marry at a more mature age. Burgess and Locke hypothesized that early age at marriage is predictive of martial unhappiness and breakups. Burchinal and Chancellor found less divorces among couples married at a later age than those married at a younger age. And, Day studying the pattern of divorce in Australia and the

United States, hypothesized that the later woman marry (and since less chance they feel have for remarriage), the less likely divorce will take place.

Table 6.3 shows the distribution of age at marriage of divorced couples in Shiraz, by year and sex. As it can be noted from Table 6.3, the age at marriage distributions for the husbands differ sharply from those for the wives. Of those who divorced in 1956, 42.0 per cent of the wives and only 5.3 per cent of the husbands had married while under 20 years of age; about 62 per cent of the wives had married while 24 or less than 24 years old. Of those who had divorced in 1966, 7.1 per cent of the husbands and 47.3 per cent of the wives had married at age under 20 years; 24.7 per cent of the husbands and 65.9 per cent of the wives had married at age under 25 years. In 1973, the proportion of marriages at an early age had further increased. About 11.0 per cent of the men and 57.0 per cent of the women had married while under age 20. That is, the majority of the divorcees had married while in their teen years. Of those who had obtained the Certificate of Irreconcilability from the Family Protection Court in 1978, 55.1 per cent of the wives and 5.7 per cent of the husbands had married at ages below 20, with 40.4 per cent of the wives below age 18. It is significant to notice that the percentage of those who had married at ages 15 to 17 years does not vary greatly between 1956, 1973 and 1978. The year 1966 is an exceptional year, for that was the year preceding the passage of the Family Protection Act. However, long before the actual enactment of the Act, it was *de facto* enforced either by massive but inaccurate media coverage of the issues, or by the government's design to test the waters relative to the public's and religious reactions to it, and partly by government tightening its grips on the already existing laws which were not previously enforced. Consequently, during 1966 the normal patterns of marriage and divorce were disrupted. This may partly explain as to why a lower percentage (25.7 per cent) of those who had divorced in 1966 came from those who had married while 15 to 17 years old. However, in less than three months after the Act was officially put into effect, the divorce rate in Tehran had resumed its upward trend. And, exactly 14½ months later, the number of divorces registered in the city of Tehran had almost reached its pre-

Act level. This sharp disruption in the normal pattern of divorce was primarily due to the fact that it took a while for the public as well as the divorce notaries at the *Mahdars* to learn the details as well as the loopholes of the Act.

TABLE 6.3

Age at Marriage Distribution of Divorced Couples by Year and Sex in the City of Shiraz (Iran)

	1956		*1966*		*1973*		*1978*	
Age	*Husband*	*Wife*	*Husband*	*Wife*	*Husband*	*Wife*	*Husband*	*Wife*
Below 15	0.0	2.2	0.3	10.9	0.0	8.7	0.0	5.8
15-17	0.4	31.4	1.0	25.7	2.5	35.0	2.8	34.6
18	1.8	4.4	0.8	5.6	5.2	6.3	2.9	7.7
19	3.1	4.0	2.5	5.1	3.3	7.4	0.0	7.7
20	4.0	5.8	2.5	5.6	3.6	7.7	3.8	3.8
21	3.5	1.3	3.1	5.9	6.6	3.0	1.0	6.7
22-24	15.0	12.8	14.5	7.1	17.2	10.9	26.0	7.7
25-29	26.5	13.3	28.0	9.7	23.5	7.7	28.9	6.8
30-34	19.5	11.9	17.3	7.9	14.2	5.5	10.6	6.7
35-39	7.5	6.6	11.2	6.9	10.4	3.8	9.6	5.8
40-44	4.0	2.2	6.9	6.4	4.9	2.2	2.0	3.8
45 +	14.6	4.0	12.0	3.3	8.7	1.9	12.5	2.9

Age Distribution at the Time of Divorce

How old were the husbands and wives when they divorced? Table 6.4 depicts the age distribution of divorced couples in the city of Shiraz for the years 1956, 1966, 1973 and 1978, by sex.

The data shown in Table 6.4 reveal significant differences in the age distribution of the husbands and wives at the time of divorce. For instance, the percentage of husbands of age below 20 was 1.4 in 1956, 1.0 in 1966, 2.3 in 1973, and 1.0 in 1978. The corresponding proportions for the wives were significantly higher: 20.5 per cent in 1956, 27.6 per cent in 1966, 23.6 per cent in 1973, and 20.2 per cent in 1978; 46.9 per cent of the wives in 1956, 48.7 per cent in 1966, 56.2 per cent in 1973, and 46.2 per cent in 1978 where below age 20 at the time of divorce. Similar pattern is observed in other Islamic countries as shown in Table 6.4.

TABLE 6.4

Percentage Distribution of Couples Divorced in Shiraz by Year and Sex

	1956		*1966*		*1973*		*1978*	
Age	*Husband*	*Wife*	*Husband*	*Wife*	*Husband*	*Wife*	*Husband*	*Wife*
Below 15	0.0	0.9	0.0	2.3	0.0	0.1	0.0	0.0
15-17	0.3	11.1	0.1	14.9	0.3	12.4	1.0	5.8
18	0.4	3.6	0.3	3.9	1.0	5.3	0.0	7.7
19	0.7	4.9	0.6	6.5	13	5.8	0.0	6.7
20	1.0	6.1	1.2	4.8	1.6	8.0	0.0	3.8
21	1.1	5.9	1.4	4.6	1.5	7.7	1.9	7.7
22-24	8.9	14.4	7.2	11.7	12.9	16.9	7.7	14.5
25-29	27.0	18.7	21.3	15.0	19.4	16.4	25.0	25.9
30-34	26.0	12.2	20.6	9.7	19.6	8.6	21.1	7.7
35-39	9.5	11.0	14.7	12.6	14.4	7.8	12.5	6.7
40-44	7.5	4.3	14.6	7.4	9.6	4.3	12.5	3.9
45 +	17.6	6.9	18.0	6.8	18.4	6.7	18.3	9.6

As it may be noted from the age-specific data presented in Table 6.4, in the non-Islamic societies such as Israel (also in the Middle East), Denmark, West Germany, and among the European population of Algeria, the percentage of women under age 25 at the time of divorce ranged between a low of 7.6 per cent to 26.3 per cent. The figures for the Islamic societies range between a low of 34.3 per cent in Turkey to a high of 52.4 per cent in Jordan and 56.2 per cent in the city of Shiraz. As discussed earlier, a significantly higher proportion of divorced women in the Muslim societies than those in the non-Muslim societies are under 25 years of age at the time of divorce. This and the age-specific percentages presented in Table 6.5 lend support to the hypothesis that the high rate of family disruptions in the Islamic communities is partly attributed to the extremely low ages at marriage.

TABLE 6.5

Age Distribution of Divorced Couples in Some Selected Muslim and Non-Muslim Countries, by Year and Sex

Country and Year		*Husband* *Per cent Under 20*	*Per cent Under 25*	*Wife* *Per cent Under 20*	*Per cent Under 25*
1		2	3	4	5
Algeria	(1959)				
Non-Muslim-Population		0.0	1.3	0.7	7.6
Morocco	(1955)	1.5	9.0	10.5	38.2
Egypt	(1966)	2.0	16.3	18.8	48.0
Jordan	(1967)	1.9	20.3	20.0	52.4
Turkey	(1966)**	1.0	13.8	6.6	34.3
Shiraz*					
	(1956)	2.4	12.4	20.5	46.9
	(1966)	1.0	10.8	27.6	48.7
	(1973)	2.6	18.6	23.6	56.2
	(1978)	1.0	10.6	20.2	46.2
Israel	(1966)	0.4	8.6	5.0	26.3
Denmark	(1966)	0.2	9.9	1.3	16.3
W. Germany	(1966)	0.0	5.9	1.1	16.9
England & Wales	(1963)	0.0	3.1	0.1	9.9

* Shiraz is a city, not a country.

** The data for Turkey relate to statistics collected at the provincial capitals and district centres.

Source: The data for all countries, except the city of Shiraz, are from the *United Nations Demographic Yearbook*.

If this is true, then there seems to be an irony in Islam. On the one hand, Islam promotes marriages and discourages divorces as cited earlier. On the other hand, it permits marriages at extremely early ages (age of puberty) which easily become the victim of disruption, leaving behind many men, women, and children subjected to its multifaceted socio-economic as well as psychological adverse effects.

Average and Median Age at Divorce

The information obtained from the divorce decrees did not allow us to identify the divorce order. That is, whether it was the first time he/she was divorcing, the second time, or the third. Although it is safe to assume that a significant majority of the decrees examined related to divorces of first order, the mean and median age at divorce presented below relate to divorces of all orders.

	1956		*1966*	
Spouse	*Mean*	*Median*	*Mean*	*Median*
Husband (H)	34.5	31.0	36.3	33.8
Wife (W)	27.4	24.3	27.8	25.0
H-W	7.1	6.7	8.5	8.8
	1973		1978	
Spouse	*Mean*	*Median*	*Mean*	*Median*
Husband (H)	34.7	32.4	35.4	32.2
Wife (W)	26.3	23.4	27.7	24.9
H-W	8.4	9.2	7.7	7.3

As it may be seen from the above statistics, again with the exception of 1966, the average of husbands at the time of divorce remained the same between 1956 and 1978. Nor there is any significant change in the mean age for the wives. In all years studied, the median age at divorce was lower than the mean ages for both the husbands and the wives. Statistically, this happens when the distribution is positively skewed. This means that the distribution of age at divorce had relatively fewer frequencies at the high end of the distribution.

There is an important and interesting fact to be noted about the average husband-wife age differentials shown above. The average differentials are obtained by subtracting the average age of the wives from the average age of the husbands. what is important to note is that these averages reflect the *absolute* average different between the age of the couples. These averages could be very misleading if attention is not paid to the fact that not in every case the husband was older than the wife. Indeed, of the 104 court files examined in 1978, in 88 cases (84.7%) the husbands were older than their wives; but, in the remaining 16 cases (15.3 per cent) the wives were older than their husbands. When these cases were analyzed separately the following mean age and mean husband-wife age differentials were obtained.

	Husband (H)	*Wife (W)*	*(H-W)*
All 104 cases combined	35.4	27.7	7.7
The 88 cases when husbands were older than their wives	36.7	26.7	10.0
The 16 cases when wives were older than their husbands	28.3	33.3	-4.9

This shows that when husbands were older than their wives, the average husband was 10 years older than his bride. And, in cases when the wives were older than their husbands, an average husband was 4.9 years younger than an average bride. But the average *absolute difference* (i.e., irrespective of whether the husband was the older spouse or the wife) between the ages of all couples combined was found to be 7.7 years. That is, 2.3 years less than 10. Unfortunately, at the time of this writing, I do not have access to my IBM data cards (which are in shiraz), and I cannot make similar calculations for the 1956, 1966 and 1973 data. However, based on what we know from the 1978 data, it is safe to assume that the average husband-wife age at divorce differentials in 1956, 1966 and 1973 for those couples with husbands older than he wives would have been about 10 years, if not more. As demonstrated by Dixon an average gap of ten years is the highest in the world. Momeni has demonstrated that the higher the husband-wife age gap, the higher the chances for divorce. Day found that divorces were more frequent among couples where wives were older than the husbands than when the wives were slightly older or younger. This explains as to why a relatively high proportion of the 104 court files examined in 1978 included couples with wives much older (an average of 4.9 years) than their husbands.

Marriage Duration

How many years the divorced couples remained married before they divorced? Table 8.6 shows the distribution of the duration of marriage for Shiraz, United States, and the non-Muslim population of Singapore. Kephart hypothesized that the percentage of divorces drops after the third year of marriage. The data on Shiraz strongly support Kephart's hypothesis, for it can be noted that 85.8 per cent of divorces in 1956, 73.6 per cent in 1966 and 71.1 per cent of divorces in 1973 took place during the first three years of marriage. The U.S. data also supports this hypothesis. But there is a significant difference between the data for Shiraz and those for the U.S. In Shiraz the first two years seem to be most crucial year. The case of the non-Muslim population of Singapore is entirely different. As we notice from Table 8.6, only 13.4 per cent of divorces took place during the first five years of marriage. As explained by Ling this is partly due to the fact that in Singapore couples legally are not allowed to file petition for divorce during the first three years of their marriage. In view of this legal impediment of Singapore, one would expect that the fourth year of marriage be the crucial year, because all those who could not divorce during the first three years will attempt at the expiration of the 3-year period. Contrary to this expectation, based on the data presented in Table 8.6, the sixth and the seventh years of marriage seem to be the most crucial years for the non-Muslim couples in Singapore. While the average duration for Shiraz was found to be less than 5 years, that of Singapore is reported to be 9.5 years. What are the factors that make the average duration in Shiraz much shorter than that for the non-Muslim population of Singapore? There is not any single explanation for this. But to be sure, the legal impediments, proper age at marriage, husband-wife age differential, and a host of socio-economic factors play their parts.

TABLE 8.6

Distribution of Duration of Marriage for Shiraz, United States, and the Non-Muslim Population of Singapore

				Shiraz (Iran)			*U.S.*	*Singapore*
Years of Duration	*1956*	*1966*	*1973*	*1978 Husband Older*	*1978 Wife Older*	*1978 Combined*	*1970*	*1960-1971*
Under 1	68.2	46.4	48.8	14.8	25.0	16.3	4.8	0.2
1-2	17.6	27.2	22.3	31.8	37.5	32.7	17.9	2.4
3-4	6.1	8.2	9.0	19.3	12.5	18.3	16.2	9.7
5-6	2.4	5.2	6.7	11.4	6.3	10.6	12.5	20.9
7-8	2.23	3.2	3.8	7.9	6.2	6.7	9.1	18.3
9-14	2.0	6.6	5.6	6.8	6.3	9.6	17.4	33.8
15 +	1.4	3.2	3.7	8.0	6.2	5.8	22.2	14.7

Source: *Vital Statistics of the United States* (1970), vol. iii, pp. 2-8.

Children and Divorce

Some researchers have found that divorce in associated with childlessness. Others have disputed this position. Monahan concluded that the alleged association between divorce and childlessness has been statistically spurious and may not exist at all. Parsons and Bales point out that the couples with children are less likely to dissolve than the childless couples. Pitts contends that sterility (which amounts to childlessness) is more likely to be an important cause of divorce in places where high value is placed on fertile woman. Or, Kirpatrick concludes that there is a positive relationship between divorce and low fertility. And, Freedman, Whelpton, and Campbell indicate that marriages with fewer children or no children at all exhibit a higher divorce rate than other marriages.

What per cent of divorces in an Islamic society are due to childlessness? This question has yet to be investigated. The data for Shiraz show a high percentage of childlessness among divorced couples as shown below:

Number of Children of Divorce	*1956 Divorces*	*1966 Divorces*	*1973 Divorces*	*1978 Divorces*
None	75.2	70.3	50.6	50.0
One	18.7	18.7	21.4	26.9
Two	4.9	7.4	16.2	12.5
Three or more	1.1	3.6	11.8	10.6

As it can be noted from the above data, 75.2 per cent of divorces in 1956, 70.3 per cent in 1966, 50.6 per cent in 1973, and 50.0 of divorces in 1978 were childless, showing the association of divorce with childlessness. But, what is more important to note is that the proportion of childless couples as a factor causing divorce steadily declined between 1956 and 1978. The percentage of couples with one chile-increased from 18.7 in 1956 to 21.4 per cent in 1973 and 26.9 per cent in 1978. Perhaps, the most notable change relates to those with three or more children. The percentage of divorced couples with three or more children increased from a low of 1.1 per cent in 1956 to 11.8 per cent in 1973 and 10.6 per cent in 1978. This is, almost a 10-fold increase in the proportion of couples with three or more children.

In order to ascertain the relationship between divorce and childlessness, in a separate tabulation, not shown here, duration of marriage was divided into three categories (under one year; 1-2 years; and, 3 or more years) and divorces by number of children involved (those with no children; those with children). The contingency analysis of the resulting table produced a highly significant chi-square ($X^2 = 24.32$ with 3 degrees of freedom), providing evidence in support of the hypothesis that duration of marriage before divorce is related to the number of children involved. The observations in Shiraz lead us to hypothesize that childlessness is associated with short duration of marriage.

In terms of percentages, of all those who divorced within the first year of their marriage, 88.2 per cent were childless couples; and of those who had divorced during the second year of marriage, 85.7 per cent were childless. This amounts to the fact that more than three out of every four childless couples divorced during the first two years of their marriage.

We may recall that in 88 out of the 104 court files examined, the husbands were older than their wives. The chi-square resulting from contingency analysis for his group was also highly significant ($X^2 = 19.6$, with 3 degrees of freedom). In terms of percentages, 11 (84.6%) of the 13 couples whose marriage had no survived the first year were childless; and, 10 (83.3%) of the 12 couples whose marriage had survived the first but not the second year were also childless.

Of the 16 couples when the wives were older than their husbands, four had divorced during the first year of marriage. All of these (100%) were childless couples. Two additional couples had divorced during the second year of marriage; these were also childless. These statistics clearly support the hypothesis put forward by Freedman, Whelpton, and Campbell that marriages with fewer children are more likely to be dissolved by divorce than others. Childlessness may be due to infertility of either spouses. Thus, a corollary of the above hypothesis is that divorce is more likely to occurs if the wife is barren (especially true in the Muslim culture). However, according to the Islamic principles and even according to the existing civil laws in most Islamic countries, when the wife is proved to be barren, the man can choose a second wife without having to divorce the first one. The problem is that many men choose divorce to the first wife in such situations.

Based on the detail data, not shown here, the total number of children of divorce were calculated for different years in Shiraz. The 699 divorces in 1956 involved a total of 225 minor children; the 694 divorces in 1966 involved a total of 319 minor children; the 678 divorces in 1973 involved a total of 696 minor children; and, the 104 court files for those who were granted Certificates of Irreconcilability in 1978 involved a total of 94 minor children. These statistics reflect a significant increase in the number of children per divorce as shown below:

	1956	*1966*	*1973*	*1978*
Number of cases	699	694	678	104
Number of cases involving children	173	206	335	52
Percentage of cases involving children	24.7	29.7	49.4	50.0
Total number of children involved	2.5	319	696	94
Number of children per 100 cases	32	46	102	92
Mean number of children per case	0.32	0.46	1.02	0.92
Mean under of children per case for couples with children	1.30	1.55	2.08	1.81

As the above calculations show, the number of children per divorce decree increased from 0.32 in 1956 to 1.02 in 1973. That is, more than triple in less than two decades. The number of children per decree for divorces involving children increased from 13 in 1956 to 2.08 in 1973. The figure for 1978 is somewhat lower than that of 1973. But, we may recall that the 1978 data are based on the information from the first 104 couples who were granted Certificates of Irreconcilability in 1978. If we had the data for the entire year, the figure would have been different. The average number of children of divorce per decree in Shiraz is significantly lower than those for the U.S., however, which was 1.93 in 1956, 2.23 in 1966, and 1.93 in 1973.

The divorce decree for 1956, 1966 and 1973 issued in Shiraz did not specify the age and the sex of the children of divorce. But, of the 94 children involved in the 104 court files examined in 1978, 50 (53.2 per cent) were boys, and 44 (46.7 per cent) were girls. Based on their ages recorded to the nearest month, they had an average age of 5.7 years. The average age for the boys was 6.24 years, and the average age for the girls was 5.0 years. That is, most divorces took place at the time when the majority of the children were in their tender age, and thus the greatest adverse effect on them as well as their parents.

Custody of Children

The only Qur'anic injunction relative to custody is Verse 233,

Surah II, presented in the section on "Legal Aspects of Divorce in Islam," of this paper. According to this Qur'anic law, the custody of children irrespective of their sex, belongs to the father. However, if the child involved is under age two, and if he, the husband, desires and she (the wife) is capable the agrees (e.g., if she has not remarried), the mother can be the care-taker of the child for the purpose of suckling till age two which is regarded as the normal age of weaning. During this period the father is still the legal guardian (custodian), and he is responsible for all the expenses incurred for the child's maintenance. The mother is not to be forced to becomes a care-taker if she is not willing to do so. According to another Islamic principle, a woman loses custody immediately upon remarriage. Thus, in view of the fact that a divorced woman is permitted to remarry after her *'iddah*, she is not granted custody in case she wants to practise her Qur'anic right.

Shari'ah, the Islamic body of laws, draws on four major sources: (1) the holy Qur'an; (2) *Sunnah*, or the collection of *hadith* (traditions of Prophet Muhammad); (3) *Qiyas*, jurists' decisions on analogous previous cases; and, (4) *Ijma*, the consensus among a group of judges. There are five major schools of laws or interpretations: The Ithna' Ashari (Twelves), Hanafi, Shafi'i, Maliki, and Hanbali. These schools have different rulings (or interpretations) regarding the God's law on custody. For instance, while the Ithna' 'Ashari law grants a mother custody of her son till age two and her daughter till age seven, the Maliki law permits the mother to keep her children, irrespective of their sex, till the age of puberty.

Shi'ah Ithna' 'Ashari is the State religion in Iran. Article 1169 of the Civil Code enacted in 1931 during the Reza Shah's regime, drawing on the Ithna' 'Ashari law granted the mother custody of her son till age two, and of her daughter till age seven. Also based on the Qur'anic verse referred to earlier, the Code distinguished between "physical custody" and "ligar guardianship." During the period that the mother was granted physical custody, based on Articles 1170-1186 of the Civil Code, the legal guardianship along with financial maintenance were with the father, or paternal grandfather, or in their absence, a mate guardian appointed by either of them. The 1967 Family Protection Act, without expressly repealing the Articles of the Civil Code, attempted to prevail whenever the two statutes were in conflict. Based on Articles 9, 12, 13, 15 and 18 of the Act, "In all cases in which a certificate of irreconcilability is issued, the court will determine the custodian and will fix the scale of child support." The Act also stipulated that even in the cases of uncontested divorces, the arrangements relative to the custody and payments of child support had to be to the satisfaction of the court

This Act, like similar laws enacted in several other Islamic nations in recent years, was regarded as a step forward toward the protection of many innocent children of divorce, and also upgrading the status of womenfolk in Iran. However, Khomeini, immediately upon his takeover of Iran in 1979, denounced the 1967 Act. It is not clear what has replaced the Act, whether he has returned to the purely Qur'anic law, or he has leaned back to the Civil Code enacted during the Reza Shah's regime.

The 1978 data were collected at the time that the 1917 Act and its 1975 amendments were still in effect. Of the 52 cases that involved children, in 34 (65.4 per cent) of them the custody was granted to women; in 14 cases (13.5 per cent) the custody was granted to men; and, in 4 cases (3.8 per cent) a joint custody were arranged.

Child Support

The realities of life are quite different from the theological prescriptions. The two often do not coincide. This is best demonstrated in the case of child support. Despite the Qur'anic injunction that the father always is responsible for the maintenance of his children, not every father abides or is able to do so.

In the previous section we indicated that in 34 cases in 1978 the mothers were granted full custody, and in 4 cases they received joint custody of their children. However, in only 24 of these 38 cases child-support were stipulated. That is, 14 or 36.8 per cent of the mothers did not receive child-support. Why? No specific answers were found in their files. But it was abundantly clear that property and/or the fathers inability to pay were the main reasons. Relative to the scale of child support in the 24 cases when such payments were stipulated, the payments ranged from a low of 1,500 Rials ($ 21.0) to a high of 40,000 Rials ($ 555.0) per month with a mean of 6060 Rials ($ 84.0) and a median payment of 3030 Rials (or about $ 42.0)

Who Initiates Divorce?

According to the Islamic tenets divorce is the man's prerogative. A women cannot repudiate her husband. But Egypt and Sudan in the 1920s, Pakistan in 1939, Jordan in 1951, Morocco in 1958, Iraq in 1959, Algeria in 1959, and South Yemen in 1974 enacted Civil Codes either permitting women to initiate divorce or have exactly the same right's as the men. In Iran, for the first time in 1931 women were given the right to initiate divorce on certain grounds, by taking their grievances to the religious judge, and if the judge had recognized the reasons as valid, the husband would have been asked to divorce his wife. Insanity (Article 1121), impotence, eunuch (castration in man), or if man's male organs were removed (Article 1122) constituted valid grounds for women to initiate divorce. In addition, the husband's failure to maintain his wife (Article 1129), and if at the time of marriage either spouse had claimed to posses a particular attribute but after the marriage proved to be false were also recognized as valid reasons for the other spouse to initiate divorce proceedings (Article 1128). The 1967 Family Protection Act put women on an equal footing with men by allowing them to initiate divorce on the broadly defined ground of "incompatibility of temperament," as well as those stipulated in the Civil Code cited above. Article 11 of the Act more fully describes the grounds for divorce: "In addition to the situation mentioned in the Civil Code, the wife or husband may also in the following situations apply to the Court for a Certificate of Irreconcilability: (1) If the wife or husband is sentenced finally and definitely to a penalty of five or more years imprisonment, or to a fine involving five years imprisonment as the consequence of liability to pay, or to imprisonment and a fine which together might result in five or more years imprisonment, and if the prison sentence or fine is the course of execution; (2) affliction with any sort of addictive habit which in the judgment of the Court is capable of making the husband's and wife's life impossible and of imparting damage to the foundation of the family life; (3) when the husband takes another wife without the written consent of the first wife; (4) when any of the spouses abandons family life; and, (5) when any of the spouses behaves contrary to the honour of the family and this has been proven to the satisfaction of the Court.

Perhaps, the most interesting aspect of the 1967 Act was that in consultation with some religious figures, the Act avoided a breakaway from the traditional Qur'anic law, and still recognized the husband's power of unilateral repudiation. This was accomplished by inserting in Article 17 of the Act that: "The provisions of Article 11 shall be inserted in the marriage certificate in the form of conditions of marriage contract, and irrevocable power of attorney for the wife to execute a divorce will be facilitated. This *talaq*, according to the provision of the Civil Code, will be irrevocable." Thus, women were given the same rights as those for men without contradicting the holy Qur'an.

Based on the 1978 data, in 37 out of 88 cases when the husbands were older than their wives, divorce was initiated by the wife. And, in 5 out of the 16 cases when the wives were older than their husbands, divorce proceedings were initiated by the wives. This amounts to a total of 42 (40.4 per cent) divorces initiated by the wives.

Goode stated: "The husband more frequently than the wife is the first to desire a divorce." And, "the husband is more often than the wife the party who adopts a line of behaviour which forces the other spouse to suggest a divorce." Of the 17 marriages that had lasted less than one year, in 82.4 per cent of the cases divorce proceedings were initiated by the men. Of the 14 marriages that were dissolved during the second year of marriage, 50.0 per cent were initiated by the husbands and 50.0 per cent by the wives. These findings do provide support in favour Goode's hypotheses. We can also hypothesize that: the earlier a marriage is dissolved, the higher the probability that divorce proceeding is initiated by the husband.

Occupational Status of the Divorcing Couples

The 1956, 1966 and 1973 divorce decrees did not specify the occupation of the divorced couples. However, the court files of the 104 couples who had received the Certificate of Irreconcilability contained the occupation of both spouses.

Ninety of the 104 wives (86.5 per cent) were housewives; eleven (10.6 per cent) were civil servants; two (1.9 per cent) were school teachers; and, one (1.0 per cent) was a janitor. The occupation of the husbands were distributed as follows:

1.	Labourer	25
2.	Transport equipment operator (i.e. driver)	17
3.	Civil servant	15
4.	Military Officer and/or policeman	9
5.	Farmer and gardener	7
6.	Blacksmith	3
7.	Carpenter	2
8.	Painter (of house)	1
9.	Electrician	1
10.	Photographer	1
11.	Technician (type not specified)	1
12.	Butcher	2
13.	School teacher	2
14.	Civil engineer	1
15.	Physician	1
16.	"Employer" (type or size not specified)	1
17.	Student	2
18.	Unemployed	4
19.	Retired	4
20.	In-prison (also unemployed)	1
21.	*Kasib* (self-employed shopkeeper)	4

Goode, Pitts and Wedgwood asserted that there is a rough inverse relationship between divorce rate and economic status. If occupation is used as an index of economic status (also a good predictor of social class), an examination of the above occupational distribution of the husbands shows that most to the 104 Certificates of Irreconcilability were granted to the families in the lower occupational categories. Labourers plus the unemployed (including the one person in prison) constituted 32.6 per cent of the sample. The two school teachers, the one civil engineer, the one physician, and the one "employer," which constituted 4.8 per cent of the husbands, could be regarded as middle class in Iran; but, all the others, amounting to 62.6 per cent of the sample, belonged to the lower-middle occupational category. Of the 104 Certificates not a single one was issued to anyone who could be regarded as the member of the upper-class. (The one physician could be regarded as a member of the upper-class.) The data for Shiraz do provide evidence in support of the above stated hypothesis that roughly divorce is inversely related to socio-economic status.

Reasons for Divorce

So far we have dealt with the antecedents of divorce in the sense that we have examined some of the socio-economic and demographic factors that make the couple more prone to divorce. Most of the factors discussed so far will not be given as the reason for requesting divorce. Indeed, none of the 104 couples who received Certificates of Irreconcilability, in roughly the first two months of 1978, had given early age at marriage or the wide husband-wife age gap as the reason for requesting divorce. The 104 court files revealed the following alleged reasons for divorce:

1.	Incompatibility of temperament	80
2.	Infertility of the woman/man	5
3.	Drug addiction (husband)	6
4.	Adultery (by woman)	2
5.	Husband's failure to maintain wife/children	2
6.	Husband a student in the U.S., failure to support wife	1
7.	Husband in prison, failure to support wife	1
8.	Husband and wife living separately	1
9.	Husband having children from previous marriage, wife cannot tole rate	2

10.	Wife having children from previous marriage, husband cannot tolerate	1
11.	Desertion (of wife by the husband)	1
12.	Man wants to go abroad, wife disagrees	1
13.	Wife being sick	1

Prior to passing of the Civil Code, the traditional Ithna' 'Ashari law applied as regards the husband's right to repudiate his wife at will, however blameless she might have been. The introduction of the Civil Code in the 1930s imposed some limitations on the husband in the sense that the following grounds were established as valid for him to repudiate his wife: (1) wife's insanity, whether permanent or periodical (Article 1121); (2) if woman was lesbian, had leprosy, or vitiligo, crippled, or blind from both eyes, provided that these defects were not present at the time of marriage (Article 1123); (3) if at the time of marriage husband was led to believe that the woman possessed a certain desirable attribute, but later proved to be false—even if the particular attribute was not stipulated in the marriage contract (Article 1128). Even after the introduction of the Civil Code, a husband had a wide latitude in repudiating his wife at will (Article 1133).

As previously pointed out, the 1967 Act significantly limited man's unilateral power to repudiate his wife, and yet the Act avoided a conflict with the Qur'anic principle.

Relative to the above statistics, it may be noted that a great of the Certificates were issued on the grounds of *'adam-i tawafuq-i akhlaqi*, or the incompatibility of temperaments. What this really means is that there is no single specific reason for divorce, rather to the best judgement of the court the marriage had irretrievable broken down, and there was no possibility for reconciliation. It must also be noted that drug addiction, adultery, and husband's failure to maintain his wife and infertility were among the major alleged reasons for divorce.

7

The Intricacy of Al-'Awl

MUSA ALI AJETUNMOBI

Succession Law in Islam: An Introduction

Islam is not a mere religion but an ideology which provides practical solutions to human and non-human problems. Our concern in this article is, however, the human rather than the non-human problems. Islam is an advocate of peace, peace with Allah, with man, and with all other things in the society living and non-living. The peaceful message of Islam is discernible in all its teachings which include the succession law.

With the death of a Muslim male or female, the law of Islam prescribes that his/her possession should devolve to four types of his/her acquitance severally or jointly. Such acquitances are the relations by blood, by affinity, by slavery, and by religion through the treasury of an Islamically constituted society. However, being a relation of the deceased Muslim is not an automatic licence to inherit him. Some relations may be prohibited from the inheritance in the following circumstances:

(a) If a relation deliberately killed the deceased relation;

(b) If two relations, who could inherit each other by law, should die at the same time or at different places by which the knowledge of who died before the other became complicated and difficult to determine;

(c) If a relation is under the bond of slavery;

(d) If a divorcing couple separated through mutual imprecation (*Li'an*);

(e) If the two relations belong to different religions;
(f) If a relation is illegitimate to the deceased; and
(g) Non-acclamation of a baby after birth before its burial.

Blood relations are classified for the purpose of inheritance into agnates and sharers. The agnates are the male descendants, their sons, ascendants, collaterals, sons of collaterals, ascendants' collaterals, and sons of ascendants' collaterals. Other categories of agnate include manumitted slave and the treasury. The shares are the spouse, female descendants, female ascendants, female collaterals and some selected male heirs (the grandfather and the uterine brothers). An agnate can inherit the whole property of the deceased if he is the only survivor but inherits and residue after allotting the appropriate shares to the respective sharers. The shares allotted by the Qur'an and the Prophetic *Sunnah* are 1/2, 1/4, 1/8, 2/3, 1/3, and 1/6. If is to be noted that the grandfather can inherit in either way or both ways, i.e. as an agnate or/and a sharer. It should also be noted that when both male and female of the same class are inheriting, the female shall drop her right as a sharer and joins her male counterpart as a cognate. In such a situation each male shall take double the share of each female.

Not all blood relations of the prepositus can inherit at the same time since some relations can expel some others either permanently or partially. Out of all relations, only the father, the mother, the son, the daughter, the husband and the wife cannot be permanently expelled. All others may be expelled by some more closer relations. Partial expulsion in this context means reduction in the original allotted share and no heir is absolutely free from it.

Origin of al-'awl

It has been established from many historical records that the concept of *pro rata* reduction developed during the tenure of the caliph 'Umar b. al-Khattab, and it was never known, during the era of Prophet Muhammad nor during the reign of the first caliph, Abu Bakr. The origin of proportional reduction in the Islamic law of succession is a bit controversial. Available records reveal that the concept was first suggested to the caliph 'Umar by either al-'Abbas, 'Ali b. Abi Talib or Zayd b Thabit. So also do divergencies abound in the first case of *al-'awl* that confronted the Companions. Some records quote the case of where a husband and two germane sisters were the heirs to a prepositus, while another quotes the celebrated case of *al-Minbariyah* in which the wife, father, mother and two daughters were the heirs. Coulson quoted another case of where the husband, father and two daughters were the survivors, while Doi also quoted two other cases where the heirs were either the husband, a full sister and a uterine sister, or the husband, a full sister and the mother, as the first case of *al-'awl* treated in Islam. Whatever be the case, the doctrine of *al-'awl* applies when the estate is over subscribed.

It is also on record that since the establishment of the concept of *al-'awl* by the caliph 'Umar, the Sunnite school of thought "has consistently maintained that the burden of reduction is to be borne reteably by all entitled Qur'anic heirs." However, the doctrine did not go unchallenged by a young Companion of the Prophet named 'Abd Allah b. 'Abbas, though not during the lifetime of 'Umar b. al-Khattab. In fact, when the first case of *al-'awl* came before 'Umar, he was reported to have said: "By Allah, I do not know which of you Allah has put first so that I too may put first and which comes next so that I too may put next but I have come across an opinion if it is appropriate then it is from Allah ('s guidance) but if it is inappropriate then it is from 'Umar ('s limitation)."

Ibn 'Abbas submitted later that had 'Umar knew the order of precedence among the heirs as prescribed by Allah and had he acted accordingly, he would not have resorted to *al-'awl*, but 'Umar had already made a statement that he did not know that order of preference. It was, therefore, expected of Ibn 'Abbas who knew the order to have gone to 'Umar for its explanation but he failed to go forward. When Ibn 'Abbas was challenged on his failure in this regard, he replied that he did not want to undermine the charisma of 'Umar and hence he kept silence on the issue. Such a failure and maintenance of silence by Ibn 'Abbas is surprising because his solution to the problem of *al-'awl* is nearer to the Qur'anic teachings on the issue than putting the burden on all sharers proportionately. The silence of Ibn 'Abbas is this regard may be due to his age, which was around twenty years at that time, and also the fact that 'Umar was prominent among his teachers from whom he acquired the bulk of his knowledge. However, the suggested solution of Ibn 'Abbas to *al'-awl* has been adopted in the Shi'ite school of thought by which "the burden of necessary reduction is to be borne exclusively by daughters or agnatic sisters." Not only that, Ibn Shihab al-Zuhri had said that "if the decision of Ibn 'Abbas was not preceded by judicial authority of Sayyidina 'Umar, nobody will differ with Ibn 'Abbas."

Ibn 'Abbas explains that the Qur'anic shares are of two types: those who inherit as only sharers and those who inherit as sharers on the one hand and as agnates on the other. He argues further that the shares among the spouse and the ascendants must be satisfied with their full Qur'anic shares while the other sharers among the descendants and the collaterals who inherit as agnates along with their respective male counterparts should take the residue after satisfying the first group. Considering the eight types of *al-'awl* discussed in section two above, it is evident (as also observed by Coulson) that "there can be no case of an over-subscribed estate unless a daughter/grand-daughter or agnatic sister is an entitled heir." We are, therefore, inclined to support the view of Ibn 'Abbas on this issue, though with some amendments as presented in the examination of Qur'an which follows.

Qur'an, IV: 11, 12 and 176 Examined

Major Qur'anic injunctions on succession are found in Chapter IV, particularly verses 11, 12 and 176. Verse 11 discusses the shares of the descendants and the ascendants in detail while verse 12 explains the shares of the spouses. Verse 176 throws more light on the shares of the collaterals which have been mentioned in brief in both verses 11 and 12. A summary of what we can understand from the three verses is as follows:

(i) That sons and daughters of the prepositus are sharers, though shares of the sons are not specifically mentioned except that a son must get double the share of a daughter. The philosophy of ratio 2:1 in this regard will be discussed in detail in another article on the subject. Meanwhile, it is clear from the order of arrangement that the descendants are more entitled to inherit the deceased's property than any other(s).

(ii) That the parents of the prepositus come next to the sons and daughters in order of importance. Mother's share is one-sixth either when inheriting along with the father—in a case where the deceased is survived by children or when inheriting along with the deceased's collaterals—in the absence of children. She shares one-third when the deceased leaves neither children nor collaterals.

(iii) The express injunction of the Qur'an on the father's share is clear only in the case of where he inherits along with the mother—when the prepositus has children. The Qur'an is silent on his share when the deceased leaves no child and when there are collaterals as heirs along with him. The injunction which prescribes one-third for the mother is capable of two interpretations when related to the father's share:

(a) That the father may take the remaining two-thirds—if the ratio 2:1 for male:female prescribed for the children is used as a yard-stick; or

(b) That he may take one-third like the mother since he has been allotted an equal one-sixth with her, where the children of the prepositus inherit with them—thus both mother and father are at par in this regard (as explained later in this section).

(iv) That the couple come next in order of priority. With children as heirs the husband shares one-quarter while the wife takes one-eighth. But without any surviving child for the propositus, the husband takes one-half while the wife or wives will share one-quarter. The ratio 2:1 is also glaring in this respect.

(v) The controversial *Kalalah* which is mentioned in verse 12 and explained further in verse 176 puts the collaterals in the last ladder of heir hierarchy. Verse 12 suggests that both male and female are at par, thus they share per capita. It also puts their total share to one-third no matter how many they may be. Verse 176 explains further that female collaterals are entitled to two-thirds where no children survive the propositus or one-half in the same circumstance if the female collateral is not more than one. Qur'anic exegetes have analyzed that the collaterals mentioned in verse 12 are the uterines while those mentioned in verse 176 are the germanes.

Whatever be the case, it appears that the collaterals, male or/and female (other than the uterines), are allotted the shares of the descendants, male or/and female, in the absence of the latter, i.e. in a *kalalah* case. They, therefore, play the role of each other except that the attention of our doctors of law, past and present, has not been directed to this interpretation.

On the basis of these analyses, we feel that if a husband, a mother and some germane female collaterals survive a propositus, the husband shall take one-quarter (and not one-half which is the present practice), the mother takes one-sixth while the germane or consanguinean female collaterals shall share the residue per capita among themselves. If there are male collaterals of equal status among the heirs, the residue will still go to all of them but the formula of ratio 2:1 shall apply in sharing the residue. However, if the collaterals are uterines, both male and female, their share is only one-third of the total estate while the residue should go to *Bayt al-Mal* (Public Treasury). When the father joins the team of heirs in this example, the husband will still take his one-quarter (and not one-half) while the parents will share one-sixth each; the residue of five-twelfths or one-third of the total estate will go to the germane or uterine collaterals who stand in the position of the descendants as explained above. We are aware, firstly, that the present practice gives the father a right to expel the collaterals but such expulsion is of no basis as long as the collaterals actually step into the shoes of the descendants and as long as the Qur'an has not allowed the mother to expel the uterine collaterals! We are also aware, secondly, that the present practice allots one-half to the husband when he inherits without descendants, but we feel that his share should also be halved as long as the collaterals who inherit with him actually step into the shoes of the descendants and as long as the share of the mother, who to us is closer to the deceased, has been halved by Allah in setting for us a paradigm. We are finally aware that the present practice accords the father a privilege to take double the share of the mother but we believe that the share of both mother and father should be equal as Allah has allotted to both an equal share of one-sixth when they inherit along with the descendants, and as the mother has been recommended by the Prophet Muhammad (p.b.u.h.) for a better consideration than the father. Our suggestion above may solve the famous problem of *al-Gharra'ayn* or *'Umariyatani* where the law favours the father.

It is unfortunate that the text of the Qur'an had to be understood in a way that a resort should be made to *al-'awl* by the early Muslim. Actually, where a daughter or a sister is allotted one-half or where the plurality of each is allotted two-thirds, no spouse will be inheriting along with her or them. In that case, the parents shall take their respective one-sixth while the two-thirds residue should go tó either the daughters or the sisters, or one-half to go to either a single daughter or a single sister. Where a spouse is inheriting with either the descendant or the collateral, the latter retires to inherit as residuary whether or not the ascendants are inheriting with them, while the former's share is halved. To illustrate this, let "daughters" replace "sisters" in our former example where the husband and the two parents are inheriting. The husband takes one-quarter, the father shares one-sixth, the mother inherits one-sixth, while the residue of five-twelfths should go to the daughters to be shared among them per capita. In another way, if the wife replaces the husband, she takes one-eighth, the parents take their respective one-sixth, while the daughters shall also take the residue. The same formula will apply where a single daughter or sister is inheriting along with the ascendants and a spouse.

8

Judicial System Under 'Umar the Great

MUHAMMAD YUSUF GURAYA

Constitution

'Umar, one of the topmost Companions of the holy Prophet, became the second caliph of Islam after the death of Abu Bakr. The Qur'an was the Constitution (*al-Kitab*) and the Guidance (*Huda*) of his government.

The heads of the Muslim States are under an obligation to make decisions in accordance with the provisions of the Qur'an. All Muslims must follow the Qur'an and submit to the decisions made on its basis. The Sunnah of the holy Prophet, an excellent exemplar (*uswatan hasanatan*) was the model behaviour before 'Umar for the implementation of the Qur'an Constitution.

Adherence to the provisions of the Qur'an and the Sunnah of the holy Prophet was the most fundamental policy of 'Umar's Government. In his various proclamations, public announcements and declarations he emphasized the supreme importance of the Qur'an and the Sunnah. He included a clause to that effect in the appointment letters of his military commanders, governors and judges of provinces. He sent written instructions to his military officers exhorting them to follow the Book of God and Sunnah of the holy Prophet. The most famous and well-known judicial charter which he sent to one of his governors and heads of the provincial judiciary, Abu Musa al-Ash'ari, contains the following clause:

> Use your brain about matters that perplex you and about which you do not find clear guidance in the Book of God nor in the

Sunnah of the holy Prophet.

The same thing was repeated while discussing the duties and obligations of his provincial governors and judges. He once said:

> O God, Thou art my witness in the appointments of the provincial governors. Indeed, I have sent them to teach people their religion and the Sunnah of the Prophet, to do justice among them, to distribute booty among them, and to refer to me the issues which they find difficult of solution.

History has recorded many cases which show that as soon as an authentic Hadith of the holy Prophet was quoted on a certain issue in hand, 'Umar decided the case accordingly. On the conquest of Iraq he was confronted with the case of the Magians. The issue was whether the Magians should be treated as the People of the Book or not. He put this issue before an assembly of the senators at Madinah in the following manner:

> I do not know how to deal with the Magians?

'Abd al-Rahman b. 'Awf, one of the members of the assembly, recalled a saying of the holy Prophet and quoted it as follows:

> I bear witness that the holy Prophet said: "Treat them as you treat the People of the Book."

'Umar accepted the statement of Ibn 'Awf and decided the case accordingly. Since the case was referred to him by a provincial government of Dast Maysan (a province laying between Basra and Baghdad), he sent the decision to the governor with the following judicial order:

> Take *jizyah* from the Magians of Hajar.

After the conquest of Syria, plague broke out in the province. 'Umar called a meeting of the military commanders at its border to discuss the situation. The problem was what should be done to save the Muslim population. Different opinions were expressed. Some wanted to stay while the others wanted to free from it. 'Abd al-Rahman, a senior Companion of the holy Prophet, made the following statement:

> I have the right information about it. I heard the Prophet saying: "Whenever you hear that a land in infected with this epidemic, do not advance towards it. But if the epidemic breaks out when you happen to be there, do not flee from it for safety."

'Umar accepted the evidence of Ibn 'Awf and decided the case in accordance with it. He announced his decision and returned to Madinah.

Legislation

The clause, quoted above from the charter of judicial instructions given by 'Umar to Abu Musa al-Ash'ari, indicates that in view of the geographical expansion of the Caliphate and due to the emergence of new social, legal and judicial problems, the state had to frame legislation for the solution of such problems and to make interpretation of the texts of the Qur'an and the Sunnah of the holy Prophet. This was a crucial and critical issue which 'Umar had to face in the absence of the holy Prophet. This required the exercise of independent reasoning (*ijtihad*), on the one hand, and its acceptance by the Muslim community at large (*ijma*)', on the other. 'Umar accepted the challenge and undertook the job. It is an established fact of history that he met the challenge most successfully.

Fundamental legislative principles were provided in the Constitution of the Qur'an. The most basic principle was, "governance by mutual consultation" (*amruhum shura baynahum*). The holy Prophet himself was ordained, "consult them (the people) in the governance" (*shawirhum fi al-amr*). 'Umar implemented the above constitutional provisions during his lifetime. After assessing the historical material and going through the annals of history, the present writer has come to the conclusion that all the *ultra revelational* matters which arose during the time of the holy Prophet were decided strictly in accordance with the aforesaid Qur'anic principles. Following the Sunnah of the holy Prophet, 'Umar devised a legislative mechanism on the consultative-democratic-Qur'anic principles. 'Umar's biographers have generally held that his decisions were based on his personal independent reasoning.

The historical evidence does not support this view. No doubt 'Umar initiated many fresh laws and gave expression to many original and creative ideas, but for their implementation he had to convince the majority of the Emigrants (*Muhajirun*) and the Helpers (*Ansar*). Thus his *ijtihad* had to be converted into *ijma'* before it gained the status of a law. The greatness of 'Umar as legislator lay in his ability to initiate a new issue and get it approved by the majority of the legislators by employing persuasive measures and using convincing arguments. For the sake of illustration of the above an enactment is quoted below:

On the conquest of Iraq a very big fertile region of land called Sawad came into the possession of the Muslim army. The officers of the army, particularly the *Muhajirun*, desired that the land and the peasants should be distributed among them. 'Abd al-Rahman b. 'Awf and Bilal were the most vocal advocates of the above view. 'Umar did not agree with this view. He wanted to keep the land as state property and to make fixed payments to the army officers and soldiers. The issue was discussed and debated at length in different sessions of the *Shura* (Consultative Assembly). Finally, it was decided to refer the issue to a committee consisting of the elite of the *Ansar*, especially constituted for this purpose. Both the parties presented their views before the committee. 'Umar's statement as reported by Abu Yusuf in his *Kitab al-Kharaj* is recorded as follows:

> You have heard the arguments of these people. They think, perhaps, I am depriving them of their rights. I have distributed among them the movable property gained as booty. However, I hold that the land and the peasants should be kept as common trust under the control of the state. The peasants should pay a fixed amounts of *kharaj* over the land and *jizyah* over their heads. The *kharaj* and the *jizyah* should accrue as permanent source of common income for the Muslims. The army, the infants and the coming generations should benefit from the common trust. We have to keep a standing army to guard our borders. Cantonments are to be developed in different conquered lands. If the lands and the tillers are distributed among these people, from where the funds will come to meet the expenditure of these projects!

Continuing his statement, 'Umar also countered their arguments and met their interpretation of certain verses of the Qur'an. He said: "These people advance only those verses of the Qur'an which serve their purpose while ignoring those which support my view." Then he quoted the relevant verse "*wa ma afa Allahu 'ala Rasulihi minhum*" from the chapter *al-Hashr* and held that it was revealed in connection with the Jewish tribe, Banu Nadir, who had already met their fate and now the verse was applicable to lands in general. Then he referred to verses 7 and 8 and emphasized that the people (*Ansar*) mentioned in the verse are equally entitled to the benefits of such lands (*walladhina tabawwa'ud dara wal-iymana min qablihim yuhibbuna man hajara ilayhim*).

The opening phrase of the verse *walladhina ja'u min ba'dihim* "the coming generations" was his most decisive argument (*inni qad wajattu hujjatan*). `Umar concluded his statement by saying: How is it possible that we distribute these lands only among the present generation and deprive the coming generations of them?

After hearing the statements and arguments of both the parties the committee announced its unanimous decision:

> O the Commander of the Believers, your view is correct. Your opinion is based on the truth. Your view is the most sound and is most suitable in the context. If the army is not kept to guard the cities and the borders the enemy (*ahl al-kufr*) will again capture them.

The above decision was accepted by both the parties. Thereafter, 'Umar appointed two persons ('Uthman b. Hunayf and Hudhayfah b. al-Yaman), most experienced among the Companions of the holy Prophet, for the measurement of the land and for determining the amount of *kharaj* and *jizyah*.

The above case provides ample evidence to the fact that the laws made under 'Umar were based on the Qur'anic principles of mutual consultation (*shura baynahum*). The Emigrants and the Helpers were taken as representatives of the general will of the Muslim community

(*Ummah*). They were called into legislative session by the announcement of "the assembly for prayer" (*al-salatu jami'atun*). In response to the above summons the members assembled in the mosque of the holy Prophet and offered tow *rak'at* as prayer along with the Caliph. Thereafter 'Umar stood on the pulpit and presented the issue in hand before the assembly.

Ibn Sa'd has reported that six seniormost Companions of the holy Prophet formed the central consultative body (*Majlis-i Shura*) whom 'Umar used to consult most frequently. They were: 'Uthman, 'Ali, 'Abd al-Rahman b. 'Awf, Mu'adh b. Jabal, Ubye b. Ka'b and Zayd b. Thabit.

Legal Education

"Ignorance of law in no excuse" is a dictum recently adopted and emphasized by the modern developed countries of the West. On the contrary, no arrangements are made to give legal education to the masses. To award punishment to an innocent person is tyranny. The persons who are kept ignorant of the law, and the authorities have made no arrangements for their legal education, are considered innocent in Islam. The award of punishment to such "innocents" is also tyranny. The West has not taken upon itself to acquaint its citizens with the law before enforcing the above dictum by their courts. Islam does not subscribe to this view. The foremost duty of the holy Prophet of Islam was to teach people and Diving Law and to make them aware of the legal obligations:

> He it is who raised among the illiterates a Messenger from among themselves, who recites to them His messages and purifies them, and teaches them the Book and the Wisdom—although they were earlier certainly in manifest error.

Here *yu'allimuhumul kitab* (he teaches them the Book) has been described to make the people aware of the Divine Law (*al-Kitab*). In another verse the holy Prophet has been reminded of his duty of teaching the Divine Law in clearer terms:

> O Messenger, deliver that which has been revealed to thee from

> thy Lord! and if thou do it not, thou hast not delivered His message. And Allah will protect thee from men. Surely Allah guides not the disbelieving people.

Islam gives the benefit of ignorance to the persons concerned if the state agencies fail to perform their duty of educating the people, and making them aware of their duties and obligations. God has made accountable only those people to whom He has conveyed His message by raising prophets among them:

> O people of the Book, indeed Our messenger has come to you explaining to your after a cessation of the messengers, lest you say: There came not to us a bearer of good news nor a warner. So indeed a bearer of good news and a warner has come to you.

Before inflicting punishment the educating agencies will take account of themselves whether they have really given legal education and have ensured that the accused had duly received it.

> Whenever, a group is cast into it (the Hell), its keepers ask them: Had not a warner come to you? They say: Yes, indeed a warner came to us, but we denied and said: Allah had revealed nothing. You are only in great error.

The holy Prophet implemented the above teaching in totality. He sent teachers among the converts for acquainting them with the Divine Law. Abu Bakr also followed him most scrupulously. He gave explicit orders to his military commanders that before punishing anyone they should ensure that the message of Islam has been duly conveyed to the people on the enemy side and they have intentionally ignored it. If someone was punished by mistake or without the teachings of Islam being conveyed to him, he was duly compensated. 'Umar institutionalized the above-mentioned judicial principle and appointed *muftis* (legal experts) in different provinces of his Caliphate to teach people the law of the land lest they remain in ignorance. The following scholars were renowned legal experts available to the masses for their education:

'Ali 'Uthman, Mu'adh b. Jabal, 'Abd al-Rahman b. 'Awf, Ubye b. Ka'b, Zayd b. Thabit, Abu Hurrayrah and Abu Darda. Shah Waliyullah has pointed out that only the authorized persons were allowed to give legal opinion (*fatwa*). The unauthorized persons were prohibited to do so and were asked to refrain from it without government permission. The authorized legal experts were properly announced and the people were asked to seek legal opinion from them. 'Umar made this announcement in a public gathering held at Jabiyah.

Administration of Justice

The holy Prophet organized the judicial system within the limits of the Arabian peninsula. Under Abu Bakr some parts of Iraq and Syria were also conquered and came within the jurisdiction of his judiciary. 'Umar extended his judicial jurisdiction to the whole of Iraq, Iraq, Syria, Palestine and Egypt after their conquests. When the heat of the conquests had cooled to the normal level and peace and tranquility were established, 'Umar, the head of Islamic judicial system, found himself confronted with the two greatest legal and judicial systems, set up in the conquered lands by the Romans and the Persians. He had also to deal with multiracial, regional and religious communities. It ws a great challenge. 'Umar accepted it and met it most successfully. He developed and elaborated the judicial system inherited from his predecessors, and evolved a very effective and efficient judiciary to meet the requirements of his time.

Due to the rapid expansion of the Islamic state and the emergence of numerous problems, organization of justice during his regime necessarily took a more formal shape. He did not only organize the judiciary on sound footings, but also made it more independent of the executive. Complete separation of powers in a government has not been possible, nor can it add to the efficiency and stability of a state. The greatness of a civilization is, however, always measured in terms of independent working or, otherwise, of the legal system on which that civilization is based. In this respect, 'Umar's efforts to keep the judiciary immune from the evil influence of the executive authority are not only admirable but seem to be in advance of his age.

Shay Waliyullah observes that the Islamic law, in theory and practice, made such extensive strides under 'Umar that most of the later jurists, particularly the founders of four schools of law, made his decisions, principles and methods the main subject of their study. The judicial decisions of the reign of 'Umar contributed to a great extent towards the development of the Islamic legal system, for they serve as a very reliable anchor for the purpose of judicial theorizing.

'Umar as Chief Justice of Islamic Judiciary

'Umar organized the judicial system in all the provinces of his Caliphate and appointed judges and *qadis* for the dispensation of justice. The provincial and district judicial functionaries referred many difficult and complicated cases to the head of judiciary at Madinah for seeking his decision or advice. History has recorded many cases which were decided and revised by 'Umar. Appeal and writs were also submitted to him against the misconduct and offences committed by his military commanders and civil administrators. He passed judgments even against the highest officers of his administration without fear or favour. The proceedings and judgement of a case decided by 'Umar are given below to show the judicial procedure as it prevailed under 'Umar:

Al-Tabari in his annals under the events in A.H. 17 has reported this case: Mughirah b. Shu'bah, a Companion of the holy Prophet, was governor of Basra. In Rabi's al-Awwal, A.H. 17, Abu Bakrah, a resident of the town lodged a written complaint against the governor with 'Ummar at Madinah. He stated in the complaint that Mughirah had committed the offence of adultery and he could prove it in the court of justice.

One the basis of the *prima facie* evidence contained in the complaint, the head of Islamic judiciary felt that it fulfilled the legal requirements for hearing. The accused Mughirah was charge-sheeted and was deposed from the office of governorship. Abu Musa al-Ash'ari, the newly appointed governor of Basra, was given Mughirah's deposition orders and was sent to Basra to take charge from Mughirah and send him to Madinah for trial.

On receipt of the deposition orders Mughirah handed over the charge to Abu Musa. Thereafter in compliance with the orders of the court the complainant along with his witnesses and the respondent proceeded to Madinah to appear in the court of the Chief Justice of the Islamic judiciary.

First of all the accused was called in the court and was served with the charge sheet and was asked to explain his position. Mughirah denied the charge and requested the court for permission to cross examine the complainant and the witnesses on the following points:

The first question was: From which side did they see me (the accused), from the side of my face or from the side of my back? The second question was: How did they see the woman and how did they recognize her? If they saw me from the side of my face then it (the sexual intercourse) was hidden from them? If they saw me from the side of my back, how was it possible for them to see me in my house in the sexual act with my wife? At the end of his statement Mughirah stated: "By God I did not have sexual intercourse except with my wife who resembled the alleged woman (Umm-i Jamil)."

After the explanation of the accused, the complainant Abu Bakrah was the first to make his statement. He stated: "Mughirah b. Shu'bah and I are neighbours. There is a street between us. We were in our attics (garrets) builds opposite to each other in our houses. Each of the attics has a window opposite to each other. A few persons came to me and we were chatting in my attic. The wind blew and the door of the window opened. I stood up to close it. I saw Mughirah, because the wind had also opened the door of the window of his attic. He (Mughirah) was between the legs of a woman. I asked the persons: 'Stand up and look.' They stood up and looked. Then I asked them to bear witness. They asked: `Who is this woman?' I said, 'She is Umm Jamil bint al-Afqam.' Umm Jamil was from Bani `Amir b. Sa'sa'ah. She used to visit Mughirah and she also used to visit other chiefs and eminent persons. Some other women also used to do the same in her time. They (the persons) said: 'We have seen only the rumps (backsides) and we do not know what the face is like?' However, they agreed when she stood up. When Mughirah proceeded to lead the prayer I prevented him from leading the prayer or saying prayer with us. Then we wrote about it to 'Umar." On receipt of the above complaint 'Umar called for Abu Musa and said: "I appoint you as governor and send you to a province where the Satan was born and grew up. Hold fast what you know and do not change, otherwise God will change you." He requested: "O Commander of the faithful, help me with some of the Companions of the holy Prophet from among the Emigrants and the Helpers. I find them in this *Ummah*, and among these affairs like salt, the food will not be cured except with it (salt)." He (ʿUmar) said: "Help yourself with those whom you like." He chose for help twenty-nine persons. Anas b. Malik, 'Imran b. Hasin and Hisham b. 'Amir were among them. Thereafter Abu Musa proceeded along with them and halted at al-Mirbad. The news of his halt reached Mughirah, who remarked: "By God! Abu Musa has come neither as a visitor nor as a trader. But he has come as governor." They were still pondering over it when Abu Musa reached them. He handed over to him a letter from 'Umar. It was the most concise letter consisting of four sentences only:

> I received stupendous news. I have sent Abu Musa as governor. Hand over to him what is in your hand. And hurry up.

In compliance with the summons of the court al-Mughirah proceeded to madinah. Abu Bakrah along with other witnesses, Nafi'b. Kaldah, Ziyad and Shibl b. Ma'bad al-Bajali, also proceeded thither and appeared before 'Umar.

Abu Bakrah stated in the court that he saw the accused between the legs of Umm Jamil. He was inserting and pulling out (his penis) like kohl stick in the kohl container.

The Chief Justice asked, "From which side did you see them?" The complainant replied, "From their back side," The Chief Justice asked, "How did you recognize her head?" The complainant replied, "I kept myself in waiting." Then the Justice called Shibl b. Ma'bad. He also bore witness like the witness of Abu Bakrah. The Justice inquired, "Did you see them from their back side or from their front side?" He replied, "I saw them from their front side." The third witness Nafi' also bore witness like the evidence of Abu Bakrah. However, the fourth witness, Ziyad, did not bear witness like other witnesses. He stated: "I saw him (Mughirah) sitting between the legs of a woman. I also saw falling of dyed and bare feet and heard violent breathing." The Justice inquired, "Did you see him doing like the kohl stick in the kohl container?" He said, "No." The Justice inquired, "Did you recognize the woman?" He said, "No, although there was some resemblance with her." The Justice remarked, "You have backed out."

According to the Qur'anic law of evidence four witnesses are required to prove the offence of adultery. If complainants do not produce four witnesses then punishment is awarded to them for false charge:

> And those who accuse a free woman and bring not four witnesses, flog them (with) eighty stripes and never accept their evidence, and these are the transgressors.

It is evident from the proceedings of the case that the fourth witness Ziyad did not support the evidence of the complainant and his two companions. Therefore, the evidence was not complete. In accordance with the Qur'anic lay they were declared false witnesses and were punishment with eighty stripes each.

Judicial Procedure Under 'Umar

We have quoted the proceedings of the above case with details to show the judicial procedure and methodology which was evolved and practised under 'Umar. The following salient features can be noted from the foregoing:

1. Justice was administered regardless of the rank, race and religion of the complainant or the respondent.
2. A common man could lodge a complaint against the governor of his province and could get redress for his grievance.
3. The court of chief justice of the Islamic judiciary at Madinah was easily accessible to all citizens of the Caliphate, where justice was administered without difficulty and without expenses.
4. On receipt of complaint, its contents were investigated and scrutinized. On the basis of the *prima facie* evidence of the case a charge sheet was prepared and served on the accused for clarifying his position.

5. If the offence was committed by a military or a civil officer, he was deposed from his office so that he could exercise neither influence nor pressure on the proceedings of the court.
6. The accused was given the fullest opportunity to vindicate his position with regard to the allegations levelled against him.
7. The circumstances and issues raised in the statement of the accused were given due importance and they were kept in view during the proceedings of the case and also during cross examination of the witnesses.
8. The complainant and the witnesses were free to state the actual circumstances and to help the court in finding truth.
9. During cross examination the complainant and the witnesses had to answer all the questions put to them and given minute details of the circumstances under which of offence was committed.
10. The Qur'anic law was held supreme with regard to the evidence and judgements. In case the complainant and the witnesses fell short of the Qur'anic law of evidence, they were punished for bearing false witness and the accused had not to lodge a separate complaint in the court of justice in this respect.

In his capacity as head of the Islamic judiciary, 'Umar decided many cases referred to him for Madinah and other provinces of his Caliphate. A few more instances are quoted in the following:

Murder Committed by More than one Person

Five men murdered an unknown person in San'a, a district in Yaman. The case was referred by the local judicial authorities to the court of the Chief Justice of Madinah. 'Umar heard the case and the circumstances under which the murder was committed. The evidence revealed that all the five accused were equally responsible for the murder. He, therefore, awarded death sentence to all of them. He further remarked that if all the people in San'a had participated in the murder, he would have extended the same punishment to all of them.

Judgement on a Murder Case wherein One of the Heirs Forgives the Murderer

A murder was committed and the case was referred to the Chief Justice, 'Umar, for adjudication. After hearing the trial the accused was convicted for the murder. 'Umar announced his judgement wherein the murderer was sentenced to death. On the announcement of the judgement one of the heirs of the murdered person declared that he forgave the murderer and abandoned the share of his claim. 'Umar, however, persisted in his judgement. A legal expert and a jurist, 'Abd Allah b. Mas'ud was present in the court at that time. With the permission of the court he expressed his opinion as follows:

> All the heirs have their right against the murderer. If one of them forgoes his right and the others do not, the judgement cannot be enforced except with the agreement of all.

After hearing his opinion, 'Umar asked him: "How should the case under reference be settled?" He submitted, "The murderer should pay the blood-money to the heirs and the share of the person who has given up his claim be deducted." 'Umar accepted his opinion, revoked his first judgement and passed orders accordingly.

Advocacy in Islam

The proceedings of the above-mentioned murder case show that the Chief Justice of the Islamic judiciary, 'Umar b. al-Khattab, allowed a legal expert to express his opinion in the law court. The legal expert interpreted the law exercising his independent judgement, and expressed his opinion. His opinion was accepted by the court. Can it not be inferred from the above that qualified legal experts (advocates) can be permitted to appear in the courts of justice and help the court in clarifying legal issues involved in the case by interpreting law from their point of view?

Decision in the Absence of Witnesses and Swearing

A horseman of the tribe of Sa'd b. Layth, while racing, crushed the toe of a person of the tribe of Juhaynah. The hurt proved fatal and the person died. The case was filed in the court of 'Umar. He summoned some leading men of the Sa'd. They were asked to swear that the deceased was not killed because of the injury. They refused to do so. He, then, asked the heirs of the deceased to swear that the deceased had died because of the injury. They also refused. On the refusal of both parties, the Chief Justice announced his judgement that the accused should pay half of the blood-money to the aggrieved party.

Complaints and Investigations

Proper investigation of complaints is a pre-requisite of justice. 'Umar was fully aware of its importance. The holy Prophet had initiated the establishment of the investigation office which was further developed by 'Umar. He set up a permanent bureau of investigation at Madinah. He appointed Muhammad b. Maslamah al-Ansari as the head of the department. Under this office investigations were made of the complaints of the subjects lodged against the governors and other high ranking officers posted in different provinces of the Caliphate. On receipt of a complaint the head of the investigation department, Muhammad b. Maslamah, was ordered by the Caliph to proceed to the provincial capital concerned and to hold an inquiry. According to the procedure of investigation, he held general meetings in the great mosque of the capital after prayer and inquired about the complaint in public gatherings. Every citizen was allowed to express his opinion and give his arguments against or in favour of the matter. A few instances are quoted below as an illustration:

In A.H. 17 the new city of Kufa was founded. Sa'd b. Abi Waqqas was its governor. A governor's house was constructed for him and a gate was put before his office. The background of the gate was that the governor's house was situated in the middle of the city which was thickly populated. Commercial markets and trade centres were situated around the governor's house. Due to the noise outside the governor's house, Sa'd could not do his official work peacefully and quietly. Hence, the governor ordered the construction of a gate in front of his office. A complaint was lodged with the Caliph, 'Umar, that Sa'd had built a palace which was named after him and he had also constructed a gate in front of it. This resulted in preventing the complainants to appear in his court directly.

On receipt of the complaint, the Caliph immediately ordered Muhammad b. Maslamah to proceed to Kufa and to investigate the matter. He was further instructed that in case the contents of the complaint were found correct then the gate be burnt. He was also given a latter addressed to Sa'd which stated:

> I have been informed that you have build a palace. You use it as a fortress. It is called Sa'd's palace. You have built a gate keeping the people away from you. Come down therefrom and close it down. Do not build a gate at your palace preventing the entry of people to you, and denying thereby their rights. It is important so that they become equal to you.

With the above orders Muhammad b. Maslamah proceeded to Kufa. He investigated the matter and found a gate installed before Sa'd's palace. He bought firewood and went to the palace and burnt its gate. News of this reached Sa'd. He sent a messenger to the investigation officer requesting him to come to his office. He refused. Then Sa'd himself went to him and requested him to dismount (from his horse) and to come in. He refused. Sa'd then presented to him his tour expenses. He declined to accept the amount and handed over to Sa'd the letter of 'Umar referred to above. After completing the action as directed by the Caliph, Muhammad b. Maslamah immediately returned to the capital. When he reached the vicinity of Madinah his funds were exhausted. He had to live on the fibre of trees. In this condition he reached 'Umar, and submitted complete report of his activities. 'Umar asked, "Why did you not accept the amount of expenses from Sa'd?" He replied, "If you had desired it, you should have given me permission in writing, or you should have permitted me verbally." Thereupon 'Umar remarked: "The most perfect men of opinion are those who, in the absence of a mandate from competent authority, act most cautiously."

It may be gathered from the foregoing that 'Umar always gave priority to the facility and convenience of the complainants and the aggrieved, and removed and imaginable impediment which, in his opinion, could cause them difficulty. Delay in accepting and receiving complaints by the authorities and prolonging decisions thereupon defeat the very idea of justice. Delay, in 'Umar's opinion, is tantamount to "denying the rights." Quick and correct decision is the basic and fundamental criterion for judging the efficiency sophistication and development of any judicial system. Comparison of 'Umar's judicial administration with any modern judicial system with reveal that 'Umar's system was more advanced in meeting all the legal requirements of a case and in receiving complaints and their efficient disposal. There is an excellent example in the conduct of Muhammad b. Maslamah for the Muslim officers who proceed on official tour on government expenses.

Supremacy of Justice over all National Issues

That persons should submit to principles and no person is above law, was the supreme judicial principle of 'Umar's judicial system. Personal interests should be subordinated to the ideology of the state. Any person howsoever great he may be, ideologically, socially and politically, he is not above justice. In the Islamic context Muslim nations and nationals can be sacrificed for the sake of Islam. Only those persons are given charge of public offices, particularly of the judiciary, who are of impeccable character. If an allegation is levelled against a persons in charge of a public office, the allegation must be thoroughly investigated regardless of the state of emergency prevailing at the time of the accusation. It is necessary because only men of spotless character and of high moral standard can lead the nation to the right direction during a crisis. To substantiate the above statement, a case against one of the greatest Companions of the holy Prophet and one of the most respectable governors and conquerors of 'Umar is quoted below which was duly investigated by Muhammad b. Maslamah.

Some men from Kufa came to Madinah and lodged a complaint with the Caliph, 'Umar, against S'ad b. Abi Waqqas, the Governor of Kufa. They were violently agitated and levelled serious allegations against him. It was a state of emergency in thc province of Kufa. The Persians had gathered an army of about 1,50,000 soldiers from all over Persia and from the provinces of Sind, Khurasan and Hulwan at Nahawand to fight a decisive battle against the Caliphate. Sa'd b. Abi Waqqas, the Governor of Kufa and Commander-in-Chief of the Muslim forces in Iraq and Persia, was seriously engaged in collecting men and ammunition and in making preparation to march towards the battlefield at Nahawand. At this most critical moment 'Umar entertained the complaint against the Commander of the Muslim forces. The Caliph addressed al-Jarrah b. Sinan, one of the complainants and remarked: "The *prima facie* evidence and the state of emergency are not in favour of your complaint. However, by God, it will not prevent me from investigating the matter you have brought with you." Thereafter 'Umar ordered Muhammad b. Maslamah to proceed to Kufa and hold an inquiry into the matter.

Muhammad asked Sa'd to have a round along with him among the people of Kufa, while the troops were departing towards Nahawand. He took him to all the mosques of Kufa. He did not inquire into the matter secretly, because the matter was not a confidential nature. In every mosque he stood up among the public gathering and asked the people about Sa'b. Everywhere the people said: "We know nothing except goodness. We do not want his removal from office. We have nothing to say in the matter." Al-Jarrah b. Sinan and his companions kept silent. Neither did they say anything against Sa'd nor did they confirm what others had said. They deliberately suppressed the appreciation (of Sa'd) expressed by the people. At last the investigation team reached Banu 'Abd. Muhammad said, "State on oath by God that you would say nothing about the man except the truth." Usama b. Qatadah said, "I swear by God that he (Sa'd) does not distributed equally, and he does not rule the subjects justly, and he does not go out for fighting." Banu Asad also alleged that Sa'd did not say his prayers with perfection.

After recording the statements of the complainants and their supporters, Muhammad b. Maslamah completed his investigation. Thereupon he proceeded to Madinah along with Sa'd and the complainants to present them in the court of justice at Madinah. The inquiry officer submitted his investigation report of the Caliph. After hearing the details of the complaint from Muhammad, 'Umar put certain questions to Sa'd for further clarification of the issue. He asked: "O Sa'd, woe unto you; how do you say prayer?" Sa'd replied, "I take longer in the first two (*rak'at*) and less time in the last two." 'Umar remarked, "This was expected from you." Then he observed, "Had it not been the question of precaution, their course would have been very clear."

After going through the investigation report and hearing the statements of the complainants and their supporters and after cross-examination of the accused, the Caliph decided to remove Sa'd from governorship of Kufa. He asked, "Who is your deputy, O Sa'd, at Kufa?" Sa'd replied, "'Abd Allah b. 'Itban." 'Umar confirmed him and appointed him governor.

A complaint was received against 'Iyad b. Ghanam, governor of Egypt. He was accused of wearing fine clothes and placing a guard at his door. 'Umar asked Muhammad b. Maslamah to proceed to Egypt and bring 'Iyad in the same condition in which he would find him in Egypt. On his arrival in Egypt, Muhammad found 'Iyad in fine clothes. He caught him in the same condition and took him to Madinah, and presented him before the Caliph. He got his fine clothes removed and made him put on clothes made of a woollen blanket. He also asked for a herd of goats and ordered him, "Take this shepherd's stick and graze these goats." 'Iyad could not dare to refuse. He, however kept on saying, "Death is better than this." Thereupon 'Umar remarked, "Why do you hate this, your father was called *Ghanam* because he used to graze goats."

Annual Judicial Session at Makkah During Hajj

The most conspicuous features of the judiciary under 'Umar were: firstly, delay in the receipt and disposal of criminal complaints and civil cases was not tolerated; secondly, all people under his Caliphate were strictly treated as equals before law and no distinction was made with regard to their official status, social position, or religious tenets. The doors of his court of justice remained open round the clock at Madinah and grievances and complaints were redressed most efficiently and the accused were given every chance to vindicate their position and were awarded punishment in case they were found guilty. For further facility and convenience of the complainants and for ensuring that justice and equity was being maintained throughout the Caliphate, he held regular annual judicial session at Makkah during the *Hajj*. At-Tabari in his Annals at the end of events of the first year of 'Umar's Caliphate, reports that the Caliph attended the *Hajj* session personally every year except during the first year when he deputed 'Abd al-Rahman b. 'Awl to do so. Abu Bakr initiated the practice of holding court on the occasion of the *Hajj* to settle outstanding disputes between different parties and to redress the grievances of those who for one reason or another were not able in the normal course of circumstances to approach the door of justice. 'Umar appreciably improved this system. He ordered his governors to attend their *Hajj* every year. He held his court near *Ka'ba* and invited the people to bring before him any complaint against any governor or oppressor. On these occasions even petty complaints were brought and redressed on the spot. Once he called a general meeting during the *Hajj* and addressed the people:

> O people, I have not appointed my governors over you so that they might beat your faces, tarnish your honour and misappropriate your properties. I have appointed them so that they may teach you the Book of your Lord and the Sunnah of your Prophet. Therefore, if anyone of them exceeds this, the oppressed must refer his excess to me so that I may redress his complaint.

At this time 'Amr b. al-'As became furious and said: "O Commander of the faithful, what do you think, if some one of the Muslims who is appointed as governor has punished one of them, would you redress his grievance?" 'Umar replied: "Yes, certainly I would give him redress. Because I have seen the Prophet granting redress against himself." At this a person stood up and said: "Your governor has scourged me with hundred stripes." 'Umar ordered: "Would you flog the governor with hundred stripes? Come and flog him." 'Amr b. al-'As stood up and said: "O Commander of the faithful, if you open this door against your governors it would become difficult for them. It would become a precedent to be followed after you." 'Umar replied: "Why should I not provide redress when I have seen the holy Prophet providing redress against himself." 'Amr b. al-'As with great difficulty persuaded the person to receive two dirhams for each stripe.

King and Common Man Equal Before Law

During one of the annual judicial sessions at Makkah a case of a king and a common man was brought in the court of 'Umar for judgement. Jabalah b. Ayham, a king of the Ghassanid dynasty of Syria, accepted Islam and came to Makkah to perform the *Hajj*. During circumambulation of the *Ka'ba* a corner of his covering cloth came under a Bedouin's foot. Jabalah gave him a slap in his face. The Bedouin also returned the same to him. Jabalah became furious out of anger and insult. He went to 'Umar and complained against the Bedouin. After hearing the details of the incident 'Umar adjudged, "You received the award of your deed." On hearing the judgement he was taken by surprise the remarked, "We people are of such a high status that if anyone misbehaves with us, he is exterminated." 'Umar said, "Such was the state of affairs in the time of Ignorance. Islam has equalized the high and the low." After hearing the final judgement Jabalah said: "If Islam is such a religion which does not accept any distinction between the high and the low, then it is difficult for me to be loyal to it." Thereafter he left for Constantinople secretly. 'Umar upheld the supremacy of the law and justice and did not change the law for the sake of a dignitary.

Non-Muslim Under 'Umar's Judicial System

The entire Persian empire and the Asian and African regions of the Roman empire were incorporated into 'Umar's Caliphate. They were the most advanced and highly developed empires of the world. This vast region—Iraq, Syria, Palestine, Egypt—was the origin and birthplace of many ancient religions and legal systems. The ancient legal codes had originated, developed and were practised in those lands. They were: the code of Hammurabi, Assyrian Laws, the Hittite Laws, Hittite Instructions, Neo-Babylonian Laws, Egyptian Treaty, Egyptian Documents, Mesopotamian Legal Documents, Laws of the Sumerians, the Akkadians, the Armaeans, the Phoenicians, the Hebrews, the Arabians and the Abyssinians. The texts of these codes have become available through explorations and excavations carried on in Egypt, Mesopotamia, Asia Minor and Syria. The cuneiform studies have revealed the significance of such texts. James B. Pritchard has edited a monumental work under the title *Ancient Near Eastern Texts*

Relating to the Old Testament.

The above-mentioned codes and laws have been published in the second part of the work entitled "Legal Texts." These codes and laws served as the ancient background of the administrative, legal and judicial institutions set up in these lands by the Romans and the Persians. They were in existence at the advent of Islam. The majority of the subjects of the Roman Empire had been converted to Christianity and the subjects of the Persian rulers were made to accept the Magians' religion. A large minority of the Jews also lived in these countries. The rest of the population was pagan.

Despite the rich legal heritage and conversion to the religion of the ruler, the subjects of those empires were not given equal treatment. They were reduced merely to tax-yielding agencies and were subjected to the severest punishment in case the ruler was not satisfied with the collection of taxes. Legal and judicial institutions were mainly converted into penal agencies awarding punishment mostly to the tax defaulters, and paying little attention to the rights of the subjects.

The tyranny of the rulers and denial of the basic and fundamental human rights to the people mainly contributed to the spread of Islam in the region and its acceptance by the overwhelming majority of the people. Islam gave a well defined and clear charter of the basic and fundamental human rights regardless of religion, race and region of the people. The Caliphate acted most firmly as a guardian of the charter, and the Muslim forces and military machinery came into action in case of Roman or the Persian Emperors, visualizing the danger to and the ultimate destruction of their tyrannical rule in the spread and acceptance of the Islamic charter of human rights by their subjects, attempted to block the rising tide of Islamic ideology. The people who accepted Islam immediately were incorporated into the *Ummah* and enjoyed equal status with other Muslims without any distinction. Those who could not enter the fold of Islam at once also benefited from the Islamic charter of human rights. In case of the offence against their life, property, honour or religion, they could have recourse to an effective, efficient and impartial judicial system.

In addition to the human rights charter in the Qur'an, the non-Muslims were also given written guarantee for safeguarding their rights and religion. Such agreements were held most sacred and they were upheld and guarded in the same manner as the provisions of the constitution of the Caliphate. Thus the non-Muslims under the Caliphate enjoyed all the constitutional rights while previously they were treated as subjects who were at the mercy of the rulers. To substantiate the above, a charter of the rights of non-Muslims granted by 'Umar to the people of *Iyliya*' (Jerusalem) at the time of their surrender in A.H. 15 is given below as an illustration:

In the name of Allah, the most Beneficent, the most Merciful.

> This is an instrument of security (*al-aman*) granted by the Servant of God, 'Umar, *Amir al-Mu'minin*, to the people of Iyliya'.
>
> He grants them the security of their lives, properties churches, crosses, the sick, the healthy and to all religious denominations. Their churches shall not be occupied, not shall they be demolished. They shall not be decreased nor their confines reduced. Neither their crosses nor anything else from their properties shall be lessened.
>
> They shall not be coerced in their religion. None of them shall be harmed. None of the Jews shall reside with the people of Iyliya'; the people of Iyliya' shall pay *jizyah* in the same manner as the people of other cities. They shall expel from Iyliya' the Romans and the thieves. Those who shall leave from among them their lives and properties shall be safe until they reach their destination. Those who shall stay from among them, shall be in security. They shall pay *jizyah* in the manner of the people of Iyliya'. Those from among the people of Iyliya', who would like to accompany the Romans along with their lives and properties and evacuate their churches and crosses shall be in security with regard to their lives, churches and crosses until they reach their destination. Those among the foreigners, from other lands residing in Iyliya' before committing any murder, who would like to stay shall pay *jizyah* in the manner of the people of Iyliya.' Those

who desire to do so can accompany the Romans. From those who desire to return to their people, nothing shall be taken until their crops are reaped.

The contents of this document carry that promise of God, guarantee of His Prophet and his successors and of the believers, so long as they will pay the *jizyah*. It was witnessed by Khalid b. al-Walid, 'Amr b. al-'As, 'Abd al-Rahman b. 'Awf, Mu'awiyah b. Abi Sufyan. 'Umar concluded it and countersigned it in A.H. 15.

The above document contains the basic and fundamental rights and privileges of the non-Muslims. They were provided maximum autonomy in their religious, social and community affairs and were given guarantee for the protection of their lives, properties and religion. Constitutional and legal security was provided to their churches, and crosses. Explicit commitment has been given for safeguarding the sanctity of their places of worship and against any encroachment on the confines of their churches. With the promise of God and guarantee of the holy Prophet they were given full freedom and no compulsion was exercised on them with regard to their religion. It was perhaps on the explicit or implicit desire of the Christians that an article was included in the covenant for the expulsion of the Jews because the Christians had been seriously offended over the centuries on the crucifixion of Christ by the Jews in the holy city of Jerusalem. Their offence had not been redressed. This is a unique charter of rights and privileges in the history of the world given by a conqueror to the conquered.

As mentioned above, the document is cited as an illustration. Otherwise such guarantees were given to non-Muslims of different regions and cities who surrendered to the forces of Islam. History is witness to the face that all such guarantees, securities and convenants were duly fulfilled most conscientiously. In case the Muslim authorities were not in a position, due to unavoidable circumstances, to protect the lives, properties, honour and religion of the non-Muslims, they refunded the sum received for their protection. An example is quoted as an illustration:

After the conquest of Hims (Homs, the ancient Emesa, a city in central Syria) by Abu 'Ubaydah, the Roman Emperor gathered his entire force in Antakiyah (Antioch) for a final battle with the Muslims. Hims was not a good place for the Muslim forces to meet the combined military strength of the Romans. Under these circumstances Abu 'Ubaydah, the Commander-in-Chief of the Muslim forces, called a meeting of the military council to discuss the situation. In the meeting it was decided to retreat from Hims and join Khalid b. al-Walid at Damascus. Under such conditions, normally the retreating armies commit serious excesses and exact the maximum amount of kind and cash from the conquered people, more so, when they profess the religion of the enemy. On the other hand, Abu 'Ubaydah was worried about the rights and privileges of the Christian population of Hims. He had given them a guarantee for the protection of their lives, properties and honour. Under the existing exigency he was not in a position to abide by the commitment. At this critical juncture history has recorded the following judgement announced by the governor of Syria and the Commander-in-Chief of the Muslim army.

Abu 'Ubaydah called his treasury officer, Habib b. Maslamah and ordered him as follows:

> *Jizyah* or *kharaj* is a tax collected from the Christians for their protection from the enemy. In the present critical condition it is not possible for us to provide them their protection. Therefore, return all that has been collected from them and tell them that we still have great regard for them. Since in the present circumstances we cannot provide them the promised security, hence the *jizyah*, which is a remuneration for their protection, is returned to them.

The treasury officer implemented the above decision of Abu 'Ubaydah and returned an amount of millions to the Christians and the Jews. They were so much impressed by the sense of justice on the part of the Muslims that they wept and out of excitement cried, "May God bring you back." The Jews were even more impressed and said: "We swear by the Torah, so long as we are alive Qaysar (Caesar) cannot capture Hims." Thereafter, they closed the doors of their fortification and posted guards on strategic points. The above decision of Abu

'Ubaydah was also implemented in other cities wherefrom the Muslims had to retreat. An order was issued to commanders of other regions asking them to return the *jizyah* collected from the Christians and the Jews before retreat from their respective areas.

The Christians were treated most justly, even if some of them became traitors and betrayed the covenant. 'Arbasus, a border town between Syria and Asia Minor, was conquered by the Muslim. Its Christian population indulged in spying for their co-religionists on the other side of the border. This was a betrayal of the agreement. 'Umayr b. Sa'd, the governor of the area, reported their disloyalty to the Caliph at Madinah. It was a serious matter and entailed capital punishment. However, 'Umar dealt with them leniently mostly because they were the protected people. He sent the following order to 'Umayr:

> Prepare an inventory of their property, land, cattle and goods. Pay to them double the price of each item, and order them to migrate to some other place. If they do not agree to it, give them one year and then exile them. Since they did not comply with the warning, the orders (of banishment) were executed.

Cases have been reported wherein the lives and properties of the protected people were treated at per with Muslims. Al-Shafi'i has reported the following judgement of 'Umar:

> A Muslim of the tribe of Bakr b. Wa'il killed a Christian of Hirah. The judge of the area sought the advice of 'Umar, the Chief Justice of the Islamic judiciary. 'Umar ordered that the murderers should be handed over to the heirs of the murdered. In compliance with these orders the murdered was given in the hands of Hunayn, the heir of the murdered person, who killed him.

> A protected person from Syria came to Madinah and lodged a complaint with the Caliph. He complained that the Muslim army during its march had destroyed his crops. 'Umar passed on order and asked his treasury officer to pay him thousand dirhams as compensation.

Within the administrative and judicial jurisdiction of 'Amr b. al-'As, a protected Christian abused the holy Prophet in the presence of 'Arafah, a Companion of the holy Prophet. 'Arafah could not tolerate it and gave him a slap. The Christian lodged a complaint with 'Amr b. al-'As. 'Arafah was summoned to the court of justice and an inquiry made into the matter. 'Arafah explained the whole incident. 'Amr reminded him of the relevant article of the agreement wherein the protected people were granted security. 'Arafah submitted: "God forbid, they have not been granted permission to abuse the holy Prophet openly. The agreement provides them freedom of speech and action in their churches. They have also been provided protection against their enemies and a guarantee that the Muslims would fight against them on their behalf. They have also been given the promise that they would not be subjected to unbearable burden." 'Amr b. al-'As gave a sympathetic hearing to the complaint of the Christian and paid attention to the arguments of 'Arafah. Thereafter he decided that 'Arafah did not violate any article of the agreement. It was the complainant himself who violated the agreement and abused the holy Prophet of Islam.

From the foregoing it becomes abundantly clear that the non-Muslims under 'Umar's judicial system were given the maximum autonomy, and when they appealed to the court of justice in case they had any grievance the courts redressed their grievances most efficiently and justly. We conclude this discussion with a rule laid down by Khalid b. al-Walid, the Commander-in-Chief of the Muslim forces during the Caliphate of Abu Bakr, which was enforced throughout the territories under the Caliphate of 'Umar. The Muslims and non-Muslims were treated on an equal footing in state affairs. A Muslim was killed in lieu of a non-Muslim. Muslim were rebuked in case they rebuked the non-Muslim. The disabled and the destitute Muslims and the non-Muslims were equal in getting living allowances in their homes from the state exchequer. The relevant rule was as follows:

> I granted them the privilege that in case an old man who had become disabled or some calamity had fallen upon him, or he was rich and poverty overcame him, and his co-religionists gave him charity, such a person would be exempted from *jizyah*. He and his family would be provided an allowance from the treasury

of the Muslims, so long as they stayed in the *Dar al-Hijrah* (Madinah) and the *Dar al-Islam* (the Caliphate). If they migrate from the *Dar al-Hijrah* and *Dar al-Islam*, then the Muslims would not be under obligation to pay them the allowance.

'Umar during the Caliphate quoted the body Qur'an in support of the above rule. He passed in order and sent it to his treasury office: In the injunction of the Qur'an *Innama'l-sadaqat li'l-fuqara' wa'l-masakin* (Zakat is only for the poor and the needy) the word *al-fuqara'* applies to the Muslims and *al-masakin* includes the People of the Book, the Jews and the Christians (*wa'l-fuqara' humu'l-Muslimun wa hadha mina'l-masakin min ahl al-kitab*). The following event and judgement of 'Umar thereon was the back-ground of the above order.

'Umar once saw an old non-Muslim beggar. He asked him, "Why do you beg?" He aid, "To pay *jizyah* and to meet necessity of life and old age." 'Umar took him to his residence and gave him some money. Thereafter he passed an order and sent it to his treasury office. He ordered: "Look at this man and others like him. By God we have not done justice to him. We have eaten his youth and have disgraced him in his old age." 'Umar then exempted him from *jizyah* and others like him.

Justice without Fear

One of the most conspicuous characteristics of 'Umar's administration was that he administered justice without fear or favour. Instances of his impartial justice will be given in the following section. As regard his justice without fear, suffice to it say that neither the most powerful persons nor any state of emergency in his Caliphate ever created any anxiety or uneasiness in his mind in arriving at correct decision of cases and in the announcement of judgements. One of the striking examples of his justice without fear during a state of emergency in his Caliphate is the case wherein Sa'd b. Abi Waqqas, one of the greatest Companions of the holy Prophet, the Governor of Kufa and the Commander-in-Chief of the Muslim army in Iraq and Iran, was accused for neither distributing the spoils of war with equity, nor administering justice among the people nor participating in fighting.

The complainants lodged the complaint with 'Umar at a critical moment when the Persian Emperor had collected his forces from all over the empire at Nahawand to give a final battle to the Muslims. Under the orders of 'Umar Sa'd b. Abi Waqqas, the Commander of the Muslims, after making full preparation to meet the Emperor was marching out of Kufa. This state of emergency did not cause any fear in his mind and for upholding the cause of justice he ordered that Sa'd, instead of marching towards the battlefield at Nahawand, should march towards the court of justice at Madinah. At this time of exigency 'Umar remarked: "By God this will not obstruct me in looking into the matter faced by you." Thereupon 'Umar ordered the chief of the investigation department, Muhammad b. Maslamah, to proceed to Kufa and hold preliminary inquiries. According to the prima facie evidence the case was worth trying by the Caliphs; hence the Commander-in-Chief, who was the accused, was ordered to appear in the court of justice and vindicate his position. The trial was held, and although the complainants could not produce substantial evidence in their support, yet 'Umar decided to depose the Commander-in-Chief from his office. Thus regardless of the power, popularity and reputation of Sa'd b. Abi waqqas and the state emergency due to the declaration of war and the supreme importance of Sa'd, who was the victor at Qadsiya, the decisive battle against he Persians, and who had mobilized men and material for the present battle, 'Umar tried him in the court and deposed him from his office. Can any nation produce such an example of administration of justice without fear?

Examples of other renowned commanders, conquerors and powerful governors and administrators such as Mughirah b. Shu'bah, 'Iyad b. Ghanam have already been quoted above. Abu Musa al-Ash'ari was also summoned to Madinah in connection with a complaint against him and was tried on the following allegations:

1. He has selected sixty princesses out of war captives and has taken possession of them.
2. He has delegated his powers of administration to Ziyad b. Samiyah who is all in all.
3. One of his slave-girls is provided with sumptuous food, which is generally not available to Muslims.

Abu Musa gave his statement in the law court wherein he vindicated his position. 'Umar himself recorded this statement with his own hands. After hearing the cases and examining the statement of the accused and the evidence of the witnesses, the Chief Justice announced his judgement. According to him, the first allegation was baseless and without any foundation, hence it was dropped.

On the second allegation Abu Musa explained: "Ziyad is a talented young man and is a great statesman. I therefore have appointed him as my advisor." Thereupon Ziyad was summoned by `Umar who examined him. He was really a capable man. Therefore `Umar himself appointed him as advisor to the governor of Basra.

On the third allegation Abu Musa could not give satisfactory answer; therefore the slave-girl was taken away from him.

The model example of administration of justice without fear was 'Umar's judgement on the complaint against Khalid b. al-Walid. The charge sheet contained the following allegations levelled against Khalid during his tenure as Commander of the Muslim army at the Qinnasrin sector in Syria:

1. Abu Ubaydah, the Commander-in-Chief of the Muslim forces in Syria, after the conquest of Hims appointed Khalid b. Walid as the Sector Commander of Qinnasrin. At al-Hadir, the Roman Commander-in-Chief and the topmost person among the Romans after Hiraqul (Heracles), launched an attack on the forces of Khalid. Minas was killed and the Romans were completely exterminated. The contingent of the people of al-Hadir, fighting against the Muslims along with the Romans, consisted of local Arab Christians. After their defeat, they sent an excuse to Khalid.

"They are Arabs. They were forced to join the others. They were not willing to participate in the battle." Khalid b. al-Walid accepted their excuse and left them alone.

The above action of Khalid b. al-Walid was against the Islamic military code. The code prescribed terms of agreement for the enemy who surrendered peacefully without fighting (*sulhan*). It contained different terms for the enemy who fought against the Muslims and was defeated (*'anwatan*). The above-mentioned Christian Arabs actually participated in a severe battle (*qitalan shadidan*) against the Muslims and met with a crushing defeat. Khalid applied neither of the terms of the code prescribed for the activist or the passivist enemy in the case under reference. Such an attitude was inexcusable in the Islamic military code. The activist enemy after defeat must be made war captives and treated in accordance with the terms prescribed in the code. Their release out of favour or with compensation is the prerogative of the head of state. Khalid did not follow the military code and was therefore charged with its violation:

1. When (news of Khalid's) action reached 'Umar he charged him with the accusation: "Khalid has invested himself with authority."
2. After his successful campaign of Qinnasrin Khalid in his leisurely and recreative mood entered a bath wherein he embrocated himself with a liquid containing liquor (*khamr*). On receipt of this information 'Umar wrote to Khalid: "It has reached my ears that you had a massage with liquor (*khamr*) whereas God has prohibited the patent (*zahir*) quality of the *khamr* as well as its latent (*batin*) quality and its massage. Therefore do not have its massage on your bodies." Khalid's explanation of the allegation did not satisfy 'Umar, who expressed his disapproval by remarking, "The sons of al-Mughirah (the grandfather of Khahid) are tempted to antipathy. God may not kill you on the same."
3. On the completion of the conquest of Qinnasrin Khalid b. al-Walid received a very large share of booty. Many people benefited from his bestowal. Al-Ash'ath b. Qays was one of the beneficiaries to whom he gave ten thousand (*dirhams*). It was reported to 'Umar who sent him the following instructions:

"You shall not bestow upon (anyone) a goat or a camel without my prior approval."

On receipt of the above instructions from the headquarters Khalid, instead of complying with them, replied: "Either I may be left alone and allowed to act (freely) or you proceed with your action." Ibn Hajar has cited a report which categorically says the Khalid' deposition was due to his irregularity, namely, that after the distribution of war spoils he was not in the habit of submitting its accounts to the Caliph.

With the above background in view, 'Umar ordered for the trial of Khalid b. al-Walid in an open court. He called for a messenger and handed over to him the following written order addressed to Abu 'Ubaydah, the Commander-in-Chief of the Muslim army in Syria:

> Ask Khalid to stand up. Tie him with his turban. Remove from his head his cap until he discloses to you the source wherefrom he bestowed the fit upon al-Ash'ath: Ask him whether he did it from his personal possessions or from the state property which he acquired as booty. If he maintains that he had given it to him from the state property, then he has confessed his dishonesty. If he maintains that he had given it from his personal possession, then he has committed extravagance. Depose him in either case and take charge of his command.

Abu 'Ubaydah summoned Khalid for appearance in his court. On his arrival , Abu 'Ubaydah called a general meeting of the people. He himself took his seat among them on the pulpit. The messenger of 'Umar, Bilal, stood up and asked Khalid as to wherefrom he gave al-Ash'ath (ten thousand dirhams). Khalid did not reply. Abu 'Ubaydah was silent and did not say anything. Thereupon Bilal stood up and said: "The Commander of the Faithful has ordered in your case this and this." He removed his turban. Khalid did not obstruct him for the commandment was for "hearing and obeying." He also removed his cap. Then he made to stand him up and tied him with his turban and asked: "Wherefrom did your give al-Ash'ath the gift? Did you give it from your own property or from the state property you had with you?" He confessed, "Rather from my own property". Bilal released him and restored his cap his then tied his turban with his (Bilal's) hand. Thereupon he said, "We hear and obey our rulers and respect and serve our authorities."

After the trial Khalid received orders of his deposition from 'Umar wherein he was also directed to report to him at Madinah. Thereupon he returned to Qinnasrin and then to Hims where he made a farewell address to the people and proceeded to Madinah.

'Umar ordered for investigation of the allegations levelled against Khalid b. al-Walid and held a judicial trial. As a result of the investigation, Khalid was deposed from his office. The process of investigation and judicial procedure was conducted most fairly and fearlessly. Khalid was given full opportunity to vindicate his position with regard to the allegations levelled against him. His explanation was not found satisfactory. He was then tried in an open court wherein he was convicted. 'Umar enforcement the judgement of the court without fear.

At the time of his trial Khalid was at the zenith of his power, popularity and reputation. He was the hero of the Battle of Mutah during the reign of the holy Prophet wherein he was awarded the epithet of *Sayf Allah* "the Sword of Allah" by the holy Prophet. He was the victor in the war of apostasy which spread in Arabia after the demise of the holy Prophet. He was appointed as the Commander-in-Chief in Iraq and then in Syria. He was the hero of the decisive Syria battles of Yarmuk and Damascus and was most popular and also the favourite of his soldiers during his conquests of Hims and Qinnasrin. The above heroic deeds, conquests and the resulting power, popularity and reputation of Khalid were on the one side and the enforcement of justice and the vindication of its supremacy were on the other. The official and social status of Khalid and his popularity in the army did not create any feeling of fear or anxiety in `Umar's mind when the complaint was lodged against him. He executed hid judgement against Khalid when the latter was convicted.

Before closing the above discussion it seems pertinent to refer to misunderstandings with regard to the relations of 'Umar and Khalid which according to the prejudiced reports of certain historians raise doubts on the impartiality of 'Umar's judgement. Al-Tabari, Ibn al-Athir and Ibn Kathir have recorded the following report:

'Umar removed Khalid for some remarks supposed to have been

made by Khalid against him. 'Umar was annoyed with him disapproving of his actions throughout the reign of Abu Bakr in view of his conduct in the affairs of Ibn Nuwayarah and his war operation against him. When 'Umar became Caliph, the first thing he talked about was Khalid's deposition. He said, "He (Khalid) will never hold any post under me." Thereupon 'Umar wrote to Abu 'Ubaydah: "If Khalid pleaded guilty then he would continue to be in charge of his present post. If he did not plead guilty then you should take charge of his command. Thereafter take off his turban from his head and divide his property into halves". When Abu 'Ubaydah conveyed the order to Khalid, he asked, "Allow me to consult my sister in my affair." Abu 'Ubaydah permitted him to do so. Khalid called upon his sister Fatimah bint al-Walid, the wife of al-Harith b. Hisham, and apprised her of the situation. She said: "By God 'Umar does not like you. He intends that you should plead guilt so that he would remove you." He kissed her head and said: "By God you have told the truth." He formulated his line of action and refused to plead guilty. Thereupon Bilal stood up and moved towards Abu 'Ubaydah and asked him what his order about Khalid was. He said: "I order you to remove his turban and divide his property." He divided his possessions except his shoes. Abu 'Ubaydah said, "This matter would be settled only with it." Thereupon Khalid said, "Go ahead, I would not keep anything which would results in my disobedience to the Commander of the Faithful. Complete the required action." He took one of his shoes and gave him the other one. After his deposition Khalid proceeded to 'Umar at Madinah.

The most serious objection to the authenticity of the above report is that it has been reported in two contradictory versions. According to the first version, it was the very first order of 'Umar at this take-over in A.H. 13. The other version says that this took place in the fifth year of the Caliphate in A.H. 17. Ibn al-Athir, while narrating the details of the trial and deposition, clearly mentions that Khalid at that time was a Sector Commander stationed at Qinnasrin wherefrom he obtained the property he bestowed upon the poet for which he was tried. Simultaneously he mentions the same event as the very first action of 'Umar in A.H. 13, even before the battle of Yarmuk and the conquest of Damascus, not to speak of Hims and Qinnasrin which were subdued five years later in A.H. 17.

Annoyance of 'Umar with Khalid and his disapproval of Khalid's actions throughout the reign of Abu Bakr is alleged to by based on the conduct of Khalid regarding the killing of Malik b. Nuwayarah and the former's marriage with the latter's wife. No doubt 'Umar was displeased when he heard only the statement of the complainant, Malik's brother, and showed his annoyance on Khalid's arrival in Madinah for appearing in 'Umar's court. But as soon as the court, after hearing the respondent's statement and learning the details of the incident, exonerated the accused and acquitted him honourably, 'Umar was satisfied. Thereafter Khalid held the highest army posts in the Arabian peninsula, Iraq and Syria, and conducted the most crucial and decisive military operations with success and honour. Hence his deposition by 'Umar on the charge which had been already proved baseless under Abu Bakr is without foundation.

The spurious nature of the report can be established by the fact that Khalid continued holding the most responsible and the highest military posts for five years (A.H. 13 to 17) under 'Umar, whereas the report under reference contains 'Umar's decision: "He (Khalid) will never hold any post under me." The following facts negate the authenticity of the reported version. In the beginning of A.H. 13 Abu Bakr sent the following commanders for the conquest of different regions of Syria:

Khalid b. Sa'id b. al-'As was sent to Tayma, Yazid b. Abi Sufyan to Damascus, Abu 'Ubaydah b. al-Jarrah to Hims, 'Amr b. al-'As to Palestine and Shurahbil b. Hasanah to Jordan. Hiraqul, the Roman Emperor, raised large armies, and mobilized the whole Syrian population and sent them against different but small Muslim armies under the above-mentioned commanders. On receipt of the news of the Romans war strategy Abu Bakr ordered that all Muslim armies in Syria should be united. He also ordered Khalid b. al-Walid to appoint his successor on the Persian front in Iraq and to take charge of the united Muslim armies in Syria against the Romans. In the same order he was specifically directed to return to Iraq on the completion of his assignment.

This shows that his appointment as commander-in-chief of the united forces was not permanent. It was an ad hoc assignment under urgent circumstances. On the completion of the operation he was no longer the commander-in-chief in view of the terms of his appointment. This is what actually happened. After the victory in the Battle of Yarmuk he ceased to be commander-in-chief. The only change which occurred on the death of Abu Bakr and the take-over by 'Umar was that according to the terms of his appointment in Syria he had to return to Iraq, whereas 'Umar retained him in Syria and made him join Abu 'Ubaydah. Under this united command Khalid exercised full powers in the conquest of Damascus, Hims and Qinnasrin. The above evidence is enough to prove the spuriousness of the report that 'Umar at the beginning of his Caliphate decided not to give any command to Khalid.

The report also refers to 'Umar's order asking Khalid to plead guilty or otherwise. It is an established fact of history that the above order was given by 'Umar in A.H. 17 after the conquest of Qinnasrin. Therefore, its mention in the report under discussion in A.H. 13 proves its falsity.

The details of the judicial procedure as described in the report most unambiguously indicate that Bilal conducted such investigation after the conquest of Qinnasrin. The big amount of money, reported to have been given to al-Ash'ath by Khalid, was in his possession only after the operation of Qinnasrin and not before that. On the top of its being spurious is its closing sentence wherein it is mentioned that Khalid proceeded to 'Umar at Madinah when he deposed him, whereas it has been proved with abundant historical evidence that Khalid was not deposed nor did he proceed to 'Umar in A.H. 13. In fact he stayed for five years in Syria commanding armies and conquering region after region under 'Umar.

The most conclusive proof of the baselessness of the impugned report is the argument quoted by Ibn Hajar in his *Isabah.* Ibn Hajar reports that after the deposition of Khalid he was again invited by 'Umar to resume his duties on condition that he would abide by the Islamic military code and rules pertaining to the distribution of war spoils. Khalid declined, saying that he should be left alone to do whatever he wanted to do. 'Umar refused to oblige.

It seems that to defame the impartial and independent judiciary under 'Umar the story was concocted that the first order issues by 'Umar after his take-over was not based on justice and equity. Its grounds were subjective and personal grudge and grievance. (*Innama naza'a 'Umar Khalidan fi kalamin kana Khalid takallama bihi fima yaz'umun wa lam yazal 'Umar 'alayh sakhitan wa li'amrihi karihan fi zaman Abi Bakr kullihi.*) This is not correct. This is a fabrication. 'Umar deposed Khalid in A.H. 17 when he had already served for five years under him. He held very responsible and high military posts and was the Commander of an army which defeated the Romans. After the decisive battle of Yarmuk 'Umar sent a war plan for the conquest of the entire Syria, according to which Shurahbil b. Hasanah and 'Amr b. al-'As were sent to Jordan and Palestine, and the most strategic and cold (*bardan shadidan*) region along the Roman occupations in Syria—Hims and Qinnasrin—were given in the charge of Abu 'Ubaydah and Khalid b. al-Walid. 'Umar's orders were, "*fansarif anta wa Khalid ila Hims,*" (Proceed along with Khalid to Hims). After the successful campaign of Hims, Khalid alone was sent for the conquest of Qinnasrin: *Ba'atha Abu 'Ubaydah ba'd fath Hims Khalid b. al-Walid ila Oinnasrin.* Al-Biqa was also conquered by Khalid : *inna Aba Ubaydah ba'atha Khalid b. al-Walid ula al-Biqa fatahaha bi 'l-sayf.* Khalid was actually held in respect by 'Umar who had given him authority to conclude peace agreements in accordance with the Islamic military code: *Salahahu ahl ba'labak wa kataba lahum kitaban.* Khalid was the commander of the vanguard during the campaign of Fihl in Syria.

The above historical evidence proves most emphatically that 'Umar had no personal grudge against Khalid b. Walid. Therefore, the story suggesting the deposition of Khalid through the very fast order of 'Umar is absolutely baseless and without foundation. Khalid commanded respect under 'Umar as mentioned above. When certain complaints were received against him, proper investigation was made and action was taken accordingly. This was the most just action which was taken after meeting all legal and judicial requirements. The relations of

Khalid and his family with 'Umar after Khalid's deposition continued to be cordial. On his arrival in Madinah Khalid did not adopt the rebellious attitude of a frustrated person. He only expressed his feelings and said: "I express to you my indignation among the Muslims. By God, you have not been reserved in my case, O 'Umar." 'Umar asked him, "Wherefrom this wealth?" Khalid replied, "From the booty and shares. What exceeds sixty thousand is for you." 'Umar evaluated his goods. Twenty thousand were found in excess which he deposited in the state treasury. Thereupon 'Umar addressing Khalid made the following observation:

> O Khalid, by God, you are honourable to me and very dear to me. You will not blame me for anything after today.

Thereafter 'Umar circulated an express order to all the provinces clearing doubts and misunderstandings about Khalid's deposition. The order in circulation carried: "I did not depose Khalid due to grudge or dishonesty. But the people had suggested his giving way to temptation and I feared that they might not trust him, and he suffered for that. I desired to inform them that only God is the Maker (of destiny) and they may not face any trouble."

The most conclusive proof of the warm and cordial relations between 'Umar and Khalid is the marriage of Fatimah bint al-Walid, Khalid's sister, with 'Umar. Fatimah's husband, al-Harith b. Hisham, fell a victim to the famous plague which spread in the Muslim army in Syria in A.H. 18. After al-Harith's death 'Umar married Fatimah in A.H. 20. Khalid was alive at the time of the marriage of his sister with 'Umar and died one year later in A.H. 21. If 'Umar had deposed Khalid due to his enmity and grudge, Khalid would not have allowed his sister to marry his enemy, nor would Fatimah have married the enemy of his brother. This marriage provides a clear proof of the most cordial relation between these two great personalities of Islam. It explodes the baseless story and exposes the falsity of a report prepared by the connivance of certain unreliable persons which says Khalid asked permission of Abu 'Ubaydah to allow him to consult his sister in his case. Abu 'Ubaydah allowed him. He called upon his sister and consulted her in his case. She said: "By God, 'Umar does not like you. He only wants you to plead guilty, then he would depose you." He kissed her head and said : "By God, you have told the truth." It is strange that Fatimah in the above report alerted her brother Khalid to be aware of the shrewdness of 'Umar, and Khalid kissed her head for that, and on the other hand the same Fatimah married 'Umar and Khalid gladly allowed her to do so. What a contradiction! In fact, the above story was concocted with the evil intention of attacking the impartially and independence of judgement of 'Umar which could not be done.

The recent transformation of the Arabs from tribalism into an *Ummah* was another important factor to be reckoned with, in respect of the deposition of Khalid. 'Umar was most vigilant and scrupulously conscientious and ever ready to take notice of any event or action which, in his opinion, had any tendency of tribalism. In the tribal code and chiefs and the tribemen were not subjected to any military code. They could kill men, women and children without discrimination and justification. Mutilation of the living and dead during and after a battle or a raid, inhuman treatment of the prisoners of war and treating the womenfolk as chattels were considered as chivalrous deeds and proud achievements. Islam gave a well-defined military code. The commanders as well as the soldiers were duty bound to abide by its provisions. Violation of any of its provisions was considered a serious offence and the dafaulter, regardless of his official or social position, was dealt with in accordance with law and justice. Keeping this socio-religious background in view, it would become easy to understand why 'Umar took serious notice of ordinary negligence, minor offences or impropriety committed by any of his commanders, governors and other public servants. The events related to Malik b. Nuwayarah and his wife, insistence on the submission of accounts of war spoils, bestowal of spoils upon al-Ash'ath, and finally the open trial and Khalid's deposition should be read in the light of the above-mentioned policy of 'Umar.

Justice without Favour

'Umar succeeded in establishing a well-organized judiciary and its successful administration due to the fact that he considered himself always to be under the law and submitted himself to the legal and judicial procedure whenever it was so required. Once a Bedouin saw that 'Umar was wearing a shirt made of a Yamani sheet of cloth, received by 'Umar as share along with other Muslims. One sheets was not enough to make a shirt of 'Umar's size. The Bedouin interrupted 'Umar during a public address and asked him to explain how it was possible for 'Umar to wear a shirt of his size out of one sheet of his share. 'Umar stopped his address and asked his son 'Abd Allah b. 'Umar to answer the question raised by the Bedouin. Ibn 'Umar explained that the sheet of 'Umar's share was not enough to make his shirt, therefore, he also gave the sheet of his share to 'Umar and thus his shirt was completed. Thereupon the Bedouin became satisfied and allowed the Caliph to resume his address.

In a fit of anger 'Umar once inflicted a number of lashes on a Bedouin who came seeking his succour against an oppressor. 'Umar soon repented and asked the Bedouin to inflict the same number of lashes on him. But the latter refused. Thereupon 'Umar returned home with the following soliloquy:

> O son of al-Khattab, humble thou wert and Allah hath elevated thee! Thou wert astray, and Allah hath guided thee; thou wert weak, and Allah hath strengthened thee. Then he caused thee to rule over the necks of the people; and when one of them came seeking thy aid, thou didst strike him. What preventest thyself before him?

'Umar never allowed his dependants and his closest relatives to interfere in the public administration. If any member of his family indulged in indecency or committed an offence, legal action was immediately taken. 'Ubayd Allah his son, indulged in drunkenness. He was beaten with lashes. He succumbed to the lashes and died.

'Abd Allah and 'Ubayd Allah, two sons of 'Umar, were once with the Muslim troops in Iraq. Abu Musa al-Ash'ari, the governor of Basra, gave them some money on loan from the state treasury. They invested the money in business and earned some profit on it. When this report came to the notice of 'Umar the summoned both of his sons to his presence. He asked them, "Did Abu Musa give such loans to every soldier or only to you?" They replied, "Only to us." "He gave it to you specially," said 'Umar, "because you were the sons of the Commander of the Faithful," and ordered that the original amount with the entire profit, accruing from it, be deposited in the state treasury. On the announcement of the judgement, 'Abd Allah kept silent, but 'Ubayd Allah requested: "O Commander of the Faithful, you should not decide this case in this way, because in case of loss we were responsible to return the entire amount to the treasury." 'Umar did not pay any attention to this plea and simply repeated his first decision. One of the audience stood up and suggested, "O commander of the Faithful, would it not be better to take it as a partnership business." 'Umar accepted this suggestion and ordered that half of the profit be deposited in the state treasury and the other half be given to 'Abd Allah and 'Ubayd Allah.

Qudamah b. Maz'un, the brother-in-law of 'Umar and a Companion of the holy Prophet, was arrested on charge of drunkenness. 'Umar without any hesitation passed order for his punishment and he was beaten with lashes (*'azala Qudamah b. Maz'un 'an al-Bahrayn wa haddahu fi shurb al-khamr*).

9

The Status of Islamic Law in Nigeria

SULIEMAN KUMO

Strictly speaking, it is only in Northern Nigeria that Islamic Law has a status. In the South Islamic law has no status of any kind within the applicable legal system. However, the fact that Islamic Law does not have (and never has had) any status in the South of Nigeria does not mean that there are no Muslim in the region. Far from it. From a purely statistical point, I believe I would be right in saying that nearly 60% of the Yoruba population are Muslims and they have been so for a long time. But, due to historical and sociological reasons, the Western Nigerian Muslims never lived as subjects of any kind of Islamic government and never operated an Islamic polity. There, custom held sway, and when the British conquered the region the English Common Law supplemented, and sometimes supplanted, customary law.

Coming to Northern Nigeria, on the other hand, one has to bear in mind that not only in the bulk of the population a Muslim population, but the fact that Northern Nigeria, along with parts of Cameroun, Niger and Chad formed the heart of the historical "Western Sudan" and the core of what was an African Islamic Commonwealth. Thus, Islam has roots there which go very deep.

Islam reached Northern Nigeria, according to available evidence, in the 10th century of the Christian Era, through the trans-Saharan trade routes. It began to take a firm hold in the 14th Century C.E. and the *Sharia* began to supplant customary law in the 15th Century C.E. in some parts of the region. After the Sokoti *Jihad*, of the early 19th Century C.E., a fully fledged and uncompromising Islamic government replaced the then existing Habe Kingdoms. This government continued in existence, deteriorating in quality, until the British conquest of what is now Nigeria. It is perhaps needless to say that before the British conquest, the *Sharia* in its entirety was the law of the land and was enforced in the various judicial and quasi-judicial tribunals—i.e., ranging from the ordinary courts of the *qadis*, which constituted the mainstream of the administration of justice, to the Emir's courts which exercised *mazalim* and *siyasa* jurisdiction.

When the British took over, after their conquest, they decided to leave intact the whole machinery of government which they found in existence and to administer the country through that machinery. This was their famous policy of Indirect Rule. As a result of this policy, the *Shari* and the whole machinery of justice was left alone, untampered with except minimally. In theory the *Sharia* was now subject to the supremacy of the new foreign laws introduced by the colonial conquerors; but in real practice the *Sharia* only suffered a diminution in penal jurisdiction and occasional administrative interferences, but was otherwise left along. This led to the existence of two parallel legal systems—in other words, two streams of justice running parallel one with the other, never meeting at any point. Here is how the policy was applied.

Lugard, who was the British High Commissioner for "the Protectorate of Northern Nigeria", laid down the policy in the following terms in his address to the Northern Emirs:

> "...in the matter of law and justice, Mohammedan law, so long as it was not contrary to the law of the Protectorate, would not be interfered with, and the Emir's and Alkali's courts would be upheld and strengthened under the supervision of the Resident. Mutilation and imprisonment under inhuman conditions would not be allowed, and no death sentence would be carried into execution without the prior concurrence of the Resident.."

This general statement of policy was given effect to by a Proclamation on the administration of justice to "the general native population." The Proclamation empowered the Resident to establish native courts in his Province which were to administer the native law and custom prevailing in the areas of jurisdiction of each court, in both civil and criminal matters; but this was subject to the proviso that no inhuman punishment could be awarded and—

> "a death sentence could only be executed on the approval of the Resident. The Resident was also given the power to inspect the courts in his Province and to review a case or transfer it from one court to another or to order a retrial or to modify the sentence or the finding of the court."

This is the gist of the provisions of the Proclamation so far as the status and organization of native courts was concerned. I should only add first that "native law" is defined to include all non-English law, including the *Sharia*, so that in the great majority of these courts the *Sharia* was applied as the law prevailing in their areas of jurisdiction. Secondly, the native courts were expressly deprived of territorial jurisdiction in all areas reserved by the British for their offices and residences. They also had no jurisdiction over non-natives and they could not deal with cases governed by English Law (or statutory enactments). To deal with all these matters new English courts were established. Thus, from the outset, there were two systems as pointed out above—the native courts having jurisdiction in well over ninety per cent of all the cases tried. The courts were subject to the administrative interference of the Resident, but appeal did not lie from them to the English courts. This was the original colonial setting. We may also note that in the colonial days interference by the Resident was minimal.

Another Proclamation, in 1906, introduced additional changes the most noteworthy of which was the provision for appellate jurisdiction within the native courts system. Thus the two parallel streams of justice (i.e., the native and the English) continued in operation, with no connection of any kind between them. This duality continued until 1933. In that year two Ordinances were promulgated which marked the beginning of an integration of the two systems. First, the Protectorate Courts Ordinance established a High Court for the whole Protectorate of Nigeria with jurisdiction throughout the Protectorate (except in matters of land which were subject to native law and custom—and in 1945 this exclusion was extended to cover what we may call family law). Second, the Native Courts Ordinance of the same years empowered the High Court to hear appeals from the native courts in certain cases. Thus, a clean break was made with the past and as from then on the judicial system became integrated and subsequent enactments confirmed this process, merely introducing minor adjustments.

Without dwelling too much on the history, let me briefly describe the present judicial system in Nigeria. In doing this I should point out that the present system is essentially the full crystallization of the colonial historical process with mainly cosmetic changes here and there, with the foundation laid down in the colonial era having suffered no radical transformations.

Nigeria has a federal system of government in which the Central Government has certain powers and the component States have the residue. The Nigerian judiciary, therefore, comprises the Federal courts—the Supreme Court of Nigeria, (the highest tribunal of the country), the Federal Court of Appeal and the Federal High Court on the one hand; and on the other State courts. State Courts comprise (in each of the nineteen States) the State High Court, the State *Sharia* Court of Appeal (in some states) and State Customary Court of Appeal (in some States) and "Area Courts" and "Customary Courts".

The State High Courts have both original jurisdiction and also hear appeals from the lower courts. The *Sharia* Court of Appeal has only appellate jurisdiction to hear appeals from the area courts mainly in matters of Islamic family law.

The "area courts" (which replaced the former "native courts") have mainly original jurisdiction, but the higher grades amongst them also hear appeals from the lower grade courts before further appeals go to the *Sharia* Court of Appeal or, as the case may be, to the High Court.

Thus, briefly, we have the following network of courts: (a) at the base, the different grades of "Area Courts". These have jurisdiction in both civil and criminal matters. Appeals from their decisions to go to the High Court or the *Sharia* Courts of Appeal. (b) From the High

Court (and the *Sharia* Courts of Appeal) appeals lie to the Federal Court of Appeal and from there to the Supreme Court of Nigeria.

This is the judicial system, the structure. What about the law to be applied? As I pointed out earlier, when the British established their colonial administration in Northern Nigeria they allowed the institutions of Government (including the judiciary) which they found in existence to continue. I think it is to their credit that they refrained from substantial interference with either the law to be applied or the machinery for its application. As a result, the *Sharia* continued to apply throughout most of Northern Nigeria, in respect of both civil and criminal matters, as was the case before the colonial intervention — except that in the case of *zina* and theft the full *hadd* punishments were not not applied. Apart from this the *Sharia* was applied in full in respect of everything else by the native courts. The native courts, as I have pointed our earlier, deal with well over 90% of all judicial cases, civil and criminal, in the North. Thus, it can readily be seen that they are, in terms of value of work, the most important part of the judicial system.

The native courts derived their authority to apply the *Sharia* first in the early colonial Proclamations and "Ordinances", which provided that the native courts were to apply the native law prevailing in their respective areas of jurisdiction. From the British colonial view point, Islamic law was just another "native law" and therefore throughout the Muslim North it was the *Sharia* which applied. In point of fact, later enactments in the matter categorically defined "native law" to include "Moslem Law". The High Court and the Magistrates Courts, on the other hand, were primarily enjoined to apply English law and such statutory enactments as were in existence or were to be promulgated from time to time.

This position of the application of the *Sharia* in all matters in the native courts continued until 1960. In 1959, when Nigeria was getting ready for independence on the basis of a newly negotiated Constitution, the then legislature of Northern Nigeria was obliged to promulgate a new Code of Criminal Law in order to conform with the Constitution. The new Constitution had provided that with effect from the date of its coming into operation (1960) no person could be convicted of any offence unless such offence was defined and the punishment for it provided in a written law. In other words, statutory criminal law had to replace native as well as *Sharia* Criminal Law. Faced with the dilemma, the Northern Nigeria Legislature promulgated the Northern Nigeria Penal Code—which was based on the Sudanese and the Indian models. It was felt that since Islamic Criminal Law comprises, apart from the *hudud*, mainly *ta'azir* offences, all that was necessary was to transfer the *qadi's* discretion to the legislature—which prepared a catalogue of offences and their punishments for application by the courts. But it is important to note two things here: first, before the Penal Code was prepared extensive consultations took place with learned *ulama* both within and outside Northern Nigeria in order to ensure that the Code would, as much as possible, conform with the *Sharia*. Secondly, all the *hudud* were defined as crimes in the Code, except that the punishments for some of them were varied. Clearly, the legislature were anxious not to depart too much from the *Sharia*.

In civil matters, the native courts retained their jurisdiction as in pre-Independence days, and they continued to apply the *Sharia*. The courts themselves went through reforms and reorganizations, but the applicable law has remained the same. The Native Courts Law of 1963 (and its successor the Area Courts Law of 1968) provide that in civil matters the courts are to apply the native law prevailing in their respective areas of jurisdiction except in "mixed causes." Mixed causes are cases where the litigants are governed by different laws—e.g., a Muslim and a non-Muslim. In such cases, the court is required to apply the law (or the combination of laws) which the parties may have agreed before hand to apply to them, or the law which the court thinks they had, or must have had, in their contemplation. In the last resort the court is to have recourse to justice, equity and good conscience.

Appeals from these courts go to the State High Court in all cases not governed by the *Sharia* and to the *Sharia* Court of Appeal in cases governed by the *Sharia*, especially in all matters of family law and personal status.

Now a further word about the *Sharia* Court of Appeal. The

Northern Nigeria Constitution of 1963 and the Northern Nigeria *Sharia* Court of Appeal Law of 1963, both confer appellate jurisdiction on the court in respect of the following matters if they emanate from the native courts:

(a) all issues relating to Marriage concluded under Muslim Law. This includes all the incidents of marriage—i.e. its dissolution, family relations depending on it, custody of children, maintenance, etc.

(b) all issues relating to guardianship of infants, prodigal persons or persons of unsound mind and generally all questions relating to the guardianship or maintenance of Muslims suffering from physical or mental infirmity; and,

(c) where the parties to the proceedings at the lower court, whether they are Moslems or not, have made a written request to the lower court to determine their dispute in accordance with the *Sharia*, any other matter.

This was the jurisdiction conferred on the *Sharia* Court of Appeal. It may be noticed that the jurisdiction did not cover all civil cases which are generally by the *Sharia* at the first instance. The position was that in all such matters appeals go to the High Court, but the High Court had to include a *Sharia* Court of Appeals judge on its bench when it heard such appeals. This position was later changed in some States. In 1976, a Committee appointed by the then Federal Military Government recommended the tidying up of the situation by transferring appeals in all civil cases governed by the *Sharia* as the court of first instance to the *Sharia* Court of Appeal. This recommendation was accepted, but before it could be implemented the new Nigerian Constitution came into existence. It is at the point appropriate to note the fact that in respect of what may be agreed are the most important matters—i.e., all matters affecting the family—the *Sharia* applies and it is applied by judges who are specially qualified in the *Sharia*, i.e. judges trained and learned in this field. In short, in these matters, there is a clear and unambiguous demarcation between the *Sharia* and *Sharia* judges on the one hand, who deal with these matters without interference, and the English law and the English branch of the judiciary on the other hand, who have no jurisdiction of any kind in such matters. The importance of this demarcation will be discussed later.

It can therefore be shown that in Northern Nigeria the *Sharia* enjoys a separate and distinct life and identity both in respect of the substantive law and procedure and in its administration. Unfortunately this was the position only until October 1979. With effect from the 1st of October, 1979, the new Constitution has introduced one important change in this matter. This was done in respect of appellate jurisdiction.

Before October, 1979 the *Sharia* Court of Appeal of each State was the final court of appeal from which no appeal could lie to any other court in the matters under its jurisdiction. This position was due to the historical fact that under the former Northern Region of Nigeria Constitution there was one *Sharia* Court of Appeal for the whole Region since, as I have pointed out at the beginning, it was only in the North that the *Sharia* applied. But with the break-up of the North into ten States it was felt that a higher *Sharia* Court of Appeal was required. During the Constitution drafting debates in the Constituent Assembly, a Federal *Sharia* Court of Appeal was proposed by a large number of members of that body. It was felt that a Federal *Sharia* Court of Appeal was desirable so that appeals from the States' *Sharia* courts could end up there. But this was rejected by the majority of the Assembly and the new Constitution provided, instead, that appeals from the State *Sharia* Courts of Appeal are to go to the Federal Court of Appeal (this position is now enshrined in S. 223 of the new Constitution of Nigeria). This provision marks a fundamental departure from the previous position already stated. Now that the Federal Court of Appeal has jurisdiction to hear appeals from the State *Sharia* Courts of Appeal Nigerian common law judges have been given the opportunity of hearing pure *Sharia* cases decided by *Sharia* judges. This, as was pointed our earlier, had never been the case previously and we have to wait and see how the new arrangements will work.

But having said this, it must be pointed out that are amongst the judges of the Federal Court of Appeal some who are learned in the *Sharia* and who could, in their own right, qualify as *Sharia* judges. In fact one of them was, at one time, a judges of the *Sharia* Court of Appeal. It is also reasonable to assume that those Federal Court of

Appeal judges who are learned in the *Sharia* may have been appointed partly because of their additional *Sharia* qualifications so that they can deal with cases coming from the *Sharia* free from what we may call extraneous interference, steps have been taken, administratively, to ensure that improper interference is guarded against.

This is a convenient point to stop and consider the relative merits of keeping the administration of the *Sharia* solely in the hands of a purely *Sharia* judiciary and the alternative of enabling the general non-*Sharia* judiciary to take part in the administration of the *Sharia*.

One must begin here by observing that the ordinary courts in Nigeria—just like English counterparts—do have a well-known procedure for applying, in specific cases, laws other than their own. It is a well established principle in both the English and the Nigerian High Courts, that whenever, because of the prior agreement of the parties, what is known as foreign law is to be applied in a particular case, that foreign law has to be proved before the court as though it were a matter of "facts". In other words, the parties will not be denied their right of choice of law, where appropriate, just because the court is not learned in that law; but the parties concerned have to call witnesses who are learned in that foreign law (preferably lawyers) to guide the court. Now, in Nigeria, the Evidence Act, and State Evidence Laws have clearly laid down this position—i.e., native law and custom (which includes Islamic Law) is to be treated as fact and has to be proved in the High Court.

One may say that really no substantial harm can be done where the High Court judge is guided by expert *ulama* as to what the *Sharia* is in any particular issue before such a judge. And this may well be true; but the fact remains that where you have a full-fledged *Sharia* judiciary it is hardly justifiable to by-pass that arm of the judicial system and provide a rather complicated procedure for deciding *Sharia* cases by what one may call second-hand means.

The other alternative, what I would call the Indian alternative—and by India I mean the whole of the sub-Continent comprising India, Pakistan and Bangla Desh—is to provide that all courts regard both the English and native (and *Sharia*) laws as directly applicable by all the courts. This has always been the case in India, where both the *Sharia* and the Hindu Law are regarded as part and parcel of the general law of the land, and the courts are expected to apply the *Sharia* (and the other laws) and lawyers are to argue it before the courts, and the question of treating it as foreign law does not arise. It may be argued that this makes for more integration and cohesion of the legal systems since all lawyers and judges will be obliged to learn all the systems. And this may well be the case. But it also leads to some undesirable consequences for the *Sharia* and its administration.

The *Sharia* is a vast and highly technical field and its administrators are required, as a rule, to devote the whole of their life to its learning, teaching, and application. Even the most learned of *ulama* have always dreaded the judicial office and have always insisted that only men who are both learned and pious may be appointed to administer the *Sharia*. We may recall the famous prophetic tradition that divides judges into three categories—two of which will go to Hell and one to Paradise. The two destined for Hell, we might recall, are the one who is ignorant of the *Sharia* and accept the office and purports to administer justice and the one who is learned but judges not in accordance with the *Sharia*. Now, taking all this into account, there can be no doubt that the ends of justice cannot be adequately served by either allowing amateurs to administer the *Sharia* or by administering it through second-hand means. What is more, when judges trained in the English legal system are called upon to apply the *Sharia* (and "take it in their stride") they cannot be blamed if their pre-conceived notions of justice and equity play a large (if subconscious) part in their application of the *Sharia*. One should also not lose sight of the fact that, due to the general ignorance of the *Sharia* amongst lawyers, there are still many common law judges whose view of Islamic law and the Islamic legal system is similar to that expressed by Justice Goddard in 1940 when he said, referring to certain provisions of the then Emergency Power Act, that his court was really put very much in the position of a *Qadi* under the palm tree: "There are no principles on which he is directed to act. He has to do the best in the circumstances, having no rules of law to guide him." This palm-tree notion of justice still dominates the minds of a good many High Court judges. But above all, the really more serious issue in the matter of non-*Sharia* judges applying the *Sharia*, concerns the possibility of either the deliberate disregard for the *Sharia* or ignorance by the bench resulting in a miscarriage of justice. To give two examples again from India: an Indian judge accepted a widow's claim for a year's maintenance in addition to her share in the inheritance of her deceased husband's estate. This judgement, which was clearly wrong, was based on the judge's misunderstanding of a Quranic verse. Now, one might say that in the first place he had no business disregarding clear and well laid down principles on the issue; but the fact is that he was either ignorant of them or he thought in all honesty the woman deserved more than her share in the inheritance. The case went on appeal eventually to the Privy Council in London.

The British Law Lords, who constitute the Judicial Committee of the Privy Council, reversed the judgement and correctly refused to be drawn into the intricacies of Quranic exegesis on the issue. They considered "it would be wrong for the Court on a point of this kind to put their own construction on the Koran in opposition to the express ruling of commentators of such great antiquity and high authority." Clearly this was a fortunate case of the Privy Council doing the right thing. Unfortunately, however, the same Privy Council in another case in 1894 had totally disregarded the *Sharia* rules and substituted for them their Lordship's own notions of English rules of equity and good conscience. This was a case of two brothers who had made a *waqf* appointing themselves as the first *Mutawallis* and making their children and descendants, generation after generation, the beneficiaries, with the poor being the ultimate beneficiaries on the extinction of the families. The judge at the first instance held the *waqf* valid, but on appeal to the High Court the decision was reversed and on final appeal to the Privy Council, the Privy Council upheld the High Court. It said that the *waqf* was merely for "the aggrandizement of a family" and the charitable part of it was merely "illusory".

This view of the Privy Council is the correct view under the general principles of the English Law of Equity; but it certainly is not the correct view under the *Sharia*. This decision, which was seen to be against the fundamental principles of the *Sharia*, led to a barrage of complaints and criticisms in India (indeed, one writer says "it created a storm in the country"). In fact, the Indian Parliament had to step in and to pass the "Musulman Waqf Validating Act" of 1913 to repair the harm done by that decision.

In short, all the foregoing shows that the best approach to the application of the *Sharia* in any plural society where the *Sharia* does not constitute the sole legal system, is the approach of giving it its own environment and leaving it in the hands of the people learned in it and devoted to it rather than in the hands of amateurs.

In this regard, I think it would be right to conclude that, although the new Constitution of Nigeria has effected a modification of the erstwhile position, Nigeria remains unique among ex-colonial countries in that it has accorded to the *Sharia* and its administration a clear place in the legal and judicial system of the country.

10

Muslim Family Law in South Asia

LUCY CARROLL

Now that Islam has dramatically impressed its political and economic presence upon the West, we are certain to be in for a spate of books exploiting Muslim subjects and written for western audiences. It would appear that even the staid and hallowed precincts of the legal world will not escape the deluge. And so we have the book under notice.

"This book describes the family laws of the Muslim world. A lot is heard these days of amputation of the hand for robbery, the stoning to death of adulterers, the flogging of intoxicants.." (Preface.) One, of course, does not flog intoxicants. If one is a pious Muslim, one pours them down the drain (as was recently demonstrated in front of the Iranian Embassy in London) and flogs the tippler (as some British citizens discovered to their discomfort in Saudi Arabia a year or so age). The mental vision of Muslim purists lining up bottles of the best wine, gin, brandy, whisky, etc. and publicity flogging them in the market perhaps provides some light comic relief. But, in fact, that is a most inauspicious beginning for a most inauspicious book.

Errors of grammar and punctuation arc unhappy; monotonous repetition of inelegant expressions (e.g., "not least becausc") is tedious; awkward and sloppy sentence structure and poor paragraph organisation are tiresome.

The book obviously would have greatly benefitted from the careful attentions of an editor skilled in the correct and aesthetic use of the English language.

Another—and extremely disconcerting—matter that necessitates comment is the careless, or non-existent, footnoting and citation. The first instance a seventeenth century document concerning British legal administration in Bombay, and in the second instance an eighteenth century document concerning British Administration in Madras. There is no footnote citation whatsoever; nor is there any identification of these documents is the text. If Dr. Pearl's research had been sufficiently thorough as actually to bring him into personal contact with these documents, they should have been fully cited, including file or reference number and the archive in which they were to be located. If the quotations were taken from a secondary source, i.e., the report of a scholar's research, they should have been cited as cited by that author, followed by "as quoted by (name of author) in (name of work, place of publication, name of publisher, date of publication)."

(Including the long quotations referred to above, as well as several other uncited quotations) resembles nothing so much as a crude patchwork of bits and pieces "borrowed" from Sir Charles Fawcett's very important and exceedingly well-researched volume, *The First Century of British Justice in India*, strung together with neither credit to the scholar nor acknowledgment of the source, and, to all intents and purposes, put forward as the author's own work. Amazingly, Fawcett's volume, to which the author is obviously very greatly indebted, is not even listed in the author's bibliography.

Clearly the book would also have greatly benefitted from the careful attentions of an editor familiar with the subject, the sources, and the protocol of scholarly prose. Serious as such literary and scholarly failings undoubtedly are, criticism as this level may perhaps be laid aside on the assumption that considerations of literary and grammatical style and the ethics and responsibilities of scholarly writing are beyond the purview of a lawyer.

But surely statutes and cases are grist for the lawyer's mill—or so one might assume. Unfortunately, this assumption is convincingly rebutted in the instant case. A very few examples must suffice.

Child Marriage Restraint Act and the Muslim Family Laws Ordinance

Dr. Pearl states that "the minimum ages" for marriage specified in the Child Marriage Restraint Act 1929 (CMRA) "have been raised to under 16 for a girl and under 21 for a boy in Pakistan and Bangladesh." The Muslim Family Laws Ordinance 1961 (MFLO), section 12(1) (c) is cited as authority for this statement.

Section 12 of the MFLO does indeed amend the CMRA. But subsection (1) (c) has nothing to do with the question of minimum ages; it adds a new definitional clause defining "Union Council." Section 12(1)(a) alters the definition of "child" in section 2(a) of the CMRA in the case of a female by substituting "sixteen" for "fourteen"; thus, a female child is defined in the amended statute as "under sixteen". Nothing, however, in the MFLO alters the definition of a male child, who in section 2 (a) of the CMRA is defined as a male "under eighteen".

The CMRA as originally enacted prescribed two different standards of punishment for a male who contracted a child marriage in violation of the Act: if the male contracting such a marriage were between eighteen and twenty-one, he was liable of fine; if he were over twenty-one, he was liable to both fine and imprisonment. This differential liability has been abolished in Pakistan and Bangladesh by the amendments of the earlier statute effected by the MFLO.

Thus, Section 12(2) of the MFLO deletes the provision of the CMRA imposing the lighter punishment in cases where the male contracting a child marriage is himself between the ages of eighteen and twenty-one. Section 12(3) of the MFLO changes the age in the provision of the CMRA imposing the heavier punishment of both fine and imprisonment: instead of becoming liable for this punishment at the age of twenty-one, the liability now accrues at the age of eighteen. This is the meaning of Section 12(3) of the MFLO which reads: "in Section 3 (of the CMRA), for the words 'twenty-one' the word 'eighteen' shall be substituted."

Section 12(3) of the MFLO is the only provision is that Ordinance amending the CMRA which makes any mention of the ages "eighteen" and "twenty-one"—and clearly, even without reading the CMRA to put the changes in their appropriate context, the revision is in the opposite direction from that remarked by Dr. Pearl, i.e., the change is from twenty-one to eighteen, not from eighteen to twenty-one. And, of course, this amendment of the CMRA has nothing to do with minimum ages of marriage under that Act; the definition of a male child in the CMRA has not been amended by the MFLO and remains a male "under eighteen."

It is further, and obviously, incorrect to speak of minimum ages for marriage under the CMRA as being "under sixteen" or "under eighteen". These phrases are operative in the context of defining what constitutes a "child" and a "child marriage" for purposes of the CMRA. The minimum ages for a marriage escaping the criminal sanctions of the CMRA would clearly be sixteen (female) and eighteen (male) in Pakistan and Bangladesh.

Dowry and Bridal Gifts (Restriction) Act

In reference to *mehr* (dower payable by the husband to the wife; and essential component of a Muslim marriage contract), Dr. Pearl states: "It was felt necessary in Pakistan for some governmental intervention in this area; thus a ceiling of Rs. 5,000 has now been created for *mehr* by the Dowry and Bridal Gifts (Restriction) Act, 1976, Section 3."

The suggestion that the Pakistan Government would even consider such an extreme attack an such a fundamental aspect of Muslim family law defies belief. Yet, amazingly, this proposition has been uncritically and unquestioningly accepted and asserted by Dr. Pearl.

Section 3(1) of the Dowry and Bridal Gifts (Restriction) Act 1976 (DBGRA)—and the Act's title itself gives the game away—provides: "Neither the aggregate value of the dowry and presents given to the bride by her parents nor the aggregate value of the bridal gifts of the presents given to the bridegroom shall exceed five thousand rupees." On the face of it, this provision would not appear to have anything at all to do with *mehr* or dower. The matter, however, it definitively settled by looking at the definitions set out in Section 2 of the same Act:

(a) 'bridal gift' means any property given as a gift...by the bridegroom of his parents to the bride in connection with the marriage but *does not include mehr* (emphasis added);

(b) 'dowry' means any property given.. to a bride by her parents..;

On a clear and unambiguous reading, the statute has absolutely nothing to do with *mehr*, which is, in terms, excluded from its provisions. In thus excluding *mehr*, the DBGRA follows its South Asian predecessors in the field of anti-dowry legislation: e.g., the West Pakistan Dowry (Prohibition on Display) Act of 1967 (see Section 2(ii)(a)); the North-Western Frontier Province Dowry Ordinance of 1972 (see Section 2(ii)); the Indian Dowry Prohibition Act of 1961 (see Section 2 (b)).

The DBGRA is concerned, not with dower (*mehr*), but with dowry (*jahez*) i.e., money and gifts which move in the opposite direction as does the *mehr*. Dowry (*jahez*) comes from the wife's family to the bridegroom, his family, the bride, and/or the bridal couple (local custom defining recipients) and is given at the time of the marriage. *Mehr* goes from the husband or his parents to the bride and is usually payable in part on demand after the marriage and in part at the time when the marriage is dissolved by death or divorce. Given the Muslim husband's unilateral right of dissolving the marriage at will and thus terminating any further financial responsibility towards his wife, *mehr* is an extremely important right of the Muslim wife. If the *mehr* is set at a sufficiently high amount, it may cause a husband to think twice before divorcing his wife; if she is divorced, it may help her to meet her needs.

Mehr is virtually always in the form of money or immovable property; *jahez* virtually always takes the form of material goods—jewellery, household furnishings and appliances, a motorcycle or car, etc. This is reflected in the enforcement provisions of the Pakistan Act and the Rules framed under it. Dowry and gifts in excess of the permitted value are to be confiscated and stored in a *jahez* go-down, from whence they will be distributed to impecunious fathers unable to provide their marriageable daughters with a dowry. In regard to enforcement, Dr. Pearl states: "The method of enforcement leaves a lot to be desired..." Assuming, as Dr. Pearl obviously does, that the *jahez* go-down was designed to cope with *mehr*, i.e., money and immovable property, the provisions for enforcement are not merely inadequate, they are positively ludicrous—a fact which might reasonably have caused one at least to re-read the statute before purporting to comment upon it in a "text book".

Dowry is a subject which does not appear in the texts dealing with Muslim law; it was not an Arabian custom and is unknown in classical Islamic law. But it is a very real and deeply entrenched social custom in South Asia (among both Hindu and Muslim communities) and one against which social reformers (both Hindu and Muslim) have been inveighing for at least three-quarters of a century. Surely anyone who has purportedly made his specially the study of Muslim family law in South Asia should neither be ignorant of such a prominent social fact as the practice of dowry (*jahez*), nor so careless as to confuse the institution of *jahez* with that of *mehr*. And, of course, no lawyer should be able to read into a statute that which is *expressly excluded.*

Dissolution of Muslim Marriages Act and Stipulations in a Muslim Marriage Contract

In reference to the absence of legislative reform of Muslim law in India in regard to polygamy, Dr. Pearl states: "The only protection, at the time of marriage, is a stipulation in the (marriage) contract that the husband shall not take a second wife—which is enforceable in that the wife is entitled to claim a dissolution under the 1939 legislation (Dissolution of Muslim Marriages Act) if the husband does indeed marry a second time in contravention of the stipulation."

This statement is nonsense; not surprisingly, no authority is cited in support of this assertion.

A stipulation in a Muslim marriage contract is usually enforced by another provision in the same contract whereby the husband agrees to delegate to the wife the power to dissolve the union by the pronouncement of *talaq* on his behalf (*talaq-i-tafwid*) in the event of breach of the stipulation. This enables the wife to terminate the marriage extra-judicially and without the intervention of a Court upon contravention of the terms of the stipulation. If the matter does come to Court it will be in the form of the wife's petition for a declaration that the marriage is no longer subsisting because of her exercise of the delegated right of *talaq*; in the form of a suit instituted by the wife for recovery of her deferred dower on the ground that the marriage has been dissolved by virtue of her exercise of *talaq-i-tafwid*; or in the form of the husband's suit for restitution of conjugal rights, in which the defence of the wife is that the marriage has been dissolved by her pronouncement of *talaq* under the power delegated to her by the marriage contract.

For over one hundred years, the Courts of the Indian sub-continent have upheld the wife's extra-judicial termination of her marriage in cases where there were both a stipulation in the marriage contract to the effect that the husband shall not marry a second wife during the subsistence of the first union, and a further provision authorizing the wife to dissolve the marriage by *talaq-i-tafwid* should the stipulation be violated. Reported cases of this kind go back at least to the early 1870's, i.e., nearly seventy years before the enactment of the Dissolution of Muslim Marriages Act of 1939 (DMMA). Similar cases which have arisen subsequently to the enactment of this statute make no reference to it for the simple reason that the DMMA is completely irrelevant to the situation.

If the marriage contract contains a stipulation which is not coupled with a provision entitling the wife to exercise the delegated right of *talaq* in case of its breach, the wife is not entitled to a divorce simply on the ground that the stipulation has been violated. The fact of breach of a stipulation in a marriage contract may, in appropriate cases, enable the wife to defeat her husband's suit for restitution of conjugal rights and it may, in appropriate cases, enable her to claim maintenance from her husband while not living with him. These reliefs are largely at the discretion of the Court and all the circumstances, including the breach of the stipulation, would be taken into account.

The DMMA does not assist the wife whose husband has violated a stipulation in their marriage contract in cases where the husband has not delegated to her the right of *talaq*. Breach of a stipulation in a marriage contract is not a ground for dissolution of marriage under the DMMA. Breach of a stipulation does not even constitute a ground under the general provisions of Section 2(ix), "any other ground which is recognized as valid for the dissolution of marriages under Muslim law," because the breach of a stipulation in a marriage contract (in the absence of a delegation to the wife of the right of *talaq*) does not constitute a ground for dissolution of marriage under the Muslim law of the Hanafi school as observed in the subcontinent. (And if the right of pronouncing *talaq* has been delegated to the wife, she has absolutely no need to have recourse to the DMMA for a judicial dissolution of her marriage; she can dissolve the marriage extra-judicially.)

Of course, a wife who can prove that she and her co-wife are not treated "equitably in accordance with the injunctions of the Quran" can sue for divorce under Section 2(viii)(f) of the DMMA. A wife wishing a divorce because of her husband's remarriage may also attempt to convince the Court that the fact that her husband has taken an additional wife constitutes such cruelty to her as to entitle her to a divorce on the ground of cruelty. The argument that the husband's second marriage constituted legal cruelty to the first wife was accepted by the Allahabad High Court in a 1960 case involving restitution of conjugal rights, but it has not yet been endorsed by any Court in the context of a suit for divorce. However, the important point is that both these contentions are available to a wife *whether or nor* there is an anti-polygamy stipulation in her marriage contract.

Thus, in sum, when the stipulation against the taking of a second wife is coupled with a provision delegating to the wife the right to dissolve the marriage by *talaq* should the stipulation be breached, the DMMA is totally irrelevant. And when the stipulation is not coupled with a provision for *talaq-i-tafwid* and the wife sues for divorce under the DMMA, the breach of the stipulation is irrelevant. A stipulation in a Muslim marriage contract is *not*, in any case, enforceable under the DMMA, which statute does *not* entitle a wife to divorce on the grounds of the breach of such a stipulation.

Dissolution of Muslim Marriages Act and the "Option of Puberty"

I refrain from commenting at any length on Dr. Pearl's handling of this question, because no textbook writer has ever succeeded in presenting what is a simple and straightforward situation (that is to say, a simple and straightforward situation once the requisite research has been done and the obvious variables identified) as anything other than a hopelessly confused and totally incomprehensible muddle.

Dr. Pearl deals with the matter by simply avoiding any comment at all on the Indian situation and contenting himself with a very general and uninformed remark concerning recent Pakistan cases. Given the importance of both the social problem of child marriage and the "option of puberty" recognized in Muslim law, the treatment of the latter subject is grossly inadequate and completely uninformative (e.g., readers are left totally in the dark about the Indian case-law and the present position of the Indian Courts).

Caste Disabilities Removal Act and Opostacy from Islam

In regard to the question of apostacy from Islam and rights of intestate succession, Dr. Pearl states: "In the classical systems of Islamic law, the apostate from Islam loses his or her right to inherit or in (sic) intestacy of a Muslim relative. This rule was abandoned in India, as a whole (i.e., the region now comprising the independent states of India, Pakistan, and Bangladesh), as early as 1850 when the Caste Disabilities Removal Act (Act XXI of 1850) was passed."

This statement is unexceptionable, *as far as it goes*. What is exceptionable is that it goes no further. No notice is taken of the fact that as long ago as 1963 the provisions of the 1850 statute, as they applied to precisely the situation to which Dr. Pearl is referring, were abolished in what was then West Pakistan and in now Pakistan.

The Act of 1850 in essence provided that no rights of property, including rights of inheritance, would be impaired or affected in any way by the fact of the individual concerned having renounced or having been expelled from any religious community. Thus, an apostate from Islam would no longer be deprived of his right of intestate succession to his Muslim relatives. This continues to be the case in India, where the Act of 1850 continues to govern the situation.

However, the Caster Disabilities Removal (West Pakistan Amendment) Act of 1963 imposed a severe and very important limitation on the applicability of the 1850 Act in present-day Pakistan by providing: "nothing contained in this Act shall apply to the rights of inheritance to the property of a Muslim." Thus, as far as succession to the property of a Muslim is concerned, the provisions of the Act of 1850 have been completely ousted and Muslim law has been reinstated as the governing rule—with the result that the apostate from Islam is now disinherited in Pakistan.

Maina Bibi v. Chaudhri Vakil Ahmad, (1924/25) 52 Indian Appeals 145

In regard to the *Maina Bibi* case, Dr. Pearl states: "In 1907 well before the case had been finally decided, the widow, Maina Bibi, executed gifts of the property in favour of a third party."

This statement makes no sense at all, unless one assumes that the woman was either *non-compos mentis* or completely senile; she was neither. (Incidentally, her husband died in 1890, not in 1870 as stated by Dr. Pearl.)

The case involved a widow in possession of her deceased husband's property in lieu of her dower debt which became payable to her on his death. In 1902 the husband's heirs sued for possession of the property. The trial Court held that the heirs were entitled to obtain their share of the property on payment of the respective proportion of the widow's dower debt. In the event that such payment was not made within six months, the case was to be dismissed. The heirs appealed; the decree of the trial Court was confirmed; and on failure of the heirs to pay the dower debt the case was finally dismissed in 1906. The widow and her legal advisors interpreted this dismissal of the suit as extinguishing the heirs' claim to the property and investing the widow with an absolute title in it.

Believing, on the advice of her lawyers, that she now possessed an absolute title in the property, the widow purported to gift this property and surrendered possession to her alieness in 1907. There was, in 1907, no litigation concerning the property in progress or pending. Indeed, there was no litigation in progress or pending between 1906, when the case was finally dismissed by the High court, and 1915, eight years after the widow transferred the property.

In 1915 the husband's heirs brought a new suit, founded on a new cause of action—the widow's surrender of possession of the property of her alieness in 1907. It was the suit, initiated in 1915, that was finally decided by the privy council in 1924.

Parveen Chaudhry v. VIth Senior Civil Judge, Karachi, P.L.D. 1976 Karachi 416

The Muslim Family Laws Ordinance 1961, applicable in Pakistan and Bangladesh, inter alia, imposed certain formal procedural requirements on any Muslim husband wishing to divorce his wife by *talaq*. Section 7 (1) of the Ordinance reads:—"Any man who wishes to divorce his wife shall, as soon as may be after the pronouncement of *talaq* in any form whatsoever, give the Chairman (of the local Union Council, the unit of local government) notice writing of his having done so, and shall supply a copy thereof to the wife." This requirement is enforced by criminal sanctions spelled out in Section 7(2) and, more importantly, by the provisions of Section 7(3), which provide that a *talaq* ("unless revoked earlier, expressly or otherwise,") shall not take effect until ninety days after the notice under Section 7(1) has been delivered to the Chairman. Section 7(3) is the more important because the Pakistan Courts have interpreted this section to mean that if the Chairman has not been informed of the pronouncement of a *talaq*, the legal assumption is that *talaq* has been revoked (and *all* Pakistani *talaqs* are now revocable) even before the husband got around to informing the Chairman of the fact that he has pronounced the formula of divorce. (E.g., *Syed Nawaz Gardesi v. Muhammad Yusuf*, P.L.D. 1963 Supreme Court 51.) Failure to inform the Chairman of a *talaq* pronouncement does not, therefore, result in an "illegal" divorce but in no divorce at all. The provisions of Section 7(1) of the Ordinance are clearly mandatory.

In regard to Section 7(1) of the Muslim Family Laws Ordinance, Dr. Pearl states: "The ordinance states that the husband *shall serve* or the wife a copy of the notice of *talaq* which he serves on the Chairman. This provision, also, has caused considerable difficulty, and there is conflicting authority on whether notice to the wife is mandatory or permissive." (Italics in source).

It is impossible to understand just who has been put to any difficulty in interpreting the mandatory provision of Section 7(1) of the Ordinance—certainly it has not been the Courts of Pakistan. In *Inamul Islam v. Hussain Bano* (P.L.D. 1976 Lahore 1466) and *Rashida v. Ghulam Raza* (P.L.D. 1977 Lahore 363), it has been clearly indicated that service of the notice on the wife is just as mandatory as it service of the notice on the appropriate public official.

The case cited by Dr. Pearl as authority for the contrary view, *Mst. Parveen Chaudhry v. VIth Senior Civil Judge* (P.L.D. 1976 Karachi 416), would not, in fact, appear to support that position at all. What was apparently at issue in *Parveen Chaudhry* was the contention that notice to the wife of the *talaq* pronouncement itself, as distinct from and in addition to notice of the communication to the Chairman informing him that the formula of divorce had been uttered, was necessary. The Karachi Court found as a fact that the divorce deed had been sent to the wife. It further held that no separate communication to the wife of the pronouncement of *talaq* was required; it did *not* hold that service on the wife of a copy of the notice to the Chairman was not mandatory. "On behalf of the petitioner (wife) objections were filed ...mainly on the ground that the divorce had not been communicated by the respondent to the petitioner and for such reason there was no valid divorce in existence..." "(S)ubsection (1) of Section 7 .... only provides for giving a notice of *talaq* to the Chairman and a copy thereof to the wife... (I)t is very clear to us that *the mere fact of absence of communication of the divorce before moving the Chairman* under sub-Section (1) of Section 7 of the Ordinance *does not invalidate the divorce.*" (P.L.D. 1976 Karachi 416, pp. 418, 420 emphasis added).

A copy of the notice to the Chairman would scarcely be sent *before* the original had been dispatched; "communication of the divorce" clearly refers to communication of the pronouncement itself, as opposed to notice of (i.e., a copy of) the notification to the Chairman. And, of course, under Hanafi law no communication to the wife of the *talaq* pronouncement itself is necessary in order to effect a valid divorce; the Ordinance has not altered this and merely requires that the wife be served with a copy of the notice informing the Chairman that a *talaq* has been pronounced in relation to her.

This particular matter is of more than academic interest to English lawyers, as the question has been raised in more than one English case. The English Court (of the basis of the "expert evidence" presented to it) reached conclusions that are, to my mind, directly contrary to the judicial authority emanating from the Courts of Pakistan, which Courts are, after all, the authoritative interpreters of Pakistan Law.

Nur Ali v. Malka Sultana, P.L.D. 1961 Lahore 431

This was a case concerning (as far as is relevant to the present discussion) succession to the estate of a Muslim deceased. The Quranic shares of the propositus' female survivors amounted, in sum, to less than unity; in the absence of a male agnate, the residue was distributed according to the principles of *radd*. Dr. Pearl states that the widow "was held to be entitled only to a fixed Quranic portion of one-eighth which cannot be increased by any 'return' of the residue." He then adds: "This is contrary to the general jurisprudence on the Indian subcontinent which was allowed the spouse relict to participate in a return."

One would have certainly appreciated some authority for this remarkable statement. None is forthcoming; I would suggest that none exists.

Generally in India, as in the classical Sunni law (excluding Maliki law, according to which the propositus can never be without a residuary heir, the public treasury stepping into this role in the absence of any other claimant) only the blood relations of the propositus participate in *radd*. The exception introduced in South Asia concerns the situation where the deceased leaves *no blood relatives at all*. In such a case, in the Indian sub-continent, the spouse relict takes the whole estate, not so much by *radd* (although this is the term generally employed) as on the basis of possession of what is regarded as a claim superior to that of the public treasury, which would otherwise claim the residue to the estate by escheat. Thus, in the subcontinent, the spouse relict does not participate in *radd* in the presence of any other heir and only takes precedence over the public treasury in case of a competition between the spouse relict as the sole surviving heir of the propositus and the state claiming by escheat.

As the deceased in the *Nur Ali* case left him surviving a daughter, a granddaughter, and a mother, in addition to a widow—and thus obviously did not depart this earth totally bereft of any blood relatives—of course, his widow was not entitled to participate in *radd*, even according to the rule applicable on the subcontinent. This decision is completely in keeping with the juridical traditions of the Indian subcontinent and does not constitute, as Dr. Pearl suggests, an exception to them.

Were time and space unlimited, the enumeration of this book's failing might be considerably prolonged. However, the constraints of the former must necessarily restrict the recitation of the latter. For present purposes is it sufficient to indicate that the subject has not been sufficiently mastered, that the approach is sloppy and undisciplined, and that the results is, therefore—and not surprisingly—highly unsatisfactory.

The format of the book is curious; so also is the title. In spite of the misleading generality of the title, the text is basically comprised of a very superficial treatment of Muslim family law in South Asia (and even this is too broad a description give, for example, the fact that India is completely ignored in the discussion of the "opinion of puberty" while the Pakistan amendment to the Caste Disabilities Removal Act passes unnoticed). The text of the volume constitutes 201 pages. The total text of 201 pages, however, includes historical chapters (concerning which the less said the better) amounting to 41 pages, and a concluding chapter on conflict of laws (again, the less said the better) amounting to 22 pages. The substantive law is thus handled in less than 140 pages; needless to say, the subject is scarcely done the justice it deserves, in terms of quantity no less than in terms of quality of treatment.

The text is followed by another 105 pages of appendices. The major appendix, comprising not less than 90 pages, consists of statutes and extracts of statutes from various and sundry Muslim countries. This appendix is virtually useless, as it is nowhere indexed and the only way to ascertain what is therein contained is to go page by page through the 90 pages—a task few will bother to undertake. One may perhaps be forgiven for venturing the opinion that this lengthy and needless section has been included merely to "pad" the volume out to a reasonably respectable length.

Besides students, the Preface refers to "lawyers with cases to argue before the courts" in defining the public for whom the book is aimed. One can only hope that "lawyer with cases to argue before the courts" will ignore this book. There are much more reliable works on the subject ready to hand; if to consult them necessitates an excursion to the library rather than to the bookseller, and if reference must be had to several volumes rather than to one—indeed, if reference must be had to, of all things, the reported case-law and legislation—so be it.

11

The Development of Muslim Law in Sri Lanka

DR. M.N.M. KAMIL ASAD

The law forms the basis of a system of social control established for the purpose of maintaining an ordered society about man and women. In Sri Lanka, the various communities developed different legal systems. Islamic law is traditionally based on the Qur'an and the *hadithes* (traditions of the Prophet Muhammad P.B.H.). It is viewed as the framework of Islam itself. Although the religion describes what the ideal life should be, it is the law which indicates the right road to follow (indeed the term *Shari'ah* bears this meaning) in order to arrive at the ideal life. Thus, the law of Islam, the *Shari'ah*, has the character of the religious obligations. At the same time, it constitutes a political sanction for the religion. As a consequence, the *Shari'ah* has greater practical importance to Muslims so much so that the creed and its study is ranked higher than a superogatory prayer by Al-Shafi'i (the founder of the Shafi'i school of law).

When the first Muslims came to Sri Lanka, they brought with them their personal law governed by the School of Al-Shafi'i, to which they belonged. This had special features on Marriage, Divorce and Inheritance. The Muslim community in Sri Lanka seems to have conducted its own affairs, personal and social, according to its own laws and customs. The *'ulama'* the standard works of Muslim law that were in use in South India, were introduced into Sri Lanka, from time to time. Some of these were translations from Arabic into Tamil, made in South India. Others were in Arabic manuscript copies of the *Kitabs* (books) sometimes prepared by the *'ulama'*. They were mainly the writings of the Shafieite jurists, the most important of them being the *Kitab al-Umm* by Imam Shafi'i himself.

Earlier, when the Portuguese arrived in 1505, Colombo, which was the chief port and the mart of the Island's trade, had a large Muslim population and boasted a Court of Justice to settle disputes, according to Islamic law. In the subsequent centuries, the evidence suggests that Sri Lanka's Muslim community did not value their separate legal system as much as one might suppose. There are repeated references to the absence of Muslim legal authorities. For example, in the late eighteenth century, the Dutch Governor I am Willem Falck (1765-85) found that there was no person in the whole Island who was sufficiently well-versed in Muslim law to make decisions among people of Islamic faith. He, therefore, in 1770, secured the help of the Governor-General of Batavia in getting "a short (tract)...framed by the best informed and most learned of the Mohommedan priests who resided within his Government" (i.e. in Batavia). In compliance with this request, Section 34 of the Batavian States of 1766" "by *Sondene Wettan Anngaandentooren off Mohometanen ennandere Inland Schenafien"* (special law relating to Moors or Mohammedances and other native races) was sent to Colombo. The code related to the law of Marriages, Divorce and Succession.

Governor Falck submitted it for consideration to all the Headmen of the Moorish inhabitants and thereafter it was considered part of the law by the Dutch Courts of Justice. As the Shafi'ite school of law prevailed throughout the Dutch possessions of the East Indies, there was clearly no difficulty about the application of the code to the Muslims of Sri Lanka. The introduction to this code says that "the Civil and Customary law codified therein had been compiled from Muhammedan rules of law by which the Muhammedans are guided in respect of disputes arising amongst them relating to marriage, divorce and succession and required that it should be duly observed.

The statement shows that Muslim law in Sri Lanka was in operation, if not continuously, during the Dutch period. The last Dutch Governor, J.H. Van Angel Beck (1794-96) and the Council Colombo also agreed to an arrangement, made by the Jaffna authorities, for the translation of the law of the Muslims "existing in the Arabic language with their Priests". The plan was first to translate this into Tamil and then into Dutch. At first, the Muslim elders at Jaffana were accused of not co-operating with this effort for their own selfish reasons. Later, it was found that the Dutch authorities in Jaffna had for some reasons antagonised these men and consequently they had proved recalcitrant. The same leaders subsequently compiled a list of 250 laws based on the Qur'an and gave this to the Governor. This incident indicates that atleast one Dutch Governor was anxious to preserve Muslim law in Sri Lanka.

The first British Governor of the Maritime Province of Sri Lanka, Frederick North, was also prepared to view Muslim law sympathetically. One of the instructions given to the Court of Directors on 25th May 1798 was that all Courts of Justice should observe the law and institutions that existed under the Dutch. Accordingly, the Muslims of Sri Lanka were enabled to follow their own customary law. Further developments took place in 1799. The British Government in Sri Lanka wanted to bring a Qadi from bengal or from North India because the Government had again found that there was no person in the whole Island who was sufficiently well-versed in Muslim law to act as Qadi among the Muslims of Sri Lanka. The Muslims objected to this decision. However, because the Muslims of Bengal and North India belonged to the Hanafi Sect not the Shafi'i, and they instead wanted the Qadi to be brought from Egypt or South India where the Shafi'i sect predominated. Ultimately, the Qadi was, infact, brought from South India.

The British safeguarded the customary law of the Island initially because it was an established principle of international law and of British constitutional practice the laws of a conquered territory continued in force until altered by the conqueror." This was reflected in the first British Charter of Justice in 1801, which remarks — "That in the cases of Cingalese or Musulman natives, their inheritance and succession of lands, rents and goods and all matters of contract and dealing between party and part should be determined in the case of Cingalese by the laws and usages of the Cingalese, or in the case of Musulmans, by the laws and wagês of the Musulmans, and where one of the parties should be Cingalese of Musulman by the laws and usages of the defendant.

In 1806, the Acting Chief Justice Alexander Johnston was requested by Governor Maitland to make a collection of these local customary laws which he found in the course of his judicial circuits in different partds of the Island. L:ater that year, Johnston submitted to the Governor in the Council, a Code of Muslim Law reputedly observed by Muslims in the area of Colombo, and the Governor resolved that it be published and observed throughout the whole Province.

The Code of Muslim law in Sri Lanka promulgated in 1806 was largely a translation of the special law relating to the Moors which had obtained during the Dutch period. The Code promulgated in 1806 by Ordinance was made to apply to Muslims in the whole of the Island, including the Kandyan Provinces. This law was said to have been one of the bodies of law recognised officially by Governor North's Proclamation of 23rd September 1799. However, there were limits to this recognition. Muslim Law was not thought applicable within Sri Lanka, unless, it had been adopted in the country, either by the Royal agent (as in the code of 1806) or by long established custom, recognised by the Courts. In cases where there was doubt about which was to apply, the law to customs that had been followed in Sri Lanka had to be adopted. The code of 1806 consisted of two titles, the first "Relating to matters of succession, Rights of Inheritance", the second consisted of "Matrimonial Affairs and the formation and Dissolution of Marriages." Despite the centrality of marriage custom in this code, its obsolete character and its unsuitability to the needs of the local Muslims was sharply exposed in 1871, when a judgement by Mr. Gillman, District Judge of Galle decreed that a lawful divorce could be obtained by a Muslim outside its ambit. This clearly caused embarrassment. It led to the introduction of a Motion in the Legislative Council by Mutu Coomaraswamy, inviting learned Muslims and leading priests from the Island, to offer their views on replacing the Code with a comprehensive enactment which would re-establish Muslim law relating to Marriage, Divorce and Inheritance and to the conduct of Mosques and Charitable Trusts *(Wakf)*.

The Government was somewhat reluctant to disturb the status quo, partly to avoid exposing itself to the criticism of interfering in religious laws and customs. It was not until 1875 that the draft of a proposed Muslim Law Ordinance was prepared (chiefly at the instance of Sir Charles Leyand, Government Agent of the Western Province) and published for general information. It contained an amended version of the 1806 code provision for the formal registration of Marriages and Divorces Law. The subject surfaced again in 1889 when Legislative Council felt that necessity of including amendments to the Marriage Registration Ordinance No. 8 of 1886 and No. 2 of 1888, whereby Muslim Marriages had also to be registered. Until then, registration was kept by the Priest of the local mosque in what then were called *Kaduttam.* (Kaduttam is a deed of settlement of dower among Muslims).

Yet it was not until 1926 that action resulted. In that year, the Muslim Member, N.H.M. Abdul Cader, persuaded the Legislative Council to appoint a Select Committee of the House to study and report on the Muslim Law of Inheritance, Marriage and Divorce. The Committee was composed of Justice M.T. Akbar (Acting Attorney-General) (Chairman), N.H.M. Abdul Cader (Member of Legislative Council), K. Balasingham (Lawyer), W. Duraisamy (Member of Legislative Council), T.B. Jayah (Member of Legislative Council), C. W.W. Kannangara, (Member of Legislative Council), H.M. Macan Markar, (Member of Legislative Council) A.F. Molamure (Member of Legislative Council) and E.R. Tambimuttu (member of Legislative Council). The Committee obtained various views from the Muslim public and submitted its report to the Council in 1928. Its key observations were that "The defects in the Muslim law of divorces in Ceylon have been due to the disappearance under the British administration of the office of Kathi...Such as official is required to interfere is disputes between husband and wife at the request of either of them and influence them towards an amicable settlement...(A) Kathi should be appointed for each Muslim area for the purpose of making his influence felt and exercising a limited right of veto in cases of divorces effected by Muslim husbands..(T) he office of Kathi has been instituted in the Straits Settlements. The Kathi can also play of very important part in cases of divorces by Muslim wives.

Under the Shafi'i law, an aggrieved Muslim wife has to go before a Judge before she consents (to) a divorce... (T) he Kathi can in a great majority of cases interfere to effect a reconciliation between husband and wife... What happens under the existing practice is that as soon s the wife sues for non-maintenance, the husband divorces her and it ends in the misery and ruin of the children of the union...(T) he husband should be allowed to divorce his wife only after giving three notices to the Kathi at intervals... (T) he Kathi could in the meantime use his best endeavours with the help of the relatives on both sides, to effect a reconciliation between husband and wife and to prevent the divorce. This is in accord with the spirit of the Muslim Law."

"(T) he Kathi should be empowered to inquire into and to decree a monthly maintenance, not only for the maintenance of the deserted wife, but also of the children...(He should be empowered to recover it by sending a certificate to the local Police Magistrate, who should then recover such maintenance as if it were a fine...This would prevent the necessity of Muslim women attending the Police Court, and it would also prevent many divorces from taking place... For want of this functionary a grave abuse has crept into the Muslim law and a custom was gradually being evolved, as indicated in the Supreme Court judgment reported in the New Law Reports, whereby a Muslim wife could, in fact, divorce her husband at their pleasure through the medium of her own agent. This led to an intolerable situation in Ceylon. It was finally decided by the Supreme Court that such divorces were absolutely invalid, and the Supreme Court indicated that in future divorces should only be allowed if the wife brought a case for divorce in the District Court. But the institution of such petty cases in the District Court is unthinkable, because in the great majority of cases, wives deserted by their husbands cannot afford to pay the stamp fees and the Proctor's fees. Many of these cases also end in the reconciliation of husband and wife, the divorce proceedings being instituted by the wife generally for the purpose of bringing her husband to reason, and it is in such cases that the Kathi will be most useful... The Committee feels strongly that unless Kathis are appointed as recommended by them the whole Muslim law of marriages and divorce is bound to end in failure and to lead to the through demoralization of the private life of the Muslim people of Ceylon."

The registration of marriage and divorce should be made compulsory and that a penalty should attach to non-registration, a great deal of abuses which have crept into the Muslim law of marriages is due to the fact that registration was made optional in Ordinance No. 8 of 1886. But a Marriage or Divorce valid or invalid according to the Muslim law was not to be rendered valid or invalid merely by reason of non-registration or registration.

In 1938, the Association of (Qadi's) made a representation to the British Government in Sri Lanka, suggesting that a Committee be set up to study the Muslim Marriage and Divorce Act. In 1939, the Government duly set-up such a Committee, consisting of the Registrar-General, M.T. Akbar (Chairman, ex-officio) T.B. Jayah, A.R. A Razik Fareed. M.C. Abdul Cader, M.J.M. Haniffa and M.H. M. Shamsudeen.

This Committee's recommendations (contained in an unpublished report of 11 November 1941) and the observations of the Muslim Marriage and Divorce Advisory Board were embodied in the (currently operative) Muslim Marriage and Divorce Act, No. 13 of 1951, which came into operation on 1st August 1951. This Act replaced the former legislation. Section 98 basically reinstituted the Muslim law on Marriage and Divorce. It now also specifically declared that "in all matters relating to any Muslim Marriage and Divorce, the status and the mutual rights and obligations of the parties should be determined according to the Muslim law governing the Sect to which the parties belong." The Act was amended by Act Nos. 31 of 1954, 22 of 1955, 1 of 1965 and 32 of 1969. Muslim law then has had a chequered history, it was initially treated as different customary law, brought to the Island by Muslim settlers. Kings of Sri Lanka respected Muslim customs in this matter. The laws were based on the Qur'an and on *hadithes* and had no bearing on their own. Over time, interest in Muslim law waxed and waned on occasions. It seems to have fallen completely into destitute or to have been relegated to the status of social custom. Prof. Nadaraja argues that, during the Portuguese period, Muslim law was destroyed in the cities but remained alive in more remote areas. The Dutch, and the British both interested themselves in its survival and it remains a badge of identity in the special provisions made for Muslim custom in Sri Lanka's law today.

I. The Muslim Marriage Law in Sri Lanka

In Arabic, the word used for Marriage in *nikah*, which originally meant uniting. Marriage in legal terms involves a contract, regulating both the conjugal relations between husband and wife and their procreation of children. The Qur'an often states that men and woman are two mates being created from the same source. "O mankind! Be careful of your duty to your Lord, Who created you from a single soul and from it created its mate and from them twain hath spread abroad a multitude of men and women,"

In Sri Lanka, the Muslim were guided by their own law in regard to marriage. The registration of every marriage, for example, took place immediately following the conclusion of the *nikah* ceremony. In the Marriage and Divorce Act of 1951, the Shafi'i rules are followed in terms that require the presence and approval of a *wali* or the guardian for marriage a specifical arrangement, unless the Qadi (*kathiqadi*) has given a dispensation. The bride's own consent to the marriage is required. A father is entitled to give his daughter in marriage without the consent. Under the Shafi'i rules, two witnesses are essential in order to register the marriage. Muslim marriage also involves payment of *Mahr* (dower money) a requirement when fulfilled the marriage becomes valid. After the marriage is over, the bride is conducted to the husband's house, followed by the marriage feast called *walimah*.

Islam prohibits marriage with certain relations. For instance Muslims are forbidden to marry step-mothers, one's own mother, uterine sisters, step-sisters, father's and mother's sisters, brother's and sister's daughters, foster mothers, foster-sisters, mother's in law, step-daughters, who are under one's protection and (born) of one's wife, wives of one's sons, grand mothers and their sisters; not are they are allowed to have two sisters together at one time as wives and all the married women (except the captives of war). Muslim women are not permitted to marry during the period of *'Iddah*.

In Sri Lanka in 1951 an Act of Parliament was introduced to prohibit female child marriage among the Muslims. The Islamic codes do not prescribe a minimum age of marriage. They sat that a male or female who has attained puberty is eligible to marry. As this permission makes it possible for a Registrar to knowingly violate this prohibition, Section 20 of the Muslim Marriage Divorce Act provides that the marriage of a Muslim girl who is below twelve years of age shall not be registered unless the *Qadi* has authorized the registration. By contrast, Imam Shafi'i fixed the age of consent for both males and females at fifteen years of age. Sri Lanka, therefore, deviates significantly from the usual practice.

Islamic law prohibits polyandry but allows polygamy. The Qur'an states: "If you fear that ye will not deal fairly by orphans marry of the women who seem good to you, two, three or four, and if ye fear that ye cannot do justice (to so many) than one (only), or (the captives) that your right hand possess. Thus, it is more likely that ye will not do injustice." (Ch. IV, V 3). According to this verse of the Qur'an a Muslim was allowed to marry orphan women. One reason for this was that the Muslims were engaged in a holy war (*jihad*) at that time and many Muslims were killed and women and children were left without their supporters. Therefore, Islam permits marriage to orphans in order that they may be provided for. Another reason for this was that, when a rich Muslim married an orphan, her wealth was spared by him. In Sri Lanka, the Muslim Marriage and Divorce Act of 1951, Section 24, seeks to regulate polygamous marriage by Muslims. A married male Muslim who intends to contract another marriage is required to give notice of his intention to the *Qadi* at least thirty days beforehand. The Certificate can be issue only on receipt of such notice and without it the marriage cannot be registered. The *Qadi* has to notify the existing wife and the proposed subsequent wife as well as to exhibit the information at all the Jum'ah Mosques in his area. This gives the wife time to ask for a divorce. Again, this deviates significantly from the Qur'anic injunctions.

II. Muslim Divorce Law in Sri Lanka

In Arabic, divorce is described as *Talak* (*talaq*) which literally means freeing or undoing of a knot. The Qur'an holds divorce to be the most hateful act of all things permitted. Keep they wife to thyself, and for Allah. And thou didst hide in thy mind that which Allah was to bring to light" "For if you hate them it may happen that ye hate a thing wherein Allah hath placed much good."

In Sri Lanka, divorce law for Muslims has supposedly been based on the Qur'anic law. A Muslim husbands of sound mind is permitted to divorce his wife. But Section 27 of the Muslim Marriage and Divorce Act requires certain procedures to be followed. He should give notice of his intention to the local *Qadi*, who must then attempt to effect a reconciliation with the help of the relatives of the parties concerned and of the elders and other influential Muslims in the area. Thirty days after the initial notice, if there has, in the meantime been no reconciliation, the husband may appear before the *Qadi* and pronounce *talaq* in the presence of two witnesses. This is then recorded by the *Qadi* and the wife is notified, if she is not present upon the lapse of a further period of thirty days and if the husband is still not reconciled with the wife, he must appear once more before the *Qadi* and have the fact of non-reconciliation recorded. After yet another thirty days, if he still persists in his intention to divorce his wife, he must appear for the final time, to have his divorce registered by the *qadi*. This procedure, thus seeks to provide adequate time for reconciliation. The third rule of the Marriage and Divorce Act provides that the *qadi* shall not record the alleged reasons for which, or the alleged grounds upon which the husband seeks to pronounce *talaq*. He is required however, to recover from the husband any unpaid *mahr* (dower money) owed to the wife. Any other judicial pronouncement of *talaq* without recourse to the statutory procedure is an offence punishable by a fine.

Section 28 of this act provides for divorce at the instigation of the wife. The *Qadi* has comprehensive jurisdiction to hear and adjudicate upon a wife's application for divorce on any of the ground which are admissible according to the Muslim law of the sect to which the parties belong. Another schedule sets out the procedure that must be adopted in these cases.

A wife may, under Section 28 seek divorce from her husband without his consent on grounds of ill-treatment or on account of any act which undermines the Sect to which the parties belong. Under Shafi'i law, this would include guilt of desertion or failure to maintain the wife. She may also seek divorce on any of the grounds admissible under Muslim law governing the Sect to which the parties belong. For the Shafi'i, this include *Fasah* (*faskh*) divorce on such grounds as the husband's impotence, his insanity, his contraction of leprosy or other such dire disease and his inability to maintain the wife.

Divorce is looked upon as a legal necessity, a recognition that marital relations can and do break down irrespective of moral turpitude on the part of the husband or wife. The Qur'an takes charitable view of the necessity for divorce, and recommends that it be resorted to in a spirit of mutual kindness, just as marriage should be.

III. The Muslim Law of Intestate Sussession

The Qur'an states "to the male equivalent of the portion of two females." Accordingly, a female should get only half of the inheritance of a male when a father dies in a family, his son is expected to take over the responsibility for all. The son is held, therefore, to require a bigger inheritance than a daughter in managing the day to day affairs of the family. In Sri Lanka, Muslims adopted the law but altered it to allow anyone the right to give all his property according to his own wishes, even to persons other than his immediate heirs.

The provisions of the 1806 code were based on Shafi'i law, but were nonetheless uniformly applicable to all Muslims irrespective of the sect or school of law, to which they belonged.

IV. Wakf

Wakf means detention. In Islamic law, it is applied to lands which are able and used for charitable purposes. Traditionally, mosques in Sri Lanka were maintained by individuals or sometimes groups of people either the 'descendants of the original donor or those selected by the '*Oor-kootam*'. After independence, Muslim had come around to the view that some regulation about Trustees and Mosque property was needed, so as to prevent the misuse of mosque funds. Opposition to such legislation gradually eroded as more and more educated youth came out from schools and entered adult life. The growth of welfare associations among Muslims, as well as the gathering momentum of Muslim reform movements, sapped the roots of the traditional elite, who, in the main had controlled mosques. The democratization of authority for mosques gained an irresistible momentum, culminating in the passage of the Muslim Mosque and Charitable Trustees of Wakf, Act No. 51 of 1956. This Act provides for the registration of mosques, Muslim shrines and places of religious resorts. It also prescribes the powers, duties and functions of their trustees and the trustees of Muslim Charitable Trusts or Wakfs and established a Muslim Charitable Fund.

The Act of 1956 resolves the vexed question of the status of the Beard and its Chairman and their mutual relationship by providing for the creation of an executive rather than merely an advisor body. Seven Muslim members were to be appointed by the Minister and presided over by a Commissioner for Mosque and Muslim Charitable. Trusts or Wakfs. The Commissioner and his Deputy were both to be public servants and Muslims were eligible for appointment. In 1982, an amendment to the Act, re-designated the Office of Commissioner as Director, and he was no longer to preside over the Board. This function being now assigned to one of the seven members appointed by the Minister (now, specifically of Muslim Affairs) as Chairman of the Board. The Board could, however, still delegates its powers, duties or functions to the Director. In 1982, also a Wakf tribunal was instituted composed of three Muslims appointed by the Judicial Service Commission. In it were vested exclusively and without appeal, nearly all the powers which the District Court had earlier enjoyed to hear and determine applications to enforce the provisions of a Muslim Charitable Trust of Wakf. This allowed the Muslims of Sri Lanka to control financial matters for their mosques and, where corruption arose, to eliminate it.

One of the recommendations of Akbar's report of 1928 was the appointment of Qadi (Qadi Boards). The recommendation became law only in 1954. The Qadi Boards' main function was conducting inquiries and hearing applications for divorce at the wife's instance. The Act also provides appeals to Supreme Court against the Qadi Boards' decisions. The Qadi Boards' power under this Ordinance were limited to hearing appeals, examining records of proceedings, including on pending cases, and making orders. It had the duty to advise the Registrar-General and the Qadi's on questions of Muslim law referred to them. In such cases, the Qadi's are bound by the opinion of the Board.

The Qadis' Board were empowered also to validate marriages and to grant divorces after proper application and inquiry, where the parties had been married according to Muslim law. If the husband institutes an application for divorce, it was called Talak; (*talaq*), if it was instituted by the wife, it was called Fash (*faskh*) divorce. Both of these could be obtained before a Qadi Board.

Under Section 47, the Qadi Board was empowered, inter-alia, to inquire into and adjudicate upon:

1. A wife's claim for the recovery of the *Mahr* (dower-money).
2. The claim by a wife, or on behalf of a wife for maintenance.
3. The claim on behalf of a child for maintenance (legitimate child or illegitimate child).
4. The claim of a divorced wife, asking for a maintenance until the registration of the divorce, or during the period of *'Idda* (*'iddat*) where the woman was pregnant at the time of the registration of the divorce, until she is delivered of the child.
5. The claim for the increase or the reduction of the amount of the maintenance of the child.
6. The claim for *Kaikkuli*.
7. The claim of a wife or a divorced wife for expenses.
8. The claim for mediation by the *Qadi* between wife and husband.
9. The claim for the declaration of annulment of the marriage, either by the husband or the wife.
10. The claim for granting permission for registering marriage of a girl who has not passed the age of twelve.
11. The right to investigate a complaint by a women or on her behalf against her legal guardian (*wali*) if he reasonably

withholds his consent to her marriage, and the Qadi Board can authorise the marriage after inquiry.

The Act specifically excluded the appearance of Advocates and Proctors before the Qadi.

The five Members of the Board, as well as the Qadi were to be selected from men of character, position and suitable attainments in the Muslim community.

Under the Act, a Muslim divorce could not be granted by another Civil Court. Sinhalese and the Tamils were granted divorce by the Civil Court of Sri Lanka.

The Muslim law was applicable in Sri Lanka to those who were Muslims by birth or conversion. Those converts were to considered genuine Muslims who were felt to have become Muslims merely, for example, in order to marry a second wife, without divorcing an existing wife. The question of whether the conversion was genuine or not had to be decide by the law courts on the evidence before them. In a recent case, Reid Vs Attorney-General a husband had contracted a marriage according to Muslim rites while his earlier marriage with a first wife was still existing. He was charged with the offence of bigamy. He pleaded that he was a convert to Islam and that his second marriage was a valid one. The accused and his second wife became converts to Islam in 13th June 1959 and they registered their marriage on 16th July 1959. Basnayake, A. the Chief Justice said that although the proximity of the date of the second marriage to the date of conversion gave room for the suspicion that the change of faith was with a view to overcoming Section 18 of the Marriage (General). Registration Ordinance of 1901, such circumstances did not affect that validity of the second marriage.

Section 18 of the Marriage (General) Registration enacted that "No marriage shall be valid where either of the parties thereto shall have contracted a prior marriage which shall not have been legally dissolved or declared void." Chief Justice Basnayake referred to the evidence of the Muslim Priest who had testified to the conversion. The inference that may be drawn is that if there was such a conversion, the convert would not go into the circumstances that led to such a conversion.

In Attorney-General Vs. Reid, the above decision was affirmed by the Privy Council. In the Privy Council, the inherent right of a person to change his religion was asserted.

Section 64 of the Marriage (General) Registration Ordinance has limited its operation to any marriage other than marriages contracted either according to the Kandyan Marriage and Divorce Legislation or marriages contracted between those professing Islam. Since, in the Reid case, the second marriage was held to have been a marriage contracted between persons professing Islam, it did not fall within the definition of marriage in Section 64 and was, therefore, not invalid by virtue of Section 18.

Adoption

Islam does not recognise adoption, which is foreign to Muslim jurists. Yet a Sri Lankan Muslim can legally adopt a child, and the law of the land will be applied in such cases, just as it would be to adoptions by non-Muslim citizens. The concept of adoption originated from Kandyan and Tamil customary laws. The main aim of this law was to permit the adoption of a child by a childless man or woman. Under the Kandyan law, anybody could give his child in adoption, provided the child was of the same caste as that of the adopting parent; otherwise, the adopted child could not inherit the hereditary property of the adopting parents. Tamil laws permitted the adoption of a child of a different caste.

The application of Muslim law has been to some extent haphazard. For example, if a Muslim in Sri Lanka dies intestate, the Muslim law of Intestate succession will apply; a Muslim may, however, make a will, leaving the entirety of his property to persons not contemplated by Muslim law; such a will, will the valid and effective. To this extent, a Muslim can deviate from the Islamic rule that he cannot will more than one-third of his property against the rules of Muslim succession. Furthermore, the Islamic doctrine of *Hasnat* does not apply to Muslims in the country. Under *Hasnat*, a Muslim female is always in the custody of a close male relative father, husband, son or any other. This principle will not be enforced in Sri Lankan Courts, because it is not recognized in the Constitution or any other body of law in the country. It appears to be illogical that Islamic law, which give males twice the inheritance of females, applies in Sri-Lanka, whereas the raison d'etre for such a rule, namely, the doctrine of *Hasanat*, whereby any female has to be supported by her nearest male relative, is not recognised. If *Hasnat* does not prevail, then it is difficult to see why the Muslim law of Intestate succession, which favours the male, should prevail in Sri Lanka. In Sri Lanka, unlike in Saudi Arabia, the penal law of Islam has not been practicable and only a part of the customary law of Islam applies to the Muslims of Sri Lanka.

12

The Supremacy of Shari'at Law in Islamic Society

S.M. YUSUF

Islam means 'surrender' i.e., technically speaking, surrender to the Will of Allah. The entire creation practises Islam in the sense of submission to the inexorable laws of nature, stemming as they do from the design and the Will of the Creator. Man, as part of the physical world, is also subject to the universal laws of nature albeit involuntarily.

But man is not just a part of the physical world; he has the distinction of being the best and the noblest of all the creation; the design of man is the most perfect and complex of all the designs in point of fine balance of intellectual and moral faculties, which distinguish him from, and give him mastery over, the rest of the creation. Being endowed with intellect, intuition and conscience, man is marked out to bear the 'trust of Allah', namely, to exercise his freedom of choice and make a volitional and meaningful surrender to the Will of Allah in regard to his moral conduct both individually and socially. This supreme act of volition, springing from upright thought and uninhibited intuition, is the real Islam, which distinguishes a Muslim from a non-Muslim.

The Will of Allah is embodied in the *Shari'ah*, which is the universal, eternal and all-comprehensive legal and moral code of conduct revealed through a human being (a man like other men with nothing of the Divine in him) chosen (*mustafa*) as messenger of Allah (*rasul Allah*) for the guidance of mankind. The messenger is not a soothsayer (*Kahin*) entertaining a nervous, spell-bound audience with irrational prophesies and ambiguous oracles; his function is to awaken the mind and the conscience of man and to guide him in plain language to the path of righteousness cheering him up (*bashir*) with confidence in his moral salvation and warning (*nadhir*) him against error.

The messenger is the teacher *par excellence* of the *Kitab* and the *Hikmah* to a mentally alert and morally sound people (*muttaqin*) yearning to live up to their nature (*fitrah* = the design and the will of Allah) in this present mundane world. He recites the *Kitab* (= the Book of Allah), making the believers learn its word, preserve its text,. understand its meaning and practise it in their actual everyday life. In the process of overseeing, directing and facilitating the practice (*hikmah*), the messenger-teacher complements the Book of Allah with his own words and normative example termed the *Sunnah*. Thus the Book of Allah, in conjunction with the Sunnah of the Rasul, is the repository of the Will of Allah and the primary source of Islamic Law. Loosely, they are spoken of separately (Kitab *and* Sunnah) as the two main sources of law in Islam.

The deliberate and volitional adoption of the *Shari'at* as the code of life presupposes an appreciation of, and firm commitment to, the universal morals in which the framework of the law is embedded. True moral consciousness invoked obedience to the Sacred Law while the enforcement of the Law keeps the moral consciousness alive. This organic relationship between Law and Morality in characteristic of the Divine order of society. Law without morality is like a body without soul and morality without law is like a departing soul bereft of lively influence upon an identifiable body.

Morals subsists only in the strict observance of the law and not apart from it. No wonder that in the primary sources of Islam law is wrapped up in moral admonitions like the bones in the flesh

Law and morality set 'limits' (*hudud Allah*) to human conduct, which ensure harmony among mankind similar to the harmony prevailing in the cosmos. Within these limits Islam urges man to develop the best in his nature so as to participate fully in an affirmative and active manner in the life of this world. Hence freedom within the 'limits' is an important as the prohibition against transgression of them. The *'halal'* (lawful) is as sacred as the *'haram'* (unlawful). It is equally reprehensible to tamper with the one as with the other. This fits in very well with the outlawing of monkery in Islam. If man were to renounce and withdraw from the world he would need no law and only a small set of 'don'ts'—just negative morals. Abhorrence of matter as such breeds timidity and inhibits man in making good use of the natural world.

The material things of life are the bounties of Allah—the source of sustenance, comfort and power for man. The acid test lies only in developing the material resources to the full in a spirit of humility and thankfulness and using them in accordance with the Will of Allah to further the ideals of Islam. It will be seen that the Islamic religion is but the observance of the *shari'at* in normal everyday life. Law is the essence of religion and not something apart from it.

Beliefs and ritual just conduce to and symbolize the submission to Divine Law.

When a body of Muslims (= those who have committed themselves to the *Shari'ah*) start practising the Islamic Law and enforcing the 'limits of Allah' by their collective will it marks the emergence of the Islamic Society. It is to be noted that prior agreement on law is the *sine qua non* of the Islamic Society. This is because the Islamic law is the dispensation of Allah and not the product of a society formed on an accidental basis. In the words of Spengler, 'it matters very considerably indeed in a man's feeling whether he regards law as an expression of some fellow man's will or as an element of divine dispensation.'

Further, the Islamic law is all-comprehensive, pervading in an effective, normative way all the fields of human activity—social, political, economic as well as artistic. Still the Islamic Society is far from being a monolith, enough latitude being allowed for variety in forms of external civilization. It is the same with Islamic law as with the fundamental laws of nature, which are effective in all scientific development in unlimited variety and complexity of forms of inventions.

As the Muslims collectively launch upon normal socio-economic activity uninhibited and unhindered but only guided by the salubrious limits of the Divine Law, a virile culture and a rich civilization are born immediately. The scientific spirit is purified and strengthened after is release from the stifling and degrading bondage to idolatry. The unlimited progress and expansion of trade, commerce and industry are assured by the belief in matter being the *mata*', the object of lawful exploitation for man without any odium attaching to it in itself.

On top of it all, the socio-economic activity of the Muslims soon assumes universal dimensions as Islam and the political hegemony of the Muslims spreads over new lands and new peoples. The free intermingling and frequent intermarriage of different peoples, rid of all racial and colour prejudice and hailing from various geographical climes with extremes of temperature, results in new social customs, new economic and commercial practices and new habits of daily conduct being thrown into the crucible of Islamic society.

Fundamentally, the regulative and normative process of Islamic law extends to the whole gamut of man's life. Yet the text of the revealed law, in its very nature, covers only a limited number of cases explicitly.

During the period from Adam down to Muhammad, Allah was gracious enough to sent prophets at appropriate intervals to modify and adjust the divine laws to the changed circumstances of time in the wake of the development of man's faculties.

According to the Islamic view of the historical development of religion through progression in revelation, the successive prophets, to name three of them in particular; Moses, Jesus and Muhammad, promulgated new up-to date laws (*Shari'at*) while reviving and reinforcing one and the same creed (*'aqidah*) concerning God, prophethood, moral responsibility of man, belief in life after death and retribution. In the circumstances there was not much need for man to exercise his own judgment over points of law, which, so to say, was supplied ready-made to him by the Law-giver Himself.

Even during the life time of Muhammad the Companions would

rush to the Prophet with the problems rather than pondering themselves over them. It was natural when the message had not been completed and revelation was going on. But Muhammad knew it better than his Companions that soon his followers would have to exercise their judgment when revelation was stopped with his death. So he was careful enough to train his companions in the exercise and give the guidelines of *'ijtihad* for future generations.

A few months before the death of Muhammad it was announced that the *'din'* had been completed and that revelation had been closed for ever. Muhammad was the Last Prophet and there would be no prophet after him.

In the words of Iqbal, it was the graduate day for man's intellect when the prophethood cancelled itself by itself and entrusted the growth of the Divine Law to the dedicated, creative understanding of man. The Divine Law, so far as it is revealed, is not subject to *change*, mutation, addition or subtraction. Allah is the only law-giver and He has given the Law for ever. Yet the onward march of life with the progress of civilization gives rise to new situations calling for new rulings not explicit in the texts of the Kitab-Sunnah. How then to fulfill the demands of the *shari'ah* in the ever-growing, rich and complex life of the Muslims of all times and climes? The key lies in the dynamism and the inner growth of the revealed provisions of the law without any limitation of time or magnitude.

The broad object of the Divine Law is to secure the common weal of mankind. Each and every provision of it benefits the society in many ways. Apart from the multifarious considerations of good (*masalih* sing. *maslaha*) in this world, there is always a prime efficient cause (*'illah*) governing the promulgation and operation of each law. Fortunately this *'illah* is almost invariably indicated in the source (Kitab-Sunnah) itself. Once the *'illah* is discovered and established objectively on the authority of the Law-giver Himself, the task of the jurist is made easy in extending the application of the law to all cases subject to the same *'illah*.

This illustrates the inner growth, expansion and development of the law to cover cases not explicitly mentioned in the revealed texts.

Evidently it is achieved through human intellect working on Kitab-Sunnah for deduction by analogy (*Qiyas*) and judgment inspired by a dedicated, thorough and deep study of the revealed fundamental law. This effort of the intellect is termed *'ijtihad'* (= the exertion to the fullest).

The in-built system of *'ijtihad* in a revealed law is a distinctive feature of Islam. It has been aptly termed a philosophical activity springing in Islam from within and characteristically its own as distinct from the philosophical thought taken over by the Muslims at a later period from the Greeks. Abu 'l-Hasan al-'Amiri, a savant of the fourth century H., has shown through a comparative study of the legal systems of the various religions that 'deduction' of new ruling in unspecified cases is peculiar to Islam. The dominant tendency in other religions is just to follow the revealed law only. The task of the jurist in Islam is not to devise laws for the new situations of life by his intellect outside the sphere of the religious law. Rather he would deduce laws by his intellect from the revealed texts so that nothing remains outside the purview of the religious law. As said earlier, the jurist has to beware of his subjective proclivities, which are independent of, and extraneous to the *Shari'ah*, in discovering the *'illah* of a law. The entire activity of *'ijtihad*, highly intellectual though it is, is permeated with the spirit of discovering the Will of Allah where it is not explicit indicated. Exercise of intellect in the legal sphere independently of Kitab-Sunnah is the antithesis of 'Islam (= surrender to the Will of Allah).

It is apt at this point to compare Islamic jurisprudence with classical jurisprudence which, in the words of Spengler, 'was always the product of immediate public experience—and, moreover, not the professional experience of the jurists, but the practical everyday experience of men who counted in political and economic life generally.' Hence, Spengler further points out, man-made laws are characterised by 'a political-economic tendency dependent, not upon what this man or that thinks, but upon what is practically intended by the class which in fact commands the power and, with it, the legislation. Every law is established by a class in the name of the generality'... 'The legislative acts', he concludes, 'are one and all political acts, and party political acts at that.'

In sharp contrast with it, deductions from a divine source in Islam are dependent, not upon the political-economic tendency of the jurist, but upon the Will of Allah, to which all Muslims have surrendered. No wonder that the Islamic law commands the willing obedience of each and every Muslim, there being no room for a minority in opposition trying 'to win sole authority for laws derived from its (own rival) outlook upon life'.

There is no organized church and no ordained priesthood in Islam. The function of *'ijtihad*, so vital for a society based on law, is essentially an intellectual and academic activity which is the privilege of the learned and the competent. The standards of learning and competence are very high indeed including a strict test of *taqwa* i.e., uprightness of belief and conduct dedicated to the aims of the *shari'ah*. Of course, the scripture of Islam is an open book and no individual or class of clergy or synod of 'holy' men holds the monopoly of reading or interpreting, far less revising or changing a comma in the text. At the same time no unlearned or incompetent man would venture an opinion on any legal point requiring proper investigation and expert judgment. Hence a referendum of the incompetent masses is just out of question. *'Ijtihad* is concerned with the Divine Will and not with the wishes of the people.

As individual jurists exercise their legal acumen upon Kitab-Sunnah, in course of time a consensus (*'ijma'*) is arrived at, which is given the force of law. It is, however, worth while to remember, particularly in view of the modernist tendencies in Muslim states, that *'ijtihad* and *'ijma'* are diffused among the whole community in such a way as to defy all attempts at regularization and organization into rigid mechanical institutions which, as practical experience will amply bear out, are dangerously exposed to rigging and regimentation. It is the inalienable non-transferable privilege of every Muslim possession the necessary qualities for the task to exercise his mind and form his individual judgment in regard to the new situations arising out of the forward march of life. When the individual *mujtahids* have put forward their opinions, there sets forth a process of conflict and survival of the fittest comparable to the natural selection in the physical world. Both follow certain well-known principles and laws, which are nevertheless immeasurable in mathematical terms. The process is slow, sometimes very very slow, it may take a generation or even more and nobody can set the pace for it.

The reason is that there is no silencing of the opposition or browbeating of the minority by the majority. The opposition is not killed; it is tolerated until is dies its own natural death. There is no snapping and no guillotine. Of course, it required a great deal of patience but the result—a consensus of the free will of the entire community—is worth much more than that. Once *'ijma'* is achieved there remains no dissident minority waiting for its turn to impose its own point of view. Spengler appreciates that the theory of the *consensus of the spiritually elect* was worked out to its logical conclusions in Islam. 'We seek to find the truth, each for himself, by personal pondering, but the Arabian savant feels for and ascertains the general conviction of his associates, which cannot err because the mind of God and the mind of the community are the same. If consensus is found, truth is established.'

Hence a high degree of recognition and permanence is accorded to the decisions taken collectively in the above manner. In addition to Kitab-Sunnah and *Qiyas*, this *'ijma'* is regarded as another source of Islamic law.

To sum up, it will be noted that the revealed fundamental law of Islam is final, permanent and unchangeable. Yet it is neither static nor in-adequate so as to turn to any exotic source for borrowing, supplementation, addition or sundry patch work. It has the inexhaustible vitality to grow and grow from within like tree but the taller it grows the deeper go its roots in the Kitab-Sunnah. It does not grow in a glass-house; it is exposed to non-Islam outside. But it subjects non-Islam to its own norms and values and reorientates it towards itself. In the residue, whatever is anti-islamic it rejects and throws out like a foreign body.

In modern times (the last 150 years) the failure to appreciate some of the points made above has resulted in some confusion about Islamic law:

(a) Kitab Sunnah is one entity, an integral whole. Tearing the one from the other is like cutting a body into two, rendering both parts dead and ineffective. The separate treatment of the Kitab *and* the Sunnah in the classical formulation has been misunderstood, in many cases deliberately misconstrued, to run down the normative character of the Sunnah.

(b) As a matter of fact, the setting aside of the Sunnah is only a ruse to introduce *changes* in the Islamic law, which, as we have seen, is quite incompatible with the essence of a revealed law. The modernists are also conscious of it in their heart of hearts; hence their effort to narrow down and limit the area of no-change to the text of the Quran.

(c) The modernists are not sincere in their surrender to the *Shari'at*; they would not nurture and stimulate the growth of the Islamic law from within and according to its own nature. Rather they would chop off its branches and graft upon it exotic notions borrowed from alien, mostly hostile, sources.

(d) The modernists intrude themselves upon Islamic law and jurisprudence under cover of *'ijtihad*. But they would seldom come up to the standards of learning, competence and *taqwa* prescribed so reasonably for a dedicated, expert, academic exercise like that. The western educated elite, who are entrenched in positions of political and administrative power in the newly-independent Muslim states, would ride rough-shod over the question of expertise in Islamics.

The situation has become acute since the coming into vogue of institutions of western democracy such as parliaments and legislative assemblies. With all the arrogance of political and administrative influence at their back, it has not been possible for these assemblies to arrogate to themselves the functions of legislation in Islam. In order to legitimize their acts in this field, they had to contrive Islamic Advisory

Councils but not without ensuring that they served as hand maidens to the secular parent bodies.

These councils were as good as loaded dice, being presided over and dominated by experts in modern law such as the High Court judges and legal practitioners. Obviously if the modern law were replaced by *Shari'at* law the High Court judges and legal practitioners would be out of a job and out of place in the new Islamic Society. Hence, the experiment of Islamic Advisory Councils proved a dismal failure, notably in Iran and Pakistan. Military dictators followed the dictum: 'Whatever I think must be good and whatever is good must be Islamic'. They enlisted some dubious support for their innovations of Western provenance through coercion and bribe and in the end fell a victim to the scorn and the pent-up rage of the Muslim masses.

(e) As a diversion from the law, which is the essence of Islam and the essential basis of Islamic society, the modernists boosted Islamic ideology and Islamic moral values (as if they were separable from the law). The characteristics of an Islamic society may be classified under three headings: (a) *'Aqa'id* and world-view, the so-called ideology, (b) Islamic law and morality (*Shari'ah* and *'akhlaq*), and (c) Muslim culture and civilization.

The first commitment of a Muslim is to Islamic law and *practical morality* (which again is distinct from ethereal moral values). Among the three categories this is essential to Islamic society. The few simple beliefs (*'Aqa'id*) of Islam are only a pre-condition and the pronouncement of the *kalimah* is just a formal pledge of the same effect. The relationship between ideology—(a new-fangled term which has no parallel in the dictionary of Islam and which is but derogatory when applied in the context of Islam)—and law in the same as between the Soul and the Body. The Soul cannot exist—cannot be identified in existence—except in a body with a definite shape and attributes. Similarly Islamic ideology can only exist—can only be identified—in Islamic law and morality. The moment the spirit of Islam is separated from the concrete laws and definite practical rules of conduct, the body of Islam is dead as well as the identifiable individuality of the spirit is lost. Islamic ideology or Islamic moral values are unthinkable except in the context of Islamic law. It is the prescribed punishment for theft which is the true measure of the abhorrence of the crime.

As for culture and civilization it is born only when law and morality are practised through the whole gamut of life—not without it. Of course, there is enough room for variety in the external forms of civilization—dress, for example—but variety is a manifestation of health, vigour and beauty only when it is sustained by the underlying unity of law and morality. Islamic law runs through the multiform civilization of the Muslim peoples like the natural law running through the movement of the bullock-cart on the ground and the ascent of the rocket to the moon. An Islamic Society or Islamic Culture and Civilization without Islamic Law (in its entirety) is a mere illusion.

13

Secularization of Islamic Law and Institutions in Turkey: A Socio-Historic Analysis

DOGU ERGIL

[Abstract: The *de facto* secularization of the Ottoman State occurred when the nationalities (*millets*) of the Empire ceased to be mere religious communities, and acquired their national independence. Moreover, the idea of the 'Islamic Ummet' (international community of all Muslims) collapsed with the outburst of Arab mutinies. These historic developments gave birth to Turkish nationalism as the popular ideology of the Young Turk movement.]

INTRODUCTION

The Ottoman Period

The imperial Ottoman civilization was a mixture of institutions borrowed from the Turkish, Arab, and Persian cultures, as well as from Islamic, Eastern, later Western civilizations. These institutions, although they co-existed for centuries, were not truly integrated. History provides ample evidence that in spite of the initial advantages it derives from intermingling with other ethnic groups, the politically dominant ethnic element of an Empire gradually becomes cosmopolitan, and remains above the masses if it loses its economic prominence. The story of the 'Turk' in the Ottoman Empire is a good example of a lost and retreived national identity.

The values and institutions that were later purged as contrary to modern civilization such as polygamy, the seculsion of women and their low status, fatalism, and ascetism came to be accepted by the Islamized Turks, chiefly through the infiltration of the Middle-Eastern cultures into *fikih* books, into the *mederse* tradition, into the Palace etiquette and the *divan* art that it created. These alien novelties, although they never deposed the Turkish ethos, nevertheless functioned effectively to de-Turkify the ruling Ottoman classes. That is why Turkish nationalism initially started as a cultural movement against cosmopolitan 'Ottomanism' and Western influence.

A brief look at the pre-Ottoman Middle Eastern history will reveal that, in the times of the Greater Seljuk Empire and the Mamluks of Egypt, the leadership of the polity and the Islamic *ummet* were distinctly separated from each other. The Caliph only performed religious functions for the Islamic *ummet.* Political authority was solely kept in the hands of the Sultans of both States. When Selim I from the House of Osman unified these offices in his person (1517), he was surely unaware of the dramatic historical difficulties he was about to initiate.

According to recorded history, however, Selim I and his Seyh-ul Islam were determined to differentiate between matters of piety from those of the judiciary. For they were quite aware that, if the office of *ifta* (interpretation) was given legislative function, a multiple judiciary would be created. But their fear became a reality some generations later, and there followed a struggle between the forces that wanted to hold both functions in their hand and obstruct change, and the forces that fought to separate them in order to establish a new social system.

As Gokalp has eloquently put it, the State is a political machinery; it tends to legalize and formalize any social force and institution upon which it touches. When Islam fused with various political organizations, it quickly grew to interpret and control every social force and institution, most importantly every innovation. So, in Islam there were no distinct concepts of Church and State as specifically 'religious' and/or 'political' institutions. The State was accepted as the embodiment of religion, and religion as the essence of the State.

When the Caliphate and the Sultanate were united in one person, the Ottoman State could not create an independent church organization.

First of all, there was no need for such an organization as long as the ruler was strong and remained as the ultimate juridical authority. These were the times when the rulers derived their power from the 'man of the sword'. But as the State got bigger and bigger, its administration required a large body of 'man of the school'. This group of bureaucrats grew continuously in number and power, and became a dominant element among the ruling Ottoman classes. When the *Sipahi* order collapsed and the *Sipahi* corps (feudal cavalry) were dismissed, the Sultan lost an important source of his power. But the decisive blow came to the yet unchallenged authority of the Ottoman ruler when the *Janissaries* slipped from the control of the *Padisah* as his personal professional army due to the economic difficulties of the Empire. Under the pressures of a declining economy, increasingly subdued by Western economic penetration, the *Janissaries* became a property owning *petty bourgeoisie* (traders-artisans-craftsmen). It is from this point on that, they became an armed supporter of the *medrese (ulema)*, and an additional social obstacle to change.

These developments (late 17th century) coincide with the expansion of the *Seyh-ul Islam's* power to include juridical powers parallel to the *Padisah's* rights, and even the authority to depose the ruler if his legislation was not concordant with the *Seriat.* Until then, the area left to the ruler was free from the limitations of the *Seriat.* There was no conception of legislation as distinct from the administrative and judicial branches of the government. Legislative, executive, and judicial powers belonged to the ruler. As long as he was powerful, no social force challenged his unique authority.

The *Ulema* (corps of the *Seriat* scholars), maintained the continuity of law and tradition and fought the anti-traditional tendencies which manifested themselves especially with the Western impact, after the 17th century.

With the erosion of the *Padisah's* absolute power, the highest *mufti Seyhul Islam,* became the highest ranking religious authority. His official statements grew to cover not only matters of religious policy, but also such major concerns of the State as declarations of war, taxations, and innovations like the adoption of the printing press.

In this manner, power of *fetva* gained an official political sanction. Thus, the religious outlook covered all aspects of social life, and the final word on what was good or bad on all matters passed to the *ulema.* Once the *ulema* acquired this power, they aligned themselves with the traditional Ottoman social classes which felt as insecure as they did under the impact of Western influences and social demands from the incipient worldliness and successfully combated innovations that threatened their power.

Whenever a *padisah* attempted to introduce an innovation or a social change 'from above', not supported by the *ulema*, he dramatically failed without the backing of an alternative power group. It is only after the annihilation of the *janissaries* and formation of a new and loyal army to the monarchy that Turkish modernization started. But the opening of the age of 'innovations' cost of the Ottoman intelligentsia numberous Grand Vezir heads, and the lives of two Sultans (Osman II, and Selim III). This age (18th century) also marks the emergence of absolute monarchs up to the Hemidian era, within which Turkish modernization and the seeds of secularization crystallized.

Beginning with Selim III in the 18th century, a series of reforming Sultans and statesmen attempted to make major changes in the Turkish society in an effort to cope with increasingly desperate internal and external conditions.

While changes were implemented (from above) especially in areas remote from the central strongholds of the religious law, the reforming party was so detached from the masses that it was unable to attain any ultimate legitimation in the eyes of the people. Periods of blind reaction followed periods of reformation although a fundamental change did not occur in the Ottoman social structure.

Due to the economic fetters of the 'Capitulations' imposed on the Ottoman society by Western imperialism, there was still no sign of a (middle) class or stratum with an independent economic base, to provide the driving force and creative ideology to 'pull' the rest of the society to transcend its present format. Even in the late 19th century ottoman State, there was no autonomous evolution of the religious institution apart from the political institutions. Turkish secularization in the 18th and 19th centuries took the form of a cultural dichotomy rather than a temporal (State) and spiritual (Church) duality independent of each other. Nineteenth-century Constitutionalism neither had a popular base (it was an elitist scheme) nor a national identity, because 'Ottomanism' was more international than national.

Parallel to (as well as a consequence of) the efforts of Mahmud II and various modernist statesmen to pass secular codified commercial and some penal laws (based on European models) and to create secular schools after the 18th century, the religious hierarchy gradually started loosing its intellectual and moral leadership under the impact of new values and socio-economic organizations.

The last of the reactionary periods in Ottoman history coincides with Abdul Hamid II's reign which was overthrown by the Young Turks in 1908. The Young Turks clearly understood that the dualism in thought and practice, particularly extant in law and education, should be transmuted into a major social and cultural transformation if economic, social, and political structures were to be altered.

It was the dominant Turkish faction of the Young Turk generation who concluded that, it was the Turkish people, not the Islamic community (*ummet*—the basis of Ottoman nationalism) that should be the fulcrum and driving force behind the national transformation. This resolution which was formulated by the emergent middle-class elements of the Ottoman society who rose to power with the Young Turk government at the beginning of the 20th century, and policies adopted thereafter, became the decisive motive of Turkish secularism and departure from the *ummet* pattern via nationalism.

Within the last two decades of the Ottoman Empire's existence in the present century, Sultan Mehmed (V) Resad's appeal to all the Muslims of the world to unite in *Cihad* (holy war) against the belligerent Westerners and non-Muslims in the First World War went unheeded. Indian Muslims fought on the British side, and the Muslim Arabs of the Empire revolted against their Caliph. These events cast further doubts on the much publicized function of the Caliphate to hold the

Empire together. Then the chronology of the events roughly followed the below pattern given:

When Turkey was invaded by alien powers (Allied armies) in 1918, Sultan Vahidettin found it convenient to collaborate with the occupiers to retain his throne under a Western mandate. His *Seyh-ul Islam* declared Mustafa Kemal and his nationalist followers who were fighting the alien forces as 'infidels'.

On 23 April 1920, the Nationalists convened the Grand National Assembly in Ankara as an organ of national sovereignty.

After the victory that ended the War of Liberation in 1922, the collaborator Sultan was deposed. Prince Abdul Mecid from the House of Osman was recognized as the Caliph on 18 November 1922, but was devoid of any political power.

The nameless popular regime that had been established three years ago gained its rightful title with the proclamation of Republic on 29 October 1923.

The Kemalist government of the young republic was quite alarmed soon after the declaration of the republic when Abdul Mecid's controversial behaviour coincided with massive popular sympathy for the office of the Caliphate. The Caliphate was abolished on 29 October 1924 following violent discussions in the Grand National Assembly.

The Republican Period

The young Turkish Republic was the culmination of a national *bourgeois* revolution (against a politically and economically bankrupt theocratic polity and the social forces that sustained it), as well as a national liberation movement (against the expanding Western imperial powers). The growing middle-class had at last eliminated the monarchy and the traditional *elite* to acquire its historical place in the modern Turkish society as the new social class. A perusal of the first and following term Grand National Assembly members will reveal their class affiliation with the emergent middle strata.

While this shift of power in the middle 'sectors' was occurring among the urban social classes, the rural social structure remained almost untouched. Under the impact of a relatively self-sustaining, subsistence level rural economy, and undisturbed patrimonial authority (social) relations between the dependent peasantry and the conservative landed upper-classes, the indigent agrarian masses contributed, and in return gained very little from Turkish political modernization.

From 1923 to 1950, a single party Cumhuriyet Halk Partisi (People's Republican Party), dominated by the military-civilian bureaucracy, ruled turkey. The first challenge to the Republican regime came with the Kurdish revolt in Eastern Anatolia which broke out in February 1925, and gave expression to strong conservative outbursts and demands to restore the *Seriat.* The leaders of this revolt were mainly tribal chiefs, property owners and *tarikat* (religious order) sheikhs who were severely threatened by the modernization and secularization efforts of the new regime.

The first opposition party, Progressive Republicans, that was formed in November 1924 was dissolved in June 1925 by the Government for alleged implications in the Revolt. This experience marks the first major clash between the old and the new *elite* which ended with the defeat of the former in its claim to redeem its threatened place in the new power structure. Although quickly suppressed, this massive revolt which was repeated on a smaller scale in the West (Menemen) in later years (1930) was the response of the reactionary forces of Anatolia to ongoing social change.

These forces were not eliminated by the limited power, and the *petty-bourgeois* ideology of the new leadership which preferred to pursue a 'reformist' (evolutionary) model of development. The unaltered rural structure of Turkey nested and nurtured the parasitical landlord (*aga*) and sheikhs in many of its corners that wielded the local power, and opposed any form of change for long years until the impact of commercialization, government reforms and rural mobility via capitalization of the agrarian sector started to change things. Nevertheless, their power is still evident in the Eastern and South-Eastern regions of

Turkey which have been left undeveloped and neglected for centuries, including the Republican era.

Kemal Ataturk encouraged the formation of a second opposition party: the Liberal Secular Republican Party was founded in 1930. Despite its name and a secular programme, the new Party began to attract many religious reactionaries and dissidents of the regime. It was voluntarily dissolved in the same year by its leadership.

In 1931, hard pressed by the Depression, but still unable to create a sound economic infrastructure and popular political basis, the Republican People's Party in power adopted six radical principles for his new statist politics: republicanism, nationalism, populism, statism, laicism and revolutionism. By striking out the principle of "The State religion of the Turkish Republic is Islam", these principles were incorporated into the Constitution in 1937, and remain in force today.

In 1926, the *Seriat* was replaced by the Turkish adaptation of the Swiss Civil Code. This was followed by the adaptation of French Commercial and Italian Penal Codes. This change meant that all Turkish citizens of whatever faith came under the protection of unified laws for the first time in Turkish history.

The formalization of Turkish secularism was firmly anchored by an amendment of the revised 1937 Constitution which stated that the Turkish Republic was a secular State. Other principles that were incorporated into various codes may be listed as follows :

(i) Article 9 of the Law of Associations prohibits the formation of associations on the basis of a sect or order (*tarikat*) of the Islamic Religion.

(ii) Political parties and associations were prohibited from seeking particularist religious support in their activities by the same Law.

(iii) Penal Code (1949 revision) prohibited any form of anti-secularist attack on the Republican regime, its legal system, and institutions thereof.

In the light of these principles and prohibitions, Turkish secularism was interpreted by the new regime as the disassociation of social, economic, political, and legal institutions of the State from religious principles. Hence the Republican secularism was a reaction against the idea of an Islamic polity.

The strategy of the new leadership, which is commonly referred to as *kemalism* brought an effective political style and leadership to the Turkish modernization. In a period of reconstruction without the support and partnership of a peasant or working class with enough power and political consciousness (and/or ideological vocabulary) to transform the Turkish society according to their own interests, the principles of 'solidarity' and 'nationalism' (expressed as anti-imperialism and anti-communism) constituted the ideological basis of Turkish modernization. But, Kemalism's lack of a politico-economic philosophy to be propagated as a universal ideology rendered it less effective as a (national) doctrine of social transformation and economic development especially after State initiative waned in the course of the 1940s. The ideological confusion among modern (present) Turkish intelligentsia to interpret the (past and future) Turkish transformation in great part has been an end result of this ideological poverty.

The Period of Multi-Party Politics

After three decades of peace (1923-1950) and an ambitious development policy initiated by the State (*etatisme*), social forces drastically changed in Turkey. A multi-party political system was introduced in 1945 as a reflection of these new social and economic forces in the Turkish society now seeking representation.

In the first years of the multi-party politics, some thirty parties were founded. Most of them demanded greater attention to religious expression and education in its programme. Many were outlawed for their extremism. But the most popular among them, the Democratic Party which emerged as the voice of the new entrepreneural and professional *bourgeioisie* championed for more freedom in religious matters. The Democratic Party had a wide array of supporters whose united power sustained the D.P. Government for ten consecutive years until it was overthrown by a military coup in 1960. The social forces behind this Party were mainly the vast dependent peasant populations, and traditional urban and semi-urban strata of artisans, craftsmen and petty traders who were alienated and somewhat threatened by the highly bureaucratic nature of the economic policy of the Republican administration with a bias for industrial development. But most importantly, it was the emergent economic *bourgeoisie* and the self-employed stratum of professionals who founded and led the Party to the end of its fateful career.

The hardships of inter-War years and the heavy handed control of the RPP Government in the name of 'austerity' for national development conveniently aided the Democrat's cause. Under the guise of equitable competition, free trade, and solidarity on the one hand and with its inflationist *laissez faire* economic policy on the other, the DP was actually trying to establish the optimum socio-economic *milieu* in which the economically privileged classes which it represented could easily thrive and wield the political power.

The first legislation enacted by the Democrats when they came to power was the Arabization of the *azan* (call to prayer) which was read in Turkish since the early 1930s. Within the DP's ranks there have been demands for the abolition of secularism and restoration of Islam as the official religion of the State, but the Party leadership has resisted these anachronistic demands and expelled some of its members who advocated them.

To its *bourgeois* constituents the DP, and its heir Justice Party (JP), after 1960 gave a liberal economy which was twice halted by military interventions (1960 and 1971) as a consequence of disorders arising from difficulties engendered chronic stagnation and economic dependence. To its peasant and other constituents from the traditional social strata—the bases of Islamic conservatism in Turkey—many concessions were given in the form of village *Kuran* courses, a number of *Imam*-preacher secondary schools—none of which was attended by the children of either of DP or the JP deputies—and a body of obscurantist literature.

Today, the traditional social forces behind Islamic conservatism in Turkey are thoroughly controlled, if not completely checked, by the rational secularist *bourgeoisie* who wield the political and economic power. The concessions given to the advocates of pristine Islam by various political parties have always remained at a level where it did not create a threat to their power, but retained its exploitative function.

In the final assessment, Turkish secularism has withstood, and is likely to withstand, its historical trial because—and in so far as—its power base is well anchored in the interests of new social classes. These emergent classes have attained their present leading position by eliminating a Theocratic Monarchy and its dominant Power *elite.* Hence it is inconceivable that they can be contained by the fetters of a theocratic polity where they will be fewer less privileges than they already have.

On the other hand, religious obscurantism and dogmatism perpetuated by the dominant social classes, are also being undermined by the dynamics of capitalist development which the country has been undergoing in the past half century. As the economic development breaks down the precapitalistic social and economic institutions and proletarianizes the small cultivator and *petty bourgeoisie* of rural Turkey—the two social bulwarks of Islamic conservatism—the ideology of *status quo* gives ground and paves the way for more contemporary collective ideologies.

In this process, Islam is gaining its rightful position as the sacred code of the spiritual domain as new social forces emerge and formulate their own class ideologies. Similarly, as both the declining traditional social classes and the newly emergent social strata (the white-collar strata, industrial labour force, and the urban sub-proletariat) wage their separate battles to change the existing social system, religion is becoming less effective as an ideological/institutional tool in the service of the Turkish ruling classes.

It is precisely this irreversible development that gives Turkish secularism its contemporary character.

First Manifestations of Change

The literature of the Tulip Era (1717-1730) reveals that the tastes of the period is saturated with secular interests in education, arts and sciences. The emergent materialism and incipient moral crisis can be attributed to declining economic conditions and the massive drive for military and administrative reforms. The interest in material life was by and large in contrast to the social and religious ethics of the past. The traditional morality was under the attack of new social forces.

The enlightened minds of the Tulip Era were aware of a new worldly polity rising in the West. They believed that if only the technical innovations could be implanted, the native Islamic soil would yield the same fruit. In the pursuit of grafting the externalities of the West, the reformists of the 18th century created the biggest obstacles to future change: the system of *capitulations.* The 1740 agreement with France extended the old extraterritorial privileges for foreign traders to an increasing number of foreign nations. This failure to see the new character of European economic development cost Turkey the title of a 'semi-colony' until the eve of World War I.

The Turco-Russian War (1768-74) disappointed the conservatives who believed more in the power of religion than in modern techniques which they rejected to accept. Thus, the necessity of technical improvement and institutional reorganization appeared to be more clear after the war. Reforms of Halil Hamid Pasa (1782-85) mark this change. Mustafa III invited Baron de Tott as a military consultant. The first military unit independent of the Janissary system, trained with Western methods, was created in 1774 by the French. This development fell within the scope of action recognized by the *ulema* as permissible. Within this context the reformist administrators secured the permission of establishing non-traditional educational institutions, and the translation of European works of science. But under pressure, they could not attempt to formulate an educational programme for the Janissary corps.

Staffed largely by French officers, a new engineering school was opened (1776) for naval officers. In addition to this, the abolished School of Engineering of the Tulip Era (by a conservative revolt that ended this period) was re-established in 1769. Although there were reform minded members of the military (*Janissary*) and the *ulema*, they were nevertheless the strongholds of conservatism. The frequent *Janissary* uprisings were now the rebellions of a discontented *esnaf* (petty traders and artisans) to halt innovations and re-establish the old *nizam* (order) which would perpetuate their newly won privileges. The *ulema* by and large sided with the Janissary because they could not afford the change of the social structure which provided them so much power. But with the increase in their numbers the religious literati also underwent some compositional rearrangements. The lower ranks of the ulema who could not be employed became more parasitical, whereas the higher ranks engaged in activities as selling offices, degrees, ranks, usury, tax-farming, expropriation of land, and most profitably controlling *waqf* (Turkish *vakif*=religious endowments) properties.

Even the mystic orders (*tarikats* like Bektasi with rather liberal and flexible philosophies), that once limited the power of the *ulema* and dogmatic Islamic trends either lost their power (after the collapse of the *Sipahi* order and, the bourgeoisification of the Janissary) or became ideologies of conservatism for the preservation of the old *nizam*.

The impoverished classes and strata were in mutual opposition to reform with the fear of their total extinction, under a new regime which only benefitted the upper classes. Their enemies were not so much the Western powers waiting at the borders, but the secular minded statesmen and modernly trained officer corps. The general policy of the conservatives was to dominate the ruler, and when this proved impossible to incite the military, the economic strata in decline, and the clericals, who clearly grasped that once the *status quo* was tempered with, their survival was at stake. So the call that appealed to the people so much was the return to the pristine qualities of the Ottoman system.

Indeed, under the impact of European capitalist expansion which disrupted the precapitalist *sipahi* order, together with the Ottoman agrarian system, collapsed. Turkish peasants never recovered from this disorder. When the country was opened to foreign commerce, trade flourished in the Ottoman towns. But with the discovery of international naval routes to the Orient, Turkish commerce declined drastically. When the foreign trader reappeared with European goods, the Ottoman industry and crafts slowly vanished. All these painful historical events accumulated in the folk memory as a deep lying hostility against modernization and any form of social change. The source of the power of the ottoman conservatives was this support they found among the masses.

On the other hand, the failure of the reformists lied in the fact that reformism was initiated by the rulers and the ruling class rather than by a new class with a wider social base and a new *weltanschauung*. The reformists not only did not rely on any of the existing clases but they did not encourage the birth of an economically active (entrepreneural) class that could have counteracted against minority and foreign capitalism. Their belief was that, the primary threat to Turkey was militarism of Europe. Thus, they failed to see the menace of a growing economic power in the West. For the sake of accomplishing military reforms, the Ottoman reformists allowed the organization of anti-reformism under the banner of Islam or *Seriat*.

The age of these limited reforms came to an abrupt end with a conservative reaction during with the second Turco-Russian War (1787). With the disastrous result of this venture in 1792, Selim III realized the necessity of more comprehensive reforms. Besides external threats, increasing impoverishment of lower classes, increasing financial difficulties, rise of strong local lords (*ayan*), and uprisings among the non-Muslim peoples provided the most legitimate excuses for a massive reform movement.

The reform proposals were incorporated into a report and was sent for the approval of the *Seyh-ul Islam.* A new idea for the time, receiving a loan from a European country was opposed on the ground that it was against religion. But no Muslim country was to be found able to lend money. During the reign of Selim III, Western culture and institutions penetrated the religious crust of the Ottoman society. A tiny group of secular intellectuals emerged during the eighteen years of his sovereignty. These men assumed important duties in the historical reform movement initiated by Selim. The survivors of this group after Selim's assassination by a conservative insurrection that ended his reform efforts went to Egypt and worked under Mehmet Ali. The most important event of this period is the appearance of scientific writings in Turkish and French by those who were educated in the new schools, or had contacted with European culture. The permanent embassies that Selim had installed in European capitals functioned as extremely useful training grounds for the staff that carried on the Ottoman reformation.

Selim's actual intentions were (which cost him his life) not only to modernize the army, but, by using it as a lever for his power, to crush the resistance of the *ulema.* By restricting the authority of the *Seyh-ul Islam,* he had planned to free himself from the pressures of the *ulema* and to be able to realize the secular transformation of the Ottoman society independent of the clergy. But the traditional Ottoman State had no established machinery for applying purely executive decisions and very little strength to enforce them. His decrees could always be repudiated by the *ulema.*

In the final analysis, the necessity of what must be done seemed much more clearer at this period. Besides the idea of change, a small group of secular minded reformist statesmen had showed up on the historical stage.

A mutiny in May, 1807, instigated by the *ulema*, the *Janissary* and the *petty hourgeoisie* of Istanbul) against Selim and his statesmen led to unprecedented killing, plunder and destruction. The popular slogan was that, Selim was no longer the defender of Islam but an agent of the infidels. This was one of the major struggles of the medieval mind with the ideas and cadres of modernization on a massive scale. Even though the ideals of the French Revolution had not yet reached the Muslim peoples of the Empire, the traditional ideas and institutions were already in a process of dissolution. However, contrary to the receptiveness of the non-Muslim peoples of the state, the new ideas to replace the traditional ones were far from being accepted. The devastating mutiny froze the reform movement for about a quarter of a century.

Towards a Secular State

After the downfall of the Ottoman reformation movement in 1807, important changes occurred in the national and international scene that left their mark in the scope and extent of the later Turkish reforms. Among the most significant international events were the union of Western powers and the downfall of Napoleon; the industrial revolution; and the appearance of the steamship on the international scene. On the national scene we might consider the massive efforts of the *qyan* to realize a hereditary feudality independent of the central authority, the desperate and destructive struggle of the *Janissaries* to establish themselves as a dominant political power without a viable economic base, the rise of nationalist-separatist movements among the *millets* partly as a result of Western economic and ideological penetration.

Mahmud II (1808-39), after waiting for the right time, made a very radical move toward the transformation of the Ottoman state into an entity composed of peoples of diverse nationalities and religions based on secular principles of sovereignty. Actually, the seeds of such development were sown during the year of the *Janissary* dictatorship after Selim's assassination. When the *Janissaries* invited the *ayan* to a *mesveret* (consultative assembly) with the new monarch, an *ittifak* (pact of alliance) was signed, in which the divine authority of the sultan was for the first time subjected to a written document.

The importance of this pact was that, it contained the idea of separating the government from the ruler. While all sides expressed their allegiance to the sultan, every precaution was taken to prevent the ruler, *grand-vezir* and even the *Seyh-ul Islam* (in case they sided with the progressive rulers) from deviating from the *Seriat.* Only a few of the *ayan* signed the *senet*; they had no intention of surrendering their newly won prerogatives to legal controls and losing some of their tributes they exacted from the people. The *Janissary* and the *ulema* unconditionally ruled the state for seventeen years.

At this time an intense propaganda against the Turk was carried on in the West. The Turk was no more needed as a buffer for Russian aggression. The French and Russian Governments were making plans for the partition of the Ottoman estates.

It is these internal and external threats to the existence of the Ottoman State that prodded Mahmud to create a new type of army. The *Janissary* terror and lawlessness had wiped off from the minds of the people, the last vestiges of acceptance and respect for their order. Furthermore, the achievements of Mehmet Ali (Governor of Egypt) convinced many people that the road to reforms passed through the destruction of the *Janissary* order. In 1826 Mahmud's new forces liquated this five century-old institution in a few hours. With the *Janissaries,* the armed hand of the *ulema* was also chopped off.

Mahmud is the first Turkish monarch who brought the idea of purposeful change, and better the conditions of his people rather than preserving the traditional order. However, in this venture he did not find any support from any of the traditional classes. By appearing among them and mixing in with common people, he broke down a sacred tadition and became a popular figure. He sought and found support for his innovations with the totality of the (urban) people. He advocated the principles of governing by law and equality before the law, irrespective of race and religion. This won him the title of 'infidel sultan', together with *'adli'* (lawful).

The traditional Ottoman system was designed to give each social estate its due (divinely ordered) in the interest of order and stability—this could not mean equality before a common law. Mahmud introduced the concepts of 'justice and law' to the field of legal enactments which created the declaration and execution of a body of rules outside the will of the Caliph and the *Seriat.* This new concept of justice was quite different from both the *Seriat* and *kanun,* because it was the harbinger of a source of legislation different from the 'word of God' and the Sultan. Hence, Mahmud's era changed the old concept of society to legitimize his reforms. "A modern state formed by men of different ethnic and religious compositions" became the guiding principle of his ideal polity. But foreign intervention and separatist movements among the *millets* (nationalities) of the Empire did not allow the full growth of this well-intended programme.

After silencing the religious resistance against his new policies, Mahmud circumscribed the legal zone which the *ulema* could operate.

In the traditional Ottoman state two offices stood above all the others. The *sadrazam's* and the *Seyh-ul Islam's.* These represented two supreme institutions; the first administrative and judicial, and the second consultative in terms of the *Seriat* as well as the *kanun.* They represented the ruler's dual functions as Sultan-Caliph. Mahmud ended this system by abolishing the office of the *sadrazam (grand-vezir)* as the absolute vicar of the monarch. The new government installed in its place was based on a different division of labour and authority. Under a new *basvekil* (prime minister) a number of *vekils* (ministers) were appointed to administer various departments of the government.

The office of the *Seyh-ul Islam* was placed outside the temporal realm of the government, and only religious matters were relegated to it. But, the greatest mistake of Mahmud in delineating the temporal and religious spheres in his newly established government organization has been the transfer of the *seriat* courts from the jurisdiction of the *Sadrazam* to the jurisdiction of the *Seyh-ul Islam.* Thus, although the latter's authority was only consultative—but had informally gained *de facto* control of the *Seriat* court system—in 1837 he was legally endowed with juridical powers over these courts. This change, which first seemed like a restriction of the religious authority, later caused the biggest hardships for the reformers of the Turkish-muslim element of the declining Empire in the implementation of cultural reforms regarding areas like family and education.

Besides these changes, Mahmud established a council to work on legal and judicial matters outside the realm of the *Seriat.* Through these provisions, in 1838, he promulgated the first Turkish public law outside the *Seriat.* The idea that statesmen of an absolute monarchy were in some way publicly responsible under the privisions of law, rather than to the monarch, was shockingly new to the masses. With these efforts, greater clarification between criminal and civil, secular and religious, and private and public law appeared.

Through the Board of Useful Affairs, another of Mahmud's new institutions, a report reached the mass media concernig secular education in 1838. Briefly the report declared that religious knowledge served salvation after death, but science served perfection of man in this world. Students entering new military, naval, engineering and medical schools, even lacked the proper reading of Turkish books. This was basically due to the defectiveness of the primary schools. So the means of acquiring science and bettering education actually meant giving a new order to the schools. But after submitting this report, the Board saw that elementary education was still in the religious realm dominated by the *seriat,* and even though a temporal authority could make recommendations, it could not decree the establishment of secular schools at the primary level. The report went back and forth between the Board and the office of *Seyh-ul Islam,* and the idea of reforming primary education in the end nwas converted to the rearrangement of ways and means of teaching *Kuran* and other traditional subjects. In brief, while the Turkish military pursued an autonomous, and progressive educational course, Turkish civilian primary education continued to be a communal and religious affair until the downfall of the Ottoman Empire.

After this abortive effort, the Board of Useful Affairs decided on opening *rusdiye* schools for adolescents. These were presented as the necessary link between the religious education of the primary schools and the worldly education of the scientific higher learning. Although no *rusdiye* schools were opened in Mahmud's time, a special school called *Mekteb-i- Maarif* (school of secular learning) was established in 1839 to educate a limited number of promising boys to be employed as Government functionaries. Some of the prominent figures of the *Tanzimat* era graduated from it. Besides this the *Mekteb-i- Ulum-u Edebiyye* (school of literary sciences) was opened to train government translators. The students of both schools studied Arabic grammar, French, geography, geometry, history and political science.

The importance of these schools was that it removed yet another segment of governmental affairs from the monopoly of the *medrese* and *Seriat.* It was facilitated the translation of European scientific works into Turkish.

Mahmud's reign is a crucial turning-point of Ottoman history in terms of secular transformation, because from this time onward, the concept 'religious' acquired a new meaning. But through this gradual change many Turks over generations developed a culturally split personality due to the dual culture they were raised in. *Usefulness* remained the chief criterion of the necessity for secular education for a long time, as did the view that modern institutions should be allowed only insofar as they transmitted the techniques and sciences of the West without disturbing the social structure and traditional stratification of the Ottoman polity.

While the heavy religious character of the elementary education continued, secular higher educational institutions became so successful that they constantly drained off the potential students of the *medrese.* The gradual decline of the *medrese* system must be considered as the triumph of the secular Turkish education in the 19th century.

In 1834 Mahmud opened the Military Academy with no ties attached to the religious institutions of the time. Besides its completely secular base, it found its roots in the populace and evolved as a national-popular institution. That is one of the reasons why from Mahmud's time onwards, the Turkish officers have been agents of social and political reforms (with reservations for the army's position after 1971). A new School of Medicine soon took its place besides the Military Academy.

To note the importance of these reforms for their time, let us point out what the *ulema* of Mahmud's time were doing. There seems to have been three controversies rife among the *ulema* at the time:

> The first was the disturbing claim that the earth was round; the second concerned the permissibility of taking quarantine measures against epidemics; the third concerned vaccination. Having exhausted their resources of interpretation and exegesis of religious texts, the *ulema* were peturbed by the strange ideas on these subjects creeping into the minds of some Muslims from afar. Those who were modern enough to approve of the two preventive health measures did not differ one bit from their adversaries in their reasoning; their total armory consisted of scholastic logic and medieval texts. We are told of a duality between a Tunisian Maliki *allamą* and Hanafi *mufti* in which the first rejected and

the later accepted the imposition of quarantines; the former emerged victorious with the proposition that interfering with epidemics would mean opposition of God's absolute will by the recognition of man's free will.

Mahmud founded a newspaper press in 1831, *Takvim-i Vekayi* (Calender of Events). It became a medium of forecast of Mahmud's policies. There were numerous hints in its issues to institutions still unknown to the Turks at the time. It is a historical irony that the ideas of constitutionalism in Turkey first filtered down from the vision of an absolute monarch to his people.

These diverse educational endeavours and various parties of students sent abroad for their education proved their significance later. Moreover, the Translation Bureau became in time a college of foreign languages, diplomacy and statecraft. It was there that some of the most prominent Turkish intellectuals got their 'education'. Even the roots of the present Turkish literature can be traced to this bureau.

The State as the Age of Social Change and Secularization

With Mahmud's efforts, the old Turkish ruler's right of enacting *kanun* on temporal matters gradually became more consolidated and systematized by the way of creating a body of public law separate from *seriat* law. Although there had been yet no distinction between public and private law, the new administrative, military and penal enactments established the foundation of a future body of public law. Moreover, with the increasing extension of public law, these enactments tended to alter the important position of the Islamic law.

Additionally, the medieval conception of the temporal law as an expression of the will of the ruler, or Islamic practices (*urf*), began to give way to impersonal legislation based on reason and contemporary need. This process eventually culminated in the 1876 Ottoman constitution.

But most important of all, while the medieval conception of the state was to maintain the general 'order' in accord with the traditional principles of Islamic polity, the State acquired the role of the ultimate mover and agency for change and progress in Mahmud's time. Nevertheless the weakest point of Turkish political transformation, as stated before, was that the reforms were not the product of a rising new class with modern needs and aspirations, but rather the creation of the traditional political authority struggling to maintain its existence under external and internal threats. This conspicuous character of Turkish modernization would later reveal its contradictions in subsequent periods.

Mahmud's next great service to the Turkish people has been the national economic complex he had created and, set into motion. Although he had little chance to develop a new economic policy as the major instrument for modernization, he still deserves praise for initiating the *etatist* policy of establishing leather, paper, textile and ammunition factories. The reasons why he could not further develop his economic policy that could have put Turkey in the league of 'modern' nations of our time can be summarized as follows : (i) the Capitulations; (ii) absence of external and internal peace and security; (iii) the character of the Turkish agrarian system that did not allow for the accumulation of capital in state coffers; (iv) absence of an entrepreneural middle-class, due to; (v) the existence of foreign and comprador merchants with extraterritorial privileges backed up by foreign powers; (vi) accumulation of capital in the hands of the non-Turkish elements of the empire and its escape through the partnership of these elements with foreign firms and entrepreneurs; (vii) the inability of Turkish statesmen to prosecute a viable economic policy.

The Tanzimat Period

The years that fall between 1840 and 1870 were significant in bringing Turkey into closer contact and dependent on to Europe. These years were also the crucial years of imperialist penetration of European economy into the Turkish soil.

During this period the *medrese* organization, systematically ignored, became the refute of the impoverished classes. Sponsored by their rich endowments they fed a reserve army of reaction against the *Tanzimat* (reformation).

Another important character of this period is that it marks the emergence of a Turkish middle-class, less impressive economically, but crucial from the political and intellectual points of view. This class consisted of the upper layers of the administrative, military, legal and financial bureaucracy. *Medrese* members who showed a degree of achievement were also recruited as government functionaries, and were considered among this class.

The European economic penetration at this period clearly shaped the form of the economic rift between the Muslims and non-Muslims of the Empire. The myth that the Turk does not engage in industry and trade (created by Europeans) is a legacy of this period.

Before 1838, the West was no more than a source of inspirations and modern technology for the Turks. Its political and soci-economic organization was an excrescence in terms of local needs and aspirations. But once Turkey was pulled into the Western economic and political "market" it became a part and a losing partner of it. The 'development of Turkish underdevelopment' coincides with this period.

Under the impact of pressing needs and threats that required a national policy of reform and planned change, the charter of November 3, 1839 was proclaimed. The common name of this charter is *Tanzimat* (ordering, reformation) and was given its name to the ensuing period of reforms and Westernization. With the permission of the new Sultan Abdul Mecid, this protocol was prepared by a Consultative Council (*Meclis-i- Sura*). It briefly states that:

(i) the old disarrayed system has to be substituted by a new one based on new laws and principles. But these laws must be in accord with the *Seriat.*

(ii) The new body of laws will guarantee life, property and honour of individuals as legal fundamental principles.

(iii) These laws and rules will be equally applicable to all citizens no matter what their religions may be.

Sultan Abdul Mecid took a written oath to comply with the principles of this Charter which was an embodiment of the *Seriat* and was accepted by the Council. He also promised not to abrogate the laws enacted on the basis of the *Tanzimat* Charter.

This is clearly the first constitutional document of the Islamic World, although it was not meant to be a constitution. Later equivocations in its terms would create serious problems.

In general, although it did not contain any sign of popular sovereignty, it definitely carried some provisions to limit the arbitrary power of the ruler. This meant the renunciation of the key concept of the medieval meaning of sovereignty. His prerogative to enact laws (*kanun*) according to his will (*irade*) in areas not covered by the *Seriat* was now restricted by both the principles of the Charter and the legislative powers of the Council.

The source of new legislation would be the deliberations of the Council or councils. The members of these organizations were all appointed by the Sultan. Even though they were invested with legislative powers (through discussion and mutual consent), their decisions acquired legal sanction only after ratification by the Sultan.

The most equivocal part of the Charter concerned the judiciary. There was no allusion to the independence or separation of the judicial function from the executive and legislative.

On the other hand a very important practice was instituted with the proclamation of the *Tanzimat* Charter without a *fetva* by the *Seyh-ul Islam* for its legitimization. Hence, the appearance of the Charter constituted the first formal breach between the temporal and the religious spheres which the *Tanzimat* philosophy (and practice) established.

The Charter's 'fundamentals' were bound to create the difficulty reconciling statue laws with practices based on the *Seriat* for the Muslims and other strictly religious traditions of the *millets* (the non-Muslim nationalities). Yet, complete legal equality was quite foreign for the period. *Tanzimat* falls to one of the most complicated periods of the Ottoman history in terms of its relations with Europe. While the European powers were demanding equality and a secular state to protect the rights of their business-partners (minorities), they were also pressing for the distinct identity of these *millets* through legal and political freedom within the confines of the Ottoman State. But the *millet* organization was based on religion and religious organization. A reconcilization of the overall secularization policy of the state and the preservation of the religious character of the millets became a headache of the *Tanzimat* period.

The result of the difficulties that ensued from the declaration of the Character culminated in the proclamation of the *Islahat Fermani* (Reform Edict) on 18 February 1856. Its provisions contained:

(i) complete freedom and guarantee for the exercise of all religious beliefs and practices:
(ii) confirmation of the rights granted by the *Tanzimat* Charter, but also arrangements for their fullest application;
(iii) confirmation of all previous spiritual and temporal privileges and immunities granted to the ottoman *millets*;
(iv) representation of religious communities in the discussions of the Supreme Council;
(v) Implementation of legal, political, educational, religious, economic, and moral reforms in which the freedom, equality, wealth and rational training of all citizens could benefit.

It became obvious at this period that the Ottoman state could be secularized only when the *millets* became solely religious communities rather than politically autonomous bodies, and also individually equal and responsible before the laws of the state. Only this way the *Seriat* would cease to be the basic law of the empire and become the private law of the Muslim population.

The *Tanzimat* did not bring about a substantial change in the composition of the ruling class. Except the initiation of legal reforms, its overall failure may be attributed to the absence of any real effort to launch a campaign of economic transformation. Furthermore, the *Tanzimat* provided no constitutional structure for regulating relations between the ruler and the ruled and between the legislative administrative and judicial authorities and functions.

In an overall assessment it can be said that, *Tanzimat* indicated the direction for future change when the Council of Judicial Enactments was transformed into a judiciary body. The new secular court system (*adliye*) was established upon the principle of universal justice (*adalet*) and outside the realm of religious law (*Seriat*) and the ruler's will (*kanun*).

During the *Tanzimat*, each ministry came to have a permanent council to prepare the necessary projects and establish new rules. These organizations gradually departed from the influence of the *Seriat* and *kanun* as their *ulema* members were replaced by secularly educated functionaries. These councils became the legislative organs of the government. The Council of Judicial Enactments (or Supreme Council) installed by Mahmud functioned as the supreme organ above all these. Its activity and meaning may be accepted as the first signs of parliamentary administration. Nevertheless it must be noted that representation was far from being popular. The members of the Council were all recruited among the highest civil officials, the highest ranking *ulema*, and the leaders of the *millet* organizations.

The internal strife among the *millets* after 1840 indicated the need of establishing greater articulation in the relations between the government and the people. The modernist estatesmen felt that it was time to try their ideals (parliamentary rule) in disguised form. Delegates were invited from the provincial councils founded by Mahmud to the capital to attend the meetings of the Supreme Council. These delegates were representatives of the *millet* organizations and were elected for one year. Their function was to express the needs of their religious communities. But, most importantly, as a part of the reorganization project of the provincial administration, the provincial councils were made representational bodies in 1964. From this date on, their members were elected by their local constituents.

In 1868 the Supreme Council was divided into two organs as the Board of Judicial Enactments (*Divan-i Ahkam-i-Adliye*) and the Council of State (*Sura-yi Devlet*). The first became the highest judicial organ and later transformed into the Ministry of Justice with jurisdictional authority over the secular *adliye* courts.

The Council of State was directed by the famous statesmen and reformist Mithad Pasa, and soon became the nest of the constitutional movement that created the 1876 Constitution. The function of this reorganization was aimed to the separation of the executive power from the judicial and religious powers.

It is an irony of the *Tanzimat* reformation that the Muslim Turks did not really benefit much from the *Tanzimat* secularism and the Reform Edict of 1856. This is mainly due to the fact that, the Muslims (especially Turks) did not have a communal organization outside the state machinery. Neither the reforms without a political foundation nor the *ummet* ideology-international in character—was sufficient to transmute the religious community (*ummet*) to a nationality among turks. Furthermore, the Muslims of the Ottoman state were devoid of national homogeneity. The Ottoman Turks as an unstructured political entity, now were under the state which was no more an Islamic institution (but awovedly secular) to represent them.

The reform programmes of the Ottoman state in the 19th Century brought into light the basic weaknesses for such a policy to take root in the society. First, new reforms did not create a distinct *milieu* for the independent evolution of the religious institution. Second, when the expected separation of the state and church was not realized, a dichotomy emerged among the cultural institutions. Third, 19th-century constitutionalism neither could build a popular base (it remained an elitist scheme), nor a national identity, for, the prevailing 'Ottomanism' was more international in essence than national.

These weaknesses of the *Tanzimat* created discomfort among the Turkish element who benefited least from its policy. But still this reaction was not nationalistic. Anti-*Tanzimat* movement personified by the Young Ottomans was Constitutionalist and religious in its nationality. In this sense, it was more participatory but less secular than the *Tanzimat* outlook. This new crystallization later was very wisely utilized by Abdulhamid to shape his Islamic State.

Tanzimat and Seriat

Although the *Tanzimat* Charter had declared loyalty to the *Seriat,* it also made clear the necessity of promulgating new laws. It was stated in the new government programme that, because neither the *Seriat* nor the *kanuns* were publicly announced, confusion and injustice was common. The *Seriat* was not a codified law. The *kanuns* were written and declared but they were not accessible by the people. Furthermore, they were subject to the will of each different ruler. So, codification became one of the most important aspects of the *Tanzimat* and laid down guidelines for later statesmen to differentiate between law and religion.

Whether it was based on *Seriat* or not, to formulate religious fundamentals as a positive codified law, and to do this in compliance with a non-religious criterion, and through deliberations of a secular authority, implied great strides toward secularization.

Ottoman legal secularization started with increasing commercial relations with outsiders—an area basically outside the domain of the *Seriat*. During the 1850's, the codification of a commercial law and the organization of first commercial courts, independent of both the *Seriat* courts and non-Muslim ecclesiastical courts took place. A second commercial code again borrowed from France was added to the first one in 1860. This in turn was followed by the Code of Maritime Commerce (1863).

These courts were the first secular Ottoman courts created outside the jurisdiction of the *ulema (Seyh-ul Islam*). Thus, the first encroachment on the realm of the *Seriat* and its practices started at this time. To take an oath according to one's own religious rite was one of the new innovations. The second and most important of such innovations was the effort toward codifying legal principles and procedures of areas presently covered by the *Seriat*. This attempt first experimented in the area of the Ottoman penal system. penal law was basically dependent on the *kanuns* enacted by the Sultans.

The first Penal Code was prepared and promulgated by the Supreme Council in 1840. Another one followed this in 1851 which screened and rearranged the principles of the *Seriat* and previous *kanuns*. But, after the declaration of the Reform Edict, a completely new penal code was drawn up (1858) based on the French Penal Code. This code remained in force until the end of the First World War (1918) and, was the first secular ottoman code in the area of civil law. Thus, the principles of individual responsibility and equality among citizens of diverse religions, and arrest for only specified acts, entered into the Ottoman legal system for the first time. However, the 1858 Penal Code still could not abrogate the penal provisions of the *Seriat* and its codification remained within the limits not covered by the penal and personal rights of the divine law.

The new Penal Code was pregnant with continuous conflicts between the religious and secular principles incorporated into its structure. This conflict reached to frustrating levels in the following court practices. The new codes became operational in the *adliye* or *nizamiye* (statutory) courts, which were under the jurisdiction of the Ministry of Justice. These secular courts operated by the side of *seriat* courts which were under the jurisdiction of the *Seyh-ul Islam*. Because of the interconnections and the fluid boundaries between the secular and religious domains, the application of civil law through two different court systems became increasingly untenable.

Finally the long refrained decision for establishing secular courts for civil law outside the jurisdiction of *Seyh-ul Islam* came with the creation of the *Divan-i Akham-i Adliye* in 1868 as the highest court of the new statutory court system.

There were two departments of the new *Divan*: civil and penal. Commercial and criminal cases were heard and judged according to the new procedural and statutory codes, but civil suits were heard and judged according to the *Seriat*. One major difference was introduced though; the court was placed under the control of a temporal authority.

The long dispute between the Ottoman intellectuals who advocated the adoption of the French Civil Code and those who defended the idea to codify a civil law based on Islamic jurisprudence ended by the Government's decision to adopt the second thesis. Cevdent Pasa was appointed as the head of the committee to compile a book of law called the *Mecelle,* whose provisions would be derived from the *Hanafi* school of law. When the *Hanafi* scholars disagreed, the decision closest to the *nass* (revealed commands in the holy texts) and the practices of the day would be accepted.

The *Mecelle* compiled a part of the Islamic law in its sixteen books between 1869 and 1876. Abdul Hamid rendered this committee inactive in 1876, and dissolved it in 1888, before it could codify the marriage, family and inheritance laws which were the core of the *Seriat* and its basic philosophy. The new *Seyh-ul Islam*, Hasan Fehmi declared that, any such function fell under his jurisdiction, not that of the Ministry of Justice.

The continuous conflict about the specific areas of each legal system was partially alleviated by a government statement issued in 1886. In this statement, marriage, divorce, alimony, retaliation, wills, inheritance and blood-wise were deemed to be under the jurisdiction of the *Seriat court*. Commercial and cirminal matters were exclusively given to the statutory courts. The remaining matters were left to the parties to choose between the two court systems.

With these provisions, the Ottoman legal structure was divided into three parts: (i) *Seriat*; (ii) codified parts of the *Seriat*; (iii) secular laws based on French codes. Their irreconcilable nature was a reflection of a society moving from a theocratic base to a secular and popular representation. The very meaning of the *Seriat* rendered it impossible to accommodate the interests of the new rising middle-classes, which were bogged down by the static and unchanging character of the divine law, and the traditional classes which were clinging to it as their saviour.

Tanzimat innovations did not worry the *ulema* very much, because the new laws were regarded as being outside the domain of *Seriat*. Moreover, the new laws were introduced through the traditional right of the Sultan to enact laws. But still, the preparation of the *Mecelle* was a product of a temporal authority. This was a step toward opening the gates of *ictihat* (free opinion) through the ruler's reactivated royal legislative capacity. Thus, the *ulema* corps would eventually take over only spiritual matters and constitute the basis of an Islamic church.

The Ottoman clergy and the *ulema* order understood this perfectly. They did not only fight the *Mecelle* fiercely, but they also opposed the secular university which was rapidly reducing their influence in teaching and indoctrination along religious sciences. Their efforts succeeded under Abdul Hamid when the *Seriat* once again became the central legal and moral source of daily relationships. Further codification was prohibited and the Mecelle Committee was dismissed. Hence, the *Tanzimat* secularization only reached the peripheries of the *Seriat*.

Ottoman Nationalism and Constitutionalism

Until the middle of the 19th century, Turkish was the language of the lower classes—even for some of the non-Muslim communities. There was no official 'Turkish' language; even schools did not teach it. Arabic was the language of the *medrese.* Arabic and Persian were the language requirements of the secondary schools, where Turkish was not taught. The State (official) and literary language was called Ottoman: a hybrid of Turkish, Arabic and Persian. The traditional ruling elements were inept to teach or write anything in Turkish. The *medrese* did not only oppose the translation of the *Kuran* into Turkish but also writing anything in Turkish. According to the *medrese,* the *Kuran* was not intended to be understood. It was the highest symbol of divine mystery, which could only by interpreted by them. This hiatus between the people and the *medrese* alienated the latter from the masses to such an extent that, with its different saints, superstitions and even with its religious leaders, the village (rural) communities bore allegiance to figures quite different than the *ulema* type, and principles forbidden by the classical Islamic teaching.

The impact of *Tanzimat* encouraged the cultivation of Ottoman and its adoption as the language of learning instead of Arabic. With its international character—reflecting the edifice of the state—Ottoman quickly became the language of secular education and government. This was another blow on the isolated *medrese.* Its language barrier of keep up with the latest developments around it further dislocated Islamic literati from the political and social developments of the time.

The Ottoman language-movement also functioned as an intellectual reaction against the impact of French as well as Arabic which was the symbol of religious dogmatism. The codification of the Ottoman language starts at this period.

Some Turkish intellectual (e.g., Cevdet) used the new Ottoman turkish for teaching Islam outside the *medrese* (and in his) books about the history of Islam and the Caliphate. With these efforts the gap between the language of the elites and the masses became so obvious to everyone that, not only purifying the language, but also changing the (Arabic) script became an issue.

At this time (1850's) the positive effects of the Translation Bureau, created by Mahmud II, began to show themselves in the translations outside the scientific books. This influx of translated French literature, now understandable to the Turkish people, brought new ideas, cultural values and most of all the intellectual foundations of the French Revolution.

Towards a Constitution

The *Tanzimat* Reforms clearly exposed the underdeveloped social structure of the Ottoman State under its theocratic crust. In the middle of the 19th century, the Ottoman Empire was no more a Muslim State dominated solely by Turks and Muslims. Nor was it a national State, because the Turks did not yet have gained a national consciousness, apart from Islamic identity, that could be utilized as a vehicle of social transformation.

Subdued by Western economic and political imperialism, if the Ottoman State was satisfying the economic needs of certain classes, these were definitely not Turkish. Thus the *Tanzimat* regime lacked both the traditional pillars of economic and political national sovereignty and a constitutional foundation based on the popular will of the people.

In this regard, it is safe to assert that, the first constitutional ideas in Turkey originated under the mounting impact of economic, cultural and political crises. These ideas were basically formulated by the ascending meagre national middle strata whose economic basis was state service.

At a time when the traditional religious foundation of the Empire was becoming increasingly unstable (19th century), the Western Powers were exerting more pressure on Turkey as one of their important zones of imperialist expansion. This was a period when Turkey was trying to Westernize in spite of Western aggression. Lacking a national identity and ideology, the Ottoman-turk raised the banner of Islam against this aggression. But the foreign economic penetration had been so firmly consolidated that, none of the adopted Western institutions securely took roots on Turkish 'ground' continuously drained by European capitalism. While the Turkish ethnic element became increasingly impoverished, the non-Muslim *millets* of the Empire prospered under the aegis of western economic enterprise.

The Ottoman intelligentsia searching for a viable cure for these problems found their religion the only unifying basis of social mobilization. For the, the Ottoman State had to be an Islamic polity—but a Constitutional one. In this sense, the movement voiced by the 'New (or Young) Ottomans' was anti-Western and Constitutional in character.

However, an immediate religious opposition grew among the traditional Ottoman classes against the Constitutionalist movement. One of the reactionary secret societies was the 'Society for the Preservation of the *Seriat' (Muhafaza-i Seriat)*. Their plot was exposed, and among those arrested were army officers of the old order, *medrese* members, Ulema sheikhs of various orders, and students of various religious schools.

Another secret society, which was founded in 1865 was *Ittifak-i-Hamiyet* (Patriotic Alliance). This organization later became the nucleus of the 'New Ottoman movement. The main of this Society was to fight against and try to change the absolutist Ottoman regime' into a Constitutional Monarchy.

This movement always remained as a body of intellectual opposition and an influential propaganda source for an Islamic form of national democracy.

Their basic arguments were directed to focus on the poverty of the masses, economic difficulties of the government which later (1875) had to declare its bankruptcy; Turkey's military, economic and political dependence on the West; and the arbitrary rule of the monarch which could be curbed only by fundamental laws and a popular government.

Although all of the 'New Ottomans' were unanimous on these aims, they differed in the ways of achieving them through the traditional structure of the Ottoman polity which they did not want to alter. They were very resentful of the Western anti-Muslim prejudices, and held the *Tanzimat* statesmen responsible for this.

The 'New Ottomans' were progressives but never revolutionists. They were either members or sons of the traditional Ottoman ruling classes. Only their education and social status separated them from the other traditional classes. In the absence an economically independent Turkish middle-class, they were dependent on either the government or their relatives who were no different.

The 'New Ottomans' were hostile both to the elements of their own culture that were obstacles to progress and to Western cultural elements that were too harmful to adopt. Through this process of elimination, they reached the important conclusion that religion was not an obstacle to development. Namik Kemal, one of their lot, was the first to capitulate on the economic penetration of the West and its distorting effect on the socio-economic structure of the state. Namik Kemal as their spokesman was exalting their religion by asking :

> Is there any other religion in the world which has succeeded in associating justice with moral virtue and thereby transforming moral obligations into legal obligations.

Thus, with this statement they were including everything, even the Constitution they had been the advocates of within the domain of religious legislation. It is not that they were unaware of the historical secularization of the Western states, they simply did not believe that a similar process was necessary for the Islamic state, because, in their belief, the Islamic state was closest to a Constitutional polity.

The pro-Western sentiments of the *Tanzimat* era quickly became transformed into anti-Western feelings. The anti-Turkish (and anti-Muslim) feeling of the West now met their opposite in Ottoman lands. However, this development put the Turkish reformers in very awkward position. The West's reaction to Turkish reforms undermined the emergent Turkish liberalism and Constitutionalism when they were just burgeoning, and paved the way for the Hamidian absolutism. This trend was also helped by the irresponsible expenditures of the *Tanzimat* era rulers and unlimited Western economic exploitation which culminated in the official bankruptcy of the State in 1876.

In the meantime, there was a growing sentiment among the people that the *Tanzimat* reforms had given too many concessions to the non-Muslim *millets* to the degree of jeopardizing the traditional basis of the Muslim nation.

Expressing this sentiment Sultan Abdul Aziz instructed his government that the new reforms should be crried out only in the framework of the ancient institutions and traditions, and by no means the *Seriat* should be violated.

In the final analysis, the 'New Ottoman' ideology of patriotism was pan Ottomanism shaded with an Islamic nationalism. The national and religious differences of a multitude of Ottoman peoples did not seem to attract their attention.

It is interesting to note that, their idea that reforms could only succeed if they were implemented in compliance with Islam; and their belief that Islam is essentially compatible with contemporary civilization and Constitutionalism recurred in almost all Muslim countries in later periods.

The 1876 Constitution and the Constitutional Era

President of the *Sura-yi Devlet* (Council of State) Midhat Pasa, an influencial leader of the New Ottomans, and his friends accomplished or to introduce a bill amending or changing a existing law. Thus, the Assembly was reduced to the rank of only a consultative council.

It is an irony of history that on the same day of the declaration of the Constitution (23 February 1876)—a significant Western reform—the 'Istanbul Conference' was convened. The European powers did not heed the new ottoman Constitution. Instead, they handed down a list of unacceptable demands which were rejected by the Ottoman Government. In response, Russia declared war against Turkey. Abdul Hamid's mistrust of the West was substantiated whereas Midhat and the Constitutionalist were left in a very difficult position.

After the war which ended with a major Ottoman defeat, Berlin Conference brought heavier terms than that of the Istanbul Conference. From this point on, Abdul Hamid became the absolute leader of the State until his overthrow by the 'Young Turks' in 1908.

Soon after the promulgation of the Constitution, Midhat and his liberal friends were either deported or sent in exile. With their disappearance. Turkey went into a thirty-year long period of isolation and traditionalism. During this period Abdul Hamid built the most efficient machinery of despotism in modern Turkish history, and he did this on the basis of the Constitution which gave him this right. The efficiency of this machinery nevertheless would not prevent the rise of a new movement and ideology represented by a new generation of Turks, which is commonly referred to as the 'Young Turks'.

The Hamidian Era and Reaction—1878-1908

The 19th century is the landmark of Western penetration into Muslim countries all over the world. When the French occupied North Africa, the peoples of Algeria, Tunisia, and Libya turned their eyes towards Turkey. Egypt fell to the British and became a centre of Anti-Western Muslim nationalism. A number of educated men from the Turkish-speaking regions of Asia that had fallen under Russian dominion (Azerbaijan, Caucasus, Crimea, Kazan, and Turkestan) came to Turkey. The Ottoman state was the only political rallying point on which the Muslim peoples of occupied lands in three continents could fall back.

In the 1880s Abdul Hamid was saluted as the Caliph of all Muslims then under foreign yoke, and a symbol for their anti-Western (and anti-imperialist) sentiments.

In the domestic scene, Hamid also became a rallying point as the economic measures of the reformists failed one by one, and modernization appeared to be the acceptance of European economic bondage and impoverishment of the masses by the application of Western economic policies. The people ardently hailed the Hamidian regime because it was a shield against damaging Western ideas of change which further exacerbated Turkey's underdevelopment Islamist, tradition-bound and governed and sustained by national forces. The Caliph seemed to be the *only* omnipotent ruler since the golden age of the Ottoman Empire. Nobody cared much whether the empire was being torn down everyday, or the blood of their economy was being sucked by the 'Ottoman Depts Administration' and pumped out to European metropolises, or the flood of the immigrants from occupied lands. The people were enjoying the official policy of 'escape' from worldly miseries and the virtues of their religious faith materialized in the personality of their Caliph afforded them this luxury. Hamid was so firmly established in the popular mind that at the onset of the 1908 Young Turk revolt, the revolutionaries did not even think of deposing him at once. He was deposed a year later.

Sultan Hamid created a number of special committees that advised him on military, political and religious matters. His political regime bore a resemblance to the *mesveret* system advocated by the New Ottomans as the basis of Islamic Constitutionalism. But his power was basically anchored in the support of his people. After he had either eliminated or pacified the modernist *elite* in the administrative apparatus he surrounded himself with the traditional *elite (ulema)*. His palace started to fill with *serifs, seyyids, amirs,* and sheikhs of various religious orders from Syria, Africa and Arabia. These people symbolized the link, between the Caliph and the Muslim *umma* (communities), and constituted the aristocracy of the religion. The lower echelons of the religious cadres also benefited from the new regime. Mystic orders and the *medreses* began to swell again. Not only the existing *tarikats* (orders) like *Naksibandi, Sadhili,* and *Rifai* became more popular, but new ones like the *Tijaniyya tarikat* came from North Africa and established themselves in the form of healers breath-curers and emulet-writers journeying from town to town and from village to village.

Outward religious expression became a character of this period. This religious fanfare proved to be a powerful medicine to ease the pains and problems of the troubled Turkish people in a world that was soon going to collapse on them.

Everything that was printed had to be inspected by the government agents. An army of informers were put together to convey even the simplest of the events of the Palace. For this purpose telegraph wires reached corners where there were yet no roads.

On the ideological side of the Hamidian period, a Pan-Islamic ideology started to take shape. Excluding the non-Muslim nationalities, the Pan-Islamists declared: "Only the Muslims of the empire should unite."

On the social and economic side of the reality, the European economic penetration into Anatolia, started although slowly, creating new social forms and strata. A working-class started to emerge, the appearance of women in business life coincides with this time. Rural migration to the cities increased. An educated youth of army officers, school teachers and professionals became a powerful intellectual stratum at this period.

In the midst of the Hamidian absolutism, the secular schools became centres of enlightenment and dissatisfaction. These schools shaped on the one hand Hamid's financial and foreign policies (controlled by Western powers), and on the other, destroyed the ideological and political foundations of his regime.

Under severe government control put on the publication of social and political subjects, the newspapers and magazines mostly printed novels and cultural news of Europe.

These news, often accompanied with pictures, gave the urban Turks to compare their life styles and standards with their European counterparts.

The secularizing effects of the new publications upon the traditional institutions came with the new written language which became increasingly popular. The new generations tried to avoid the complex symbolic allusions, which were meaningful only to those with classic literary training. The appearance of pictures and illustrations in new publications created a different atmosphere in a short time, and shattered the traditional views of learning emanating from classical schools and through religious instruction.

The End of the Hamidian Era

In his policy of 'escape' and relative tranquility in the home front, Abdul Hamid allowed two developments to occur that jeopardized the continuation of his rule. First,

> by establishing the omnipotence of his *devlet* (state) Abdul-Hamid imperilled the *din* (religion). There came into existence a cleavage in the minds of the intellectuals between the two.

The authority and oppression of the Hamidian *devlet* was so embracing that religion became an ideological tool in the hands of the Caliph—not an end in itself. So, the control of the religion over temporal affair came to an end during the reign of this celebrated Islamist monarch.

Secondly, the Hamidian regime brought no viable remedy to the super-exploitation of Turkish economic resources by the Europeans, and the permeation of Western control and influence into all spheres of Ottoman daily life. The customs were in the hands of the Westerners and wide open to any European artifcats that Hamid was irritated of; including revolutionary publications.

The more the Hamidian regime became oppressive, the more European cultural and ideological elements filled the vacuum. The despotism of their own government made many Turkish intellectuals believe that European patterns of government and culture was much better than their own.

The Hamidian absolutism gradually created its anti-thesis: a wide intellectual opposition which also incorporated the 'Young Turks'. Now we have enough evidence about the fact that this catch all term does not denote all the opposing factions of the Hamidian regime, for they were diverse in their ideologies and many in number. So, by 'Young Turks' we mean a group of revolutionary Ottoman intellectuals who constituted a political alternative and opposition to the Hamidian regime, and who replaced it by overthrowing Abdul Hamid in 1908.

The Young Turks and the Emergence of Turkish Nationalism

'Turks' for the Ottomans were conceived as their pre-Islamic forefathers who mainly inhabited and ruled Asia. We do not see any trace in the writings of the 'New Ottomans' about Turkism and turkological subjects. Their patriotism was Islamic and pan-Ottomanist. For them, a Turk was still a peasant or an uncivilized Tartar. This misconception was somewhat altered by European works of history and anthropology in the minds of numerous Ottoman political exiles of the Hamidian regime.

But most importantly, the emergence of Turkish nationalism occurred through two historical processes which were closely related:

(i) the decomposition of the Ottoman *millet* system, and its replacement by national-political communities;

(ii) the waning of the concept of *ummet* and, its gradual replacement by nationalism. In both cases the basic social and political concepts of the traditional polity had undergone a process of secularization, slowly shedding their religious content.

Starting with the Greek *millet,* Bulgarians, Serbians, Roumanians consecutively ceased to be religious communities and became nation-states. But the Turkish element in the beginning of the Hamidian era was still not differentiated from the Islamic *ummet* along national lines. This situation went on until the rise of nationalist movements among the non-Turkish Muslim peoples. The Arab, Albanian and Kurdish political movements played a decisive role in the secularization of Turkish nationalism. Thus, the Turkish national identity, renunciated in the name of the 'universal brotherhood of Islam' (*ummet*), gradually came back to the Turk through the differentiation (nationalization) of his co-religionists.

The first signs of this differentiation occurred in the language as a revolt against Arabic and the Medrese system which upheld it. It is interesting to note that political nationalism was still absent at a time when the Turkification of the language and literature was going on. In fact, all factions of the Young Turks at first advocated Ottomanism at a time when the Empire was being torn by national struggles and imperialist schemes of the West.

Only after the 1908 revolution, Turkish nationalism would gain strength in the battlefield, against both the Western powers and numerous Muslim and non-Muslim nationalities of the State who were fighting for their independence. The 'Turkish' viewpoint at this period seems to be most clearly defined and inspired by the Turkish nationalist who fled from Russia.

Mesrutiyet (Constitutional Rule) and 'Union and Progress' 1908-1918

The 1908 revolution that overthrew Abdul Hamid and his reactionary regime stands out as the first political movement that the Ottoman people had participated in on a massive scale. These people were not drawn in from *elite* circles like the previous movements. These people were young army officers, students, professionals, *petty bourgeoisie,* and the uprooted urban folk of the lost territories.

In the absence of national and cultural institutions separate from religion, the Turkish element of the Ottoman Empire came to identify strongly with the State whose importance was more accentuated over religion in Hamid's reign. Especially after the decline of the *ummet* concept, the Young Turks realized that their religious patriotism and Ottomanism had no social basis. It is after this realization that, they started to organize 'people's councils' and hundreds of branches all over the empire for their new political organ; Society of Union and Progress (*Ittihat ve Terakki*). Soon the Society became a national organization, and hearth of Turkish nationalism.

The society was' the organ of the emergent Turkish national *bourgeoisie.*

> . . .it did not encompass the peasantry. . . it did not gain the allegiance of the conservative geneations and classes. . . The mass basis of the Society was amorphous and evolving; this was reflected in the shapelessness of its ideology. Its class basis gradually shifted... to the esnaf (artisans) and the tuccar (merchants) of the towns—the class out of which the Party of Union and Progress sought to forge a Turkish bourgeoisie.
>
> Most of the leaders...were uprooted Turks, or Turks who had broken with tradition through education, or non-Turkish Muslims who had been Turkified by modern education. Army officers, doctors and teachers were prominent among them. By Hamidian standars, they were all *dehris* (innovators in religious matters) in their politico-religious views; they were firm believers in progress.

By gaining political power in a regime of Constitutional Monarchy, the Society became the Party of Union and Progress in 1913. The Union had two rival political parties in the Parliament: *Hurriyet ve Itilaf* (liberal), Westernist, and *Ittihad-i Muhammedi* (Mohammedan Union), Islamist. The policies and interests of these parties were contradictory, however both of them emphasized the importance of relationships between the State, and religion; and between the State and the non-Muslim millets.

The Unionists' idea of secularism meant a religiously ineffectual, but educationally and economically strong central government. In the beginning, their nationalism was still Ottomanism. But by then Ottoman *millets* had become political nationalities either by fighting or aspiring for their own nation-states. At this juncture the Unionists vacillated for years, because, in their belief the basis of Ottoman unity could not be nationalism—for there were numerous nationalities within the State. Nor could it be Islam, because there were millions of non-Muslim citizens of the Empire. Struggling with this dilemma, the Young Turks chose to reinforce the central government and economy to sustain the Ottoman unity. But the severest opposition to these policies came not from the non-Muslim nationalities but from Muslim Arabs.

The rebellion of the Muslim *millets* of the State delivered the final blow to Muslim nationalism and unity; and paved the way for Turkish nationalism separated form religion.

The Islamist position in and outside the Parliament was expressed by three groups which we will not elaborate here. They all had organs in the press and various public organizations. Mustafa Sabri, one of their outstanding figures, became the collaborationist *Seyh-ul Islam* during the Allied occupation (1918-1923) after the First World War. In one of his publications, he declared that photography was blasphemy.

A faction of this group under, the leadership of Dervis, Vahdeti, instigated the 31 March, 1908 Mutiny to reinstitute the *Seriat.* They were hanged by a court martial. Following this event, the Unionists took over the government.

The Islamists' most famous papers and reviews were *Beyan ul Hak, Sirat-i Mustakim* and *Sebil-ur Resat.* Their writers continuously attacked the changing concepts of womanhood, religious institutions, education, language and the Arabic script. But their biggest enemy were the Turkists who held that the Turkish nation would come into existence following the decline of the Islamic *ummet* through a secular nationalism and a successful liberation struggle against the West' 'colonialist' penetration. Gokalp and F. Koprulu stated clearly that Turkism did not mean breaking away form the spiritual community of the Islamic world.

Mesrutiyet Secularism and the 'Young Turk' Reforms

The disastrous results of the Balkan Wars once again brought out the urgent need for large scale social reforms. This move again revived the controversy over the share of Islamic, Western and nationalistic proportions of the new reforms.

For the Islamists, the 'appropriate' elements of the Western civilization were its science and industry. However, they were not cognizant of the fact that these elements were closely related with social and economic structures of each society that were shaped through a unique historical evolution. Nevertheless, they sensed an intrinsic danger even of these externalities of Western civilization for Islam.

No. 57 (1909) issue of *Sirat-i Mustakim* lashed at the Muslim students studying in Europe, when their pictures wearing hats appeared in the press.

The Islamist view of reforms was that anything that had not been covered by the *Seriat* was open to change and adoption of new ways. But, in the meantime, they persistently sought policies, arguments and public support for enlarging the scope of the *Seriat* to cover areas that were traditionally outside its grips. This they tried to do by including *urf* (mores) into the body of *nass* (sacred injunctions) and give them the strength of the latter. Hence, for them, change was impermissible even in matters of custom that were thought to be outside the realm of *Seriat.*

The adoption of Western sciences always remained a confusing subject for the Islamists. This confusion is very evident in their publications at the time. One of the ways they found to guard themselves from the dangers of modern science was to declare that the current scientific theories were contained in the *Kuran.* Since religion embraced everything, social reform could be achieved best by saving traditional customs and institutions from decadence, by bringing them under the sanction of religion.

With these efforts, which inevitably failed, the Islamists rendered one useful service which was ignored by the Ottoman Westernists, that is, focusing on the importance of the traditional elements of culture, and drawing attention to the limits of borrowing foreign cultural institutions.

The Turkists were in agreement with the Islamists in refusing a total imitation of the West. But the Turkists differed from the latter in pointing out that the traditional institutions were in a state of decline and were thus factors of social turmoil and cultural maladjustment. Therefore, they should be eliminated as a pre-condition of reforming those parts of life related to them.

For the Turkists, the roots of the Islamist ideology were no more anchored in the dynamic institutions of the society. The social orzanization that had created those institutions was the *ummet,* the value system of which was provided by the unchanging supreme principles of religion. But the Turkish society was in the process of transformation from an *ummet* formation to nationhood. Like all other modern societies seeking their own (new) identity, the Turkish people could now only be motivated by national ideals.

Before deciding what should be taken over from the West, it was necessary either to secularize those institutions that had been put under *Seriat* and made identical with Islam or eliminate the long decayed elements carried through the *Seriat* for centuries. On after the rejuvenation of the Turkish culture through the above process there could be a genuine reform. Thus, the Turkish reform programme came to mean secularization through Turkification. This programme was quite different from those of the Islamists and Ottoman Westernists.

In the absence of a concrete social stratum (middle-class) that would serve as the source of modernist ideology and politico-economic power, the Young turks became conscious of the need for the creation of such a stratum to provide the driving force of the historical Turkish social transformation. It was through the participation of the people in the political process that they believed the cosmopolitan Ottoman society could be transformed into nationhood.

For this purpose, the Young Turks attempted to accomplish two taks :

(i) to put out the Turkish people from the *ummet* pattern and consciousness; and

(ii) to furnish this new born national community with economic and technical enterprises to sustain its independence. Approaches to the first problem were realized in the fields of education, law, and liberation of some current customs from the grips of religion.

While these reforms were being implemented, the *Seyh-ul Islam* of the time launched a campaign to expand his authority in education, law and customary practices. Translation of R. Dozy's *Essai sur i'historie de i'Islamisme,* and the first translation of the *Kuran* (in 1914) were confiscated before they were even completed. Their further publication was prohibited. These measures, which were still within the power of the *Seyh-ul Islam,* were followed by the arrest of some teachers teaching the evolutionary theory.

The Seyh-ul Islam not only was trying to put his executive powers, to full use, but he was also striving to extend his authority over the judiciary and legislative organs that were gradually coming under complete Unionist control. These efforts eventually culminated in the Islamist-led Mutiny of 31 March to restore Abdul Hamid to full power (1908).

Although they received a heavy blow after the suppression of the mutiny, the Islamists insisted that the Parliament was not entitled by Islam to legislate, and that it was a blasphemy to do so. For them, the *Seriat* was the constitution of the Islamic polity, and the *ulema* its protectors and interpreters.

The Young Turk's answers to the Islamist's view was simple. For them, the turk had carried the burden of the Islam long enough, and still serves as its protector. Islam has become his national religion and would remain so, but for the sake of Islam he had forsaken his nationality, his language and his glorious past. This alienation had reached to such a point that the Turks national identity (in the past as well as the present) had begun to be denied—even by the Turk himself.

In the meantime, the signs of change were manifesting themselves in many ways and in diverse spheres of daily life. With the coming of the new regime in 1908, violations appeared in the traditional apparel. Some women adopted European dresses with no veil, especially when they started working during the First World War. The number of girls' schools were increased. Trade and vocational schools for girls were increased and reformed. Day and evening courses in child care, cooking, sewing, nursing were initiated. The first girls' high school was opened in 1911. Girls were admitted to secretarial and commercial courses. Women became active members in organizations and social events. They started to appear in family businesses. Thousands of women were employed in the industry during the War. The government took great pains to increase the number of female primary school teachers especially after the primary education was liberated from the control of the *ulema* during the *Mesrutiyet.* From the new generation of young female teachers, prominent figures of national liberation and the Republican era emerged.

Although these changes were slowly assimilated, women still could not go to the restaurants (even with their husbands), and they had to sit in partitioned sections of street-cars and ferry-boats. Sea bathing was still forbidden to them. Plays, lectures and concerts were repeated once more for women. They entered the University during the First World War, but sat behind curtains drawn across each classroom. Proportionately, more non-Muslim women benefited from the new freedoms.

Even this much liberty was detested by the Islamists. In *Sirat-i Mustakim* (No. 2, 1908, and No. 3, 1909) they wrote that one of the obligations of the Muslims was covering their women. Also, they propounded, women were inferior in Islam, and that was one of the great truths of Islam.

Although they differed in almost all areas, all the three major political Factions of the *Mesrutiyet* (Islamists, Turkists and liberal-Westernists) agreed that, without economic progress, the Ottoman State was doomed. The Islamists declared the permissibility of adopting Western technology and industry. The liberal Westernists blamed their own society for backwardness and never accused Western imperialism for causing it. While the Westernists firmly believed in capitalism, the Islamists defended neither capitalism nor socialism. They looked at both of them as the evil creations of the Western civilization that was based on wrong moral principles.

The Islamist economic views were basically shaped by the principles of a pre-capitalist economy: fair competition, equity, a more or less just price system and rejection of formal interest or interest transactions.

The economic classes which the Islamist ideology appealed—and still appeals—most was the small local businessmen and traders, the *esnaf*: artisans and craftsmen strata who aspired to a system free from the threats of big industry and big business. Reflecting this mentality, Haci Mustafa wrote a book to refute the materialism of Ludwig Buchner (Kraft and Stoff), in which he scoffed at insurance as the most absurd manifestation of Western materialistic mentality, because insurance meant disbelief in God's Will.

Seeing the danger in perpetuating the existing confusion in social and legal life, the Unionist Government launched a series of reforms in 1916. According to these measures :

(i) The *Seriat* Courts were transferred from the jurisdiction of the *Seyh-ul Islam* to that of the Ministry of Justice.

(ii) The *Seyh-ul Islam* was removed from the Cabinet.

(iii) The control of the *Medresses* was taken away from the jurisdiction of the *Seyh-ul Islam.*

(iv) The management of all the financial matters of religious institutions was transferred to the newly founded Ministry of *Evkaf* (Pious Foundations).

These measures not only helped to consolidate the separation of the State from the influence of religion, but also laid the foundations of judicial, legislative, educational and financial affairs of the State. With these new arrangements, religion was to a great extent confined to matters of piety. Following these measures, the Law of *Seriat* Court Procedure was promulgated in 1917 for the unification of the whole Ottoman judicial procedure. Following this, for the first time in an Islamic country, the Law of Family Rights was codified the same year. Before the Law, all civil matters relating to marriage and divorce, inheritance, will, and guardianship were still uncodified, and were subject to the interpretations *(fetva)* of the *muftis.* However, this Code not only incorporated many provisions of the *Seriat,* but also secular European legal principles and Christian and Jewish communal usages current at the time. As a consequence it was equally resented by the *millet* organizations of the Empire as well as the Ottoman Islamists. The latter criticized the Code because it transferred the prosecution of the marriage contract to the authority of the State. Secondly the Code accepted the right of women to initiate divorce in cases when: (a) the husband wanted to take second wife and, (b) the husband violated a condition which the bride had previously incorporated into the marriage contract. This code was later replaced with the Swiss Civil Code in 1926, but continued to exist in Syria and Jurdan until 1953, and to the best of our knowledge it is still used in Lebanon and among the Muslim community of Israel.

The second area that was subjected to secularization was education, especially primary education. The Unionist Government took great strides in replacing *sibyan* schools, which resembled miniature *medreses* producing little *Kuran*-reciters, with secular elementary schools for the first time in Ottoman history. This was primary education was taken from the control of the *Seyh-ul Islam* and the *ulema* class and was tied to a national authority and programme. Courses in literature, history and philosophy were introduced into secondary education for the first time. The recently founded University of Istanbul opened up new departments of philosophy, sociology, fine arts, and Turkish history and literature.

Among the political and ideological forces of the *Mesrutiyet,* the Turkists were clearer about the economic programme of Turkish modernization. Influenced by both the collectivists ideas of the day, and inspired by the great economic advances of the Turkish *bourgeoisie* in Russia (before the Revolution), the Young Turk government developed a programme of economic nationalism and statism. This programme defined two basic goals: (a) to free Turkey from European economic and military imperialism; (b) to foster the growth of a middle-class which would provide economic entrepreneurship, and be the bearer of national interests against foreign and minority elements.

The First World War—although it ended in disaster—provided the Unionists the opportunity to abolish the 'Capitulations', launch a policy of nationalization and Turkification of non-Turkish businesses, and create, with the aid of state-promoted banks, the nucleus of a national entreprencural class.

The World War defeat and consequent Allied occupation, and the War of National Liberation (1919-1922), did not allow the seeds of the Young Turk reforms to grow. But their implementation pointed the direction towards which the Turkish Republic advanced rapidly.

The Era of the Grand National Assembly—1919-1923

Unable to withstand the aggression of the capitalist giants of the West, the pre-capitalist Ottoman Empire collaposed with all its contradictory institutions and ideologies in October of 1918. Out of the *debris* of the Empire, a new Turkish nation-state emerged as a response to Western imperialism and nascent Communism.

In the holocaust of the War of National Liberation (*Istiklal Harbi*), the Turkish society also underwent a National-*bourgeois* Revolution. The newly emergent military-civilian bureaucratic class succeeded in rallying the landed upper-classes and the local commercial *bourgeoisie* of Anatolia against the Invaders and their collaborators, the Sultan-Caliph and the traditional Ottoman ruling classes, namely the *compradore bourgeoisie,* the Palace retinue and the substantial portion of the *Ulema.*

When Mustafa Kemal passed to Anatolia to initiate the national resistance, the picture of the vanquished country was as given below:

Diverse social groups had united in various un-coordinated organizations to resist aggression and occupation. It is interesting to note that the peasant masses, who constituted the backbone of Turkish armies and the bulk of the productive forces, remained outside these organizations. After eight years of continuous wars, the economic and physical exhaustion of the peasantry was so complete that they had no desire to follow either the Nationalists or the Communists, who failed to offer a cure, but to survive peacefully. It is only after the Western invasion and the unification of resistance movements by Mustafa Kemal and the Ankara Grand National Assembly that a large-scale popular mobilization of diverse social forces was accomplished.

The factors behind the successful organization and the general character of the national liberation front may be stated as follows :

(i) Western imperialism had shifted tactics from indirect exploitation to *de facto* occupation.

(ii) The Sultan-Caliph, Mehmed VI (Vahidettin) turned against the Anatolian nationalist movement because he believed that he could at least survive as the Caliph of all Muslims within a colonial state under Western protection.

Furthermore, Vahidettin abrogated all the Young Turk reforms and appointed the ultra-conservative and anti-nationalist Mustafa Sabri as his *Seyh-ul Islam* who also collaborated with the enemy.

Both these events in the end helped the nationalists in pointing out the fact that the Turks as a national entity were not really dependent on the existence of a sultanate, and that religion could be made a tool against the true believers.

(iii) The Bolshevik revolution, going on across the broder, inspired the Turkish revolutionaries not so much as an ideology and universal philosophy, but as a successful war against Western imperialism, and also the colapse of the russian Empire—an arch-enemy of the Turks. Both the make-up of the Turkish leadership and social structure and the Russian ambivalence towards the Turkish revolution caused the Turkish transformation to take a nationalistic-*bourgeois* line.

(iv) Mustafa Kemal's personality and mental capacity, and the unique leadership provided by him and his friends, were important in the victory of the National Movement. It is this strong leadership that pursued an unchallenged drive towards secularism in the following years. Furthermore, his contribution in the prosecution of policies like nationalism, populism and secularism as a response to the forces of imperialism, Communism and theocracy was substantial.

While Kemal was unsuccessfully struggling to establish a National Assembly in Ankara, the Allied Powers dissolved the Ottoman Parliament in Istanbul and deported its deputies to Malta. This event ended the first division in the nationalist movement that started on the establishment of a Parliament in Anatolia.

The Grand National Assembly convened for the first time in Ankara on 23 April, 1920. There were great differences among the representatives on the authority and the duties of the Assembly. The Kemalists and the conservative-Westernist group first clashed over the issue of instituting a revolutionary government. The second group wanted to go on with the liberation struggle, but not to transgress the Constitutional system (with the Caliphate at the centre towards the establishment of a new regime based on popular sovereignty. They looked at the National Assembly as a temporary body that would only function for the duration of the liberation movement, and that it was constituted in the name of the Sultan-Caliph. Only Kemal and his group looked at the Assembly as a permanent organisation exercising legislative and executive functions on behalf of the Turkish people.

The Kemalist-Nationalist faction not only had to struggle with the enemy on the battlefield, but also with their conservative counterparts in the Assembly, and numerous local, reactionary uprisings instigated by Sheikhs, *hocas* (clergy), and the traditional *petty bourgeoisie* in the name of the Caliph and their 'threatened' religion. The biggest of these uprisings took place in Duzee, Bolu, Yozgat, Zile, Konya, and Sivas between 1919-1921. All of these bloody events were also partly instigated, but nevertheless they received full support from the Istanbul Government.

Another of such obscurantist movements that really worried the Nationalists was initiated by a man called Esref, who posed himself as the expected *Mahdi* and the protector of the *Seriat.* Seref started a large-scale uprising in the Eastern provinces of Turkey against the ongoing liberation movement. The adverse effect of religion and the betrayal of the Caliph drew more uncommitted intellectuals into national struggle, the outcome of which was indeed very dubious at the time. Ankara became the symbol and centre of a revolutionary mentality and hope.

The social conditions of those days can be summarized in a few sentences. War-sick peasants of Anatolia were left to the mercy of nature and big landlords, living on or under subsistence level. Foresaken villages were virtually closed to the rest of the world and its realities. Constantly exploited and oppressed, this amorphous mass manifested no evident class consciousness. There was no proletariat to speak of that could have initiated a social movement and alter the character of ongoing the national-*bourgeois* revolution as happened in Russia. It was the nascent Turkish middle-class which was leading this struggle against both imperialism and the traditional legacy of the decadent Empire.

However, this class did not yet possess a solid economic base to carry on such a massive movement. So it had to seek the aid and support of the national *bourgeoisie* who, after a brief hestiation, came to the conclusion that a radical bureaucratic cadre was much easier to deal with later than the impending liquidation in the face of advancing foreign invasion.

The ensuing conservative character of Turkish political structure not only blocked the possibility of a peasant movement, but also remained totally immune from the challenge of a non-existent proletarian antagonism. All of these circumstances were successfully utilized by the nationalist leadership to rally the strategic social classes around the nationalist cause.

This successfully executed mobilization laid the foundations of the populist and 'corporatist' character of the Republican regime after the victory was achieved.

The nationalist struggle for independence also involved a constant battle against the *Seriatists* and Khilafatists. Just after the opening of the Grand National Assembly the conservative group wanted to reach a conciliation with the Sultan Caliph. But Kemal, being the inevitable leader of the movement, kept urging that sovereignty belonged to the nation and no other person could be above it. He also insisted that the Assembly would be the ultimate legislative and executive body representing the people.

During these impetuous discussions in the Assembly about the fate of the Sultanate-Caliphate, the Kemalists' view was that as soon as the Caliph was rescued from the captivity of the enemy, he would take his 'proper' place within the framework of the decisions given by the National Assembly.

In August 1920 a committee was chosen to prepare a draft constitutional bill in the framework of a project drafted by Mustafa Kemal. Completely opposite to the principles behind the formation of a sovereign National Assembly, the committee gave back a draft in which the Assembly and its government were deemed to be provisional and could only function until the Caliph was rescued. The conservatives and clericals in the Assembly ardently opposed the proposal on the grounds that Caliphate implied Sultanate. They wanted both institutions to be mentioned specifically as the foundations of the new regime. These discussions went on for days, but no one on the Kemalist side could openly say that the Sultanate existed no more and sovereignty had passed to the people.

In September 1920 Mustafa Kemal prepared and submitted a project to the Assembly which was called the 'Programme of Populism'. The bill based on this project anchored the theses of national sovereignty and people's government into the Turkish political life. The New Constitution adopted on 20 January, 1921 (after five months of tempestuous discussions) incorporated the article: "Sovereignty unconditionally belongs to the people", and the principle of "Government is based on the people's direct rule over their destiny." For the Kemalists, this was a popular government, but it was a provisional government for the conservatives, established to free the Sultanate-Caliphate from the enemy.

In the difficult years of the War of Independence, the Assembly was swayed by an amalgamation of ideologies of anti-imperialism, nationalism, populism, conservative Westernism and Islamism. There was no expression of diverting or extending the national struggle to a full scale revolution to alter the basic social structure of the society. The limited 'revolutionary changes' accomplished in this and later periods were based on compromises between the bureaucratic leadership of the nascent middle-strata and the traditional classes in the urgency of the existing conditions. Despite the acceptance of the principle of national sovereignty, the Sultanate and the Caliphate were constitutionally still existing institutions. The final duel of the progressive and conservative factions of the Assembly had been postponed by both sides until after the War of Liberation.

In the meantime, the power of Islamism frequently surfaced in the discussion of some new bills. The clerical deputies introduced proposals involving the rendering of educational matters to the jurisdiction of the new Ministry of *Seriat,* prohibiting the unveiling of women, making polygamy compulsory, etc. These proposals were tactfully postponed by the Kemalists with the excuse that time was precious to debate over these issues in the middle of a war for survival.

Towards the end of the War of National Liberation, the conservative and reactionary elements in the Assembly became so active that no substantial decision could be made without compromise. To curb their power, Mustafa Kemal gathered the progressive members into a group called the 'First Group'. After this division the conservatives were referred to as the 'Second Group'. Coinciding with this re-organization, two clerical deputies of the Assembly founded the Society for the Preservation of the Sacred Traditions *(Muhafaza-i Mukaddesat Cemiyeti)*. Mustafa Kemal himself reveals the intentions of this Society under the guise of fighting with Communism. Their aim was to preserve the rights of the Sultan-Caliph and to work for the absolute avoidance of the republican form of government which they believed would create harm to the country and Islam but most of all to their very existence.

After the war, the Allies committed the mistake of inviting the Sultan's government to Lausanne peace conference. This mistake was tactfully used by Kemal. After winning a war that lasted for three years (1919-1922), the Allied naivety to refuse the Ankara government as the only representative of the Turkish people angered all factions of the National Assembly. On 1 November, 1922, in a long and effective speech, Mustafa kemal explained how harful the Sultan's behaviour had been to the nationalist cause, and now that the sovereignty belonged to the people, the Caliphate may be detached from this title and the

Sultanate could be abolished.

The conservatives protested this proposal and propounded that the Sultanate could not be separated from the Caliphate. Mustafa Kemal responded :

> Gentlemen, sovereignty has never been given to any nation by scholarly disputation. It is always taken by force and with coercion.... The Turkish nation has now taken back its usurped sovereignty by rebellion. This is a fact. The question facing us now is not whether or not his sovereignty will be left to the nation, but the simple matter of declaring that this is the fact... If those who have assembled here recognize this natural fact like everyone else, all will be fine. If not, what is natural will happen anyhow, with the only difference that a few heads will probably have to fall off.

After this speech, the bill for the abolition of the Ottoman Sultanate was passed in a few hours.

Vahidettin was deposed as the last Ottoman ruler and Caliph on 17 November, 1922. He left Istanbul under British protection under which he had placed himself four years ago against his countrymen who were fighting to save him and his country.

The next day, Abdul Mecid (another Ottoman Prince) was elected by the Parliament as the Caliph of all Muslims. From this moment onwards, the conservatives began to look at the Caliphate as the foundation of the still not secular State, and a power to check the Kemalists. Both sides were feeling that they were at the brink of a final showdown. The time had come either to establish a new Islamic state under the leadership of the Caliph like the medieval Papacy, or the establish a Republican regime.

The protraction of the debates over *khilafatism* from within National Assembly to the press alarmed the Kemalists. The Assembly dissolved itself in April 1923 for new elections. The Kemalist group of the *khilafatist* members were back in the new Parliament. This impasse left only one alternative to solve the problem : to declare the new Turkish state either Islamic or secular-representative.

In the confusion of a long cabinet crisis, Kemal gave a speech explaining that this was not a cabinet crisis, but a Constitutional one, and with a slight alteration in the Constitution the present system could be named Republic. The conservatives were caqught defenseless. In this confusion, without allowing too much time for debates, the bill declaring the Republic was accepted on 29 October, 1923. For the price of this great victory the Kemalists had given one concession to be incorporated into the amended Constitution : Article 2 stated that "The religion of the Turkish state is Islam.

Mustafa Kemal was elected to be the first president of the Turkish Republic. Document show that the Caliphate could have survived had it stayed as a spiritual authority. But the new government became increasingly irritated by the propaganda of the new Caliph that he was the true ruler of all believers. Not only the Ottoman family occupied their palaces, but Abdul Mecid was inclined to revive the old pompous court-life and ceremonies. He also appointed envoys to foreign countries. But Kemal lashed back when the Caliph demanded the creation of a separate Caliphal Treasury. "Kemal once more used his genius arousing nationalistic sentiments over religious zeal" and after a week-long vehement struggle in the Parliament, the bill abolishing the Caliphate was accepted on 3 March, 1924.

The Republican Secularism and Social Reforms

Following the abolition of the Caliphate, two more important bills were passed. These abolished the Ministries of *Seriat and Evkaf* all religious orders *(tarikats)* and their convents.

Under the provisions of the new laws, the *Seriat* courts were closed. A law passed in 1934 prohibited the use of religious titles like *molla, haci* and *hafiz* in official business. The clericals were only allowed to wear their religious attire while conducting their duties.

Forming societies for the purpose of religious prayer and practice was not forbidden. But the 1938 'Law of Associations" prohibited political parties participating in religious activities and engaging in religious propaganda, and formation of societies based on religion sect and order. The 1926 Penal Code prohibited any propaganda against the secular laws and principles of the Republic.

Although opening religious schools or institutions for religious instruction was not forbidden, the new educational laws making secular primary education universal and compulsory (up to the age of twelve) did not leave too much room for the development of religious schools. Furthermore, after the adoption of the Latin Script (1928), teaching in Arabic alphabet was prohibited in schools now attached to the Ministry of Education.

But the final touch of secularism in Turkish social life came with the secularization of the Civil Code. After the abolition of the Caliphate, the Ministry of Justice had formed a special committee to prepare a new family law. The resulting draft was devoid of the necessary principles to produce a unified system of codes. Consequently, following heated discussions that went on for two years, the Swiss Civil Code was adopted in February 1926.

The revolutionary character of the new regime in its legal policy was to shape the traditional social relations according to a model which would create new social institutions and release the social energy heretofore 'frozen' under the old regime. The new Code brought completely new principles pertaining to the areas of property, contract, family, marriage and divorce.

With the promulgation of this code, the men of religion lost their function as agents of law. Marriage became an entirely secular contract. Under the *Seriat,* the husband had unilateral freedom in matters of divorce. He lost this prerogative with the new Code. Polygamy was abolished.

The effects of the new code on the status of women soon started to show itself in the full and equal franchise of women and their achievements in social, professional and economic life.

The process of secularization quickly expanded into cultural matters. with the 1925 'Hat Law,' the new regime launched a campaign to eliminate symbols of traditionalism. Informal measures were taken to unveil women.

After some preparations, in August 1928 Mustafa Kemal and his government opened a massive educational campaign to teach the new Turkish alphabet based on the Latin script. A law followed this vigorous national campaign prohibiting the use of Arabic script in all public affairs (after 1 December, 1928).

One of the conspicuous achievements of the new regime was the unification, consolidation and universalization of primary education. In 1924 all education came under the jurisdiction of the Ministry of Education. *Medreses* were closed. A Faculty of Divinity was opened in Istanbul which was later replicated in Ankara. The Ministry of Education opened *Imam-Hatip* schools (Minister-preacher schools) for the training of religious personnel.

In 1928, the teaching of Arabic and Persian was removed from the secondary-school syllabus. This job was given to special departments in the Universities.

As for the ideological structure of Kemalism, its basic principle, 'sovereignty of the people' took a form different from both the liberal and Communist philosophies of its time. Actually this principle, which found its official expression in 'populism,' was shaped by a radical *petty bourgeoisie* bureaucratic stratum in the push and pull of these two dominant doctrines, and developed as a reaction to both. The Turkish intellectuals and the Kemalist leadership looked at the national struggle not as a total social revolution that would abolish all dominant classes, but as a struggle to eliminate the power and privileges of certain traditional strata that had become fetters to the development of a national *bourgeoisie* and other economic classes of a modern society. Populism as a state policy came to mean national sovereignty, unity, and economic reconstruction through State initiative.

The republican leadership clearly understood that Turkey as an underdeveloped country had different problems and characteristics than the developed societies. Hence, it has to adopt different methods of development that would accomplish economic independence and self-support. At the foundation of this drive, they put the *inter-dependence of all social classes* (corporatism) and State entrepreneurship for a rapid industrialization. This contradictory political philosophy was the weakest point of the Kemalist doctrine that would cause increasing difficulties for the later Republican administrations (in the 1960s and 1970s) as the weak Turkish *bourgeoisie* grew strong enough to claim predominance over other social strata.

The Republican secularism reached its final stage when in 1928 Article 2, which stated that Islam was the religion of the Turkish State, was removed from the Constitution. However, the principle of 'secularism' would only be incorporated into the Constitution in 1937.

The Reorganization of Religion as a Spiritual Domain

One of the main goals of the new regime, specially of its leader, was to teach the principles of Islam in Turkish rather than Arabic to a people who had been practising Islam without understanding it for centuries. So religious enlightenment of the people became a government policy. This campaign was also designed to eliminate the last stronghold of the *ulema* who claimed monopoly over its interpretation as the reason of their existence.

In 1924 the Department of the Affairs of Piety was constituted (Public Law No. 430) to perform the administrative tasks of religion. Its head was selected by executive appointment from among the competent and technically qualified religious personnel. This office would confer no extratemporal or spiritual leadership to its chief. The Department was prohibited to receive donations or income from *vakifs,* now under the administration of the General Directorate of Religious Endowments *(Vakiflar Umum Mudur).* The tasks of the Department were translating, editing and publishing religious works "for the purpose of supplying the public with authentic religious information and literature." It was given no educational functions.

The religious policy of the new regime was the elimination of all kinds of anchronistic fetters on religious expression and separation of all legal and political considerations from affairs of piety.

Mustafa Kemal's personal appeal, leadership and personality to the men of religion and to the masses, soon bore fruit and without the need of promulgating any law concerning the subject, *azan* (call to prayer) and the sermons came to be delivered in Turkish starting by 1931. It is interesting to note that what Mustafa Kemal Ataturk could achieve with public consent was made a law in 1941 (three years after his death) and reverted back to Arabic by another law in 1951 by the Democrats in the multi-party political period.

Ataturk's highest goal in the religious field was the translation of *Kuran* into Turkish. When Ataturk was able to check the opposition of the Turkish Islamists, their fight was taken over by the Egyptian *ulema.* Shaikh Rashid Rida, in his *Tarjamat al-Quran* (Cairo, 1922) declared the Turks' sacrilege of translating the *Kuran* into their tongue as *Kufr* and pronounced Kemalist Turkey heretical. According to the Shaikh, these actions were expressions of Turkish nationalism, which was another heresy. Basing his claim upon twelve quotations from the *Kuran,* he believed, translating the *Kuran* was heresy...."

This resistance, and failure of the Islamists to translate the *Kuran* into Turkish made more Turks doubt the outcome of a theocratic state that these men would be running.

The first full length translation of the *Kuran* was produced in 1924. Afterwards, other and better translations followed suit.

The formalization of Turkish secularism was consolidated first by an amendment of the 1937 revised Constitution which stated that the Turkish Republic was a secular state. Other principles that were incorporated into various codes may be listed as follows:

(i) Article 9 of the Law of Associations prohibits the formation of associations on the basis of sect and order *(tarikat).*

(ii) Political parties and associations were prohibited from seeking particular religious support.

(iii) Penal Code (1949 revision) prohibited anti-secularist attacks on the Republican regime and its legal system.

In the light of these principles and prohibitions, Turkish secularism was interpreted by the new regime as the disassociation of social, economic, political, and legal institutions of the State from religious principles. Hence the Republican secularism was a reaction against the idea of an Islamic polity.

New Patterns of Secularism : Socio-economic Transformation

The Republican regime, created by a radical nationalist military/ civilian bureaucracy and headed by Kemal Ataturk, initiated a politically innovative era as evinced by the many penetrating cultural reforms accomplished. However, due to two historically significant phenomena the Turkish National Revolution basically remained socially and economically conservative in character :

(i) The radical bureaucratic/military leading cadre which had started the National Liberation Struggle (1919) did not have true popular support from the improverished masses. When this cadre sought the social and financial aid of the national *bourgeoisie*—long subdued by Western imperialism and the comprodor minority capitalists — the upheaval that gave birth to modern Turkey did not transcend the limits of an anti-imperialist national *bourgeoisie* transformation.

(ii) After the Victory (1922) and the establishment of Turkish Republic (1923), the military / civilian bureaucratic cadre that led the nationalist revolution gradually turned into a 'State *bourgeoisie.*'

In a semi-colonial socio-economic *milieu* where a strong national *bourgeoisie* could not flourish—as Third World experience amply demonstrated—a nascent middle-class used the State apparatus and the military establishment to ascend to power, and acquire a 'modernizing' leadership function as happened in Turkey. The lack of an autonomous economic basis, that could serve as a long-term source of power for this class, led it to take two historical actions that profoundly affected the future of Turkey :

(i) *Economic :* Prosecution of State capitalism as an economic policy ;

(ii) *Political :* Establishment of a corporatist/authoritarian one-party political regime.

In the long-run, such an authoritarian capitalist system which diligently protected and aided the national *bourgeoisie* could have only functioned the strengthen the private sector. However, the growing Turkish *bourgeoisie,* increasingly discontent with the restrictions of an authoritarian regime and a guided economy, started to become an effective political opposition to the regime in the Parliament during the 1940's. Nevertheless, the power of the Turkish *bourgeoisie* reached its all-time high after the Second World War when it found its most congenial companion in the partnership of U.S. Government and foreign capital. Under the pressure of internal and external forces, and already in trouble in coping with the difficulties of a stagnating economy, the Republican People's Party and its statist policies received a fatal blow at the polls in 1950.

The economic oligarchy which came to power with the Democratic Party Government in 1950 soon implemented a liberal economic policy which firmly tied Turkey to the Western capitalist system, and which remains as the guideline of Turkish economic development. An assessment of this development for the past twenty-four years does not appear very encouraging:

(i) The dependent character of Turkish development on external sources has created a snowballing foreign debt of nearly $ 4,000 million. The service of this debt not only constitutes a heavy burden on the national economy but further renders it vulnerable to foreign economic penetration.

(ii) Despite a much publicized seven per cent annual economic growth rate since the beginning of planned economic process (1963). The GNP *per capita* remains below $ 400 (the 1973 plan estimates it as $364). This poverty perpetuates the restricted size of the domestic market and creates a growing army of unemployed and underemployed labour which bypass the industrialization process and carry on a barely subsistence level existence.

(iii) On the whole, the basis of Turkish industrialization has been import substitution. This process lacks the basic ingredients necessary to eliminate its own limitations, namely : Capital of scale, technology, sufficient markets and raw material resources. Consequently, most of Turkey's dynamic industrial sectors have been increasingly penetrated—although less than many Third World countries of colonial heritage—by capital intensive foreign enterprises. This phenomenon has further limited the employment capacity of the expanding industrial sector.

(iv) Turkish development has been extremely unequal, both geographically and sectorally. While the contribution of agriculture to the GNP has continuously declined, the contribution of the industrial and service sectors has increased substantially. However, Turkish industrialization has basically flourished in major port cities, especially those of Western Anatolia. Istanbul and its vicinity alone accommodate nearly 50 per cent of the modern Turkish industry and absorb the lion's share of industrial investments and capital created in other regions of the country. What are the crucial consequences of this slow and unequal development in Turkey which benefited the urban rather than the rural strata?

First, the countryside has been left to its fate and under the control of the traditional landed oligarchy, which for decades blocked any form of social and economic change until recent capitalization of the agrarian sector. Thus, despite enormous profits reaped from agriculture, the impossibility of transferring capital from this sector to finance national economic development, that could have raised the level of indigent populations, could not be accomplished.

As a consequence, even today over 69 per cent of the peasant families live at below-subsistence level, and another 27 per cent live in subsistence conditions, sometimes producing marketable products. The rest, four per cent of the agrarian population, which constitute the rural upper class, own 28 per cent of all cultivable land and earn nearly half of the (47.2%) total annual agricultural income.

Under these conditions nearly three and one half million farm families are totally dependent on the landed upper-classes, money lenders and rural mercantile groups for land, capital, loans and the marketing of their produce. Consequently, these basic necessities lay the groundwork for their political and social dependence on the former groups. Besides this exploitative dependence, the fact that roughly 70 per cent of the Turkish peasants have land of their own on which they can rely for their livelihood in varying degrees of relatives self-sufficiency is a crucial factor in terms of the conservative attitudes and political preferences of the Turkish peasantry.

However, survey results reveal that the Turkish peasant is well aware of his poverty and powerlessness but he is incapable of linking these phenomena to the wider conditions and their external sources. This 'gap of consciousness' or politico-ideological 'isolation' is constantly reinforced by illiteracy (48%) poverty, religious obscurantism (that has no relation with the principles of Islam whatsoever) and patriarchal relations between the peasantry and the landed upper class. Political parties who derive most of their power from their 'good partner' relations with the landed upper classes also play a key role in the continuation of the *status quo* in the Turkish countryside.

Secondly, due to the underdevelopment of productive forces the bulk of manufactured goods and services in a predominant section of Turkish villages and small towns continued to be provided by a large traditional artisan-craftsmen stratum. It is these and the small local merchantile groups—often manipulated and co-opted by the dominant economic *bourgeoisie*—that sustained Islamic conservatism and 'clientele politics' *vis-a-vis bourgeois*-conservative parties in local centres of Turkey until the 1970's.

A Theoretical Approach to Turkish Secularism

When put in a theoretical context the historical data presented earlier suggest that religion (or religiously oriented beliefs) and the socio-economic infrastructure of a given society are in constant interaction with each other. In the historical continuum of a given mode of production religious beliefs and institutions function to perpetuate the relations of production that have either given birth to them or presently support them. This situation, constantly reinforced by the social forces dominant in that particular historical period, will continue until the society becomes transformed to another mode of production, creating a completely new set of institutions.

Historical evidence bears out the fact that the belief and behaviour patterns of social groups in socially and economically advanced and differentiated societies are relatively different from their less developed and undifferentiated counterparts. So a socio-historical study of this sort must never lose sight of the combined conditions of the socio-economic evolution of a society in which religious behaviour in social movements is at issue.

The case of Turkey clearly delineates that every cultural or administrative innovation introduced in suspension from corresponding qualitative changes in the mode and relations of production has remained as alien institutions unacceptable by the people. These alien institutions not only have failed to generate favourable conditions in the social and economic lives of the masses, but have created two adverse phenomena: (i) the emergence of a cultural dichotomy between the ruling classes and the rest of the society; (ii) the State's increasing economic and political dependence on Western imperial powers from which these institutions were borrowed.

In this context, one can infer a strong correlation between the emergence of nationalism and the evolution of a society along class lines—the two seed-beds of political ideologies and social movements. Both of these pehomena have emerged rather late in the historical experience of colonized and semi-colonized countries like Turkey. Given these conditions, one gains a better understanding of the importance of religion as a surrogate ideology of social protest and political action (as well as reaction) in the absence of other national or class based ideologies. In this regard Karl Mannheim propounds that "stages of historical development may be regarded as the immediate precursor of the notion of ideology."

Sundry cultural innovations, and *bourgeois* institutions borrowed from the West by the Turkish ruling classes, without the corresponding economic sub-structure that have given birth to them, have *always* engendered more adverse living conditions for the millions of subsistence level small rural / urban producers of Anatolia. Hence Westernization and modernization 'from above' which further exacerbated the deep suffering and exploitation of the masses were deemed as heresy. And their initiators, the Westernist intelligentsia, were viewed as heretics and infidels in the popular mind. Not even the great leader Kemal Ataturk and his nationalist cadre have been able to escape this ominous label.

For the small rural cultivator and the declining traditional *petty bourgeoisie* whose economic basis was rapidly waning, there was but little choice to defined their conventional ways and communal institutions in which religion has always played an important social role.

The religiously permissive Democratic Party (1950-1960) and its heir justice Party (1960-71), both hailed as being on the side of true *mumins* (believers), have successfully exploited the anxieties and religious sentiments of the lower classes and traditional middle stratum, despite the gross inequalities created and perpetuated by their liberal capitalist economic policies.

This contradiction became increasingly conspicuous as political injustices and economic inequalities mounted up until the wide popular front mobilized and manipulated by the big *bourgeoisie* for two decades began to dissolve in the turbulent years of the late 1960's and early 1970's violent strikes staged by the working-class, protest marches of the small producers, occasional land invasions by the landless peasantry, and urban guerilla warfare launched by radical urban middle-class intelligentisia followed one another until the 12 March, 1971 Military 'intervention' took place.

For our purposes, two very important social processes emerged in this period : (i) on the one hand, the organized working-class and educated white-collar stratum—in most cases together — formulated radical leftist ideologies and programmes for change : (ii) on the other hand, the fragmented and threatened small producers (due to their mode of production that isolate them from the rest of their kind) of the pre-capitalistic or early capitalistic age—artisans, craftsmen, petty mercantilist groups and small agricultural producers—sought refuge in Islam as a shield against the onslaught of social and economic change. Their conservative programme envisaged the re-creation of the golden age of Islamic *ummet :* co-existence and brotherhood of believers. In this unchanging communal structure, the rights and obligations of each social category was defined by a divine hierarchy, imminent in the religious ideology.

In this context, there appears to be two distinct manifestations of Islamic conservatism in Turkey, depending on the socio-economic *milieu* they have emanated from. In the first case, religion serves as a dynamic and radical ideology of *reaction* for *organized* traditional groups / classes in transience against forces of capitalist changes in economically and socially more developed areas. In the second case, religion, as one of the most important cultural institutions that influence social relations and attitudes is often used as an instrument of social control by the *bourgeoisie* to preserve the *status quo.* This is especially true for the landed oligarchy which acts through the influence of local religious figures to exploit religious sentiments for the perpetuation of their dominant position in economically underdeveloped or still pre-capitalistic regions of the country.

In such 'environments' where the oppressed strata lack both formal organizations and organizational consciousness to initiate a social struggle, *tarikats* become an instrument of passive dissent and escape for social groups alienated from the oppressive conditions of their lives. Hence, it is not surprising that the number and influence of *shaikhs* in various areas of Turkey evince a strong correlation with the number and influence of semi-feudal big landlords and tribal formations found in the same areas. Turkish East, South-East and various regions of the dry central plateau are such areas where *tarikats* are stronger and more popular than religious organizations/associations. In these regions land is extremely fragmented to yield a significant surplus, and/or land distribution is grossly unequal — and in both cases the mode of production is basically pre-capitalistic.

Empirical evidence presented by Dr. Yucekok reveals that while the proportion of active religious associations / organizations to the total population is 1/12338 for the nation, this ratio is almost half in the developed regions, and nearly double in underdeveloped regions of the country.

If we try to sum up the arguments presented above, it can be said that religious organizations / associations in Turkey are only 'primitive' vehicles of political action of the 'radical right.' they are anachronistic forms of political organization of the traditional strata that are caught up in the historical course of transformation from being 'classes in themselves' into becoming 'classes for themselves' in the very process of their extinction.

However, the historical dilemma of this religio-political struggle waged by declining social classes lies in their misdated imagery that envisages a return to a past 'golden age' — or the disrupted mode of production that previously afforded them an economic basis and social status. This ideal state is symbolized by the Islamic *ummet,* which has already been ground to pieces between the formidable gears of the world capitalist system.

The political mobilization of the declining social strata against the advancing modern economic system and its privileged classes in the late 1960's has marked the emergence of two extremely significant processes in Turkey : (i) the declining traditional classes which backed up the *bourgeoisie* since the late 1940's. While the economic policy implemented by the latter also benefited the lower social strata in its initial stage, it left the wide conservative coalition to wage their own struggle for survival. (ii) Secularization implemented until then 'from above' by bureaucracies alien to the masses was taken over by the oppressed, exploited and existentially thretened classes in their quest for a place in the new social order. It is in this struggle for survival that religion ceased to be merely an ideological tool in the hands of the ruling classes with which they manipulated the economically less privileged classes and blocked social/political differentiation.

The Turkish experience suggests that once the *status quo* is broken down by the dynamic forces of capitalist development religion also takes on a dynamic character as the radical ideology of declining social classes in search for a more just order. However, this stage seems to be the first phase in the historical struggle of threatened classes. World political history bears out the fact that the next stage in the irreversible evolution of the traditional economic classes towards extinction calls for the adoption of more progressive and collective ideologies as their proletarianization and marginalization gains speed.

The Culmination Point of Turkish Development : Class Conflict in the 1970's and Secularization from Below

The October 1973 National Elections that were preceded by a two-year period of military-backed unpopular government (1971-1973) brought to the fore extremely important new trends in Turkish politics.

While the bulk of the agrarian population once again voted for the conservative parties (Justice and (new) Democratic Parties), migrant peasants now crowding the anomalous shanty-towns encircling major Turkish metropolises voted overwhelmingly for the leftist Republican People's Party. This phenomenon signifies the loosening of the firm grips of the conservative forces and institutions over the ex-peasant urban slum-dweller who has been torn away from his rural habitat and the institutional constraints which it harbours.

Increasingly dissatisfied with the monopolistic trends of Turkish capitalism that basically favoured the urban industrial and big commercial *bourgeoisie*, the *petty bourgeoisie* and the landed oligarchy left the united conservative popular front which constituted the power base of the Justice Party which ruled the country from 1965 to 1971. While the Anatolian *petty bourgeoisie* formed their independent political party, the National Salvation Party (Milli Selamet Partisi), the landed oligarchy, chose to revitalize the old Democratic Party.

The National Salvation Party (NSP), which was formed only six months prior to the election date, ran on a platform of Islamic puritanism and national capitalism. Conflicting though it might appear at first instance, these ideological guidelines were nothing else than the rational programme of survival of the oppressed and declining local producers and petty mercantile groups of Anatolia. Their quest for equal competition actually meant resistance to the insurmountable pressures of growing economic corporations. Their rather naive refusal of interest in credit transactions is a strategy to ward off the domination of national financial giants that to not only neglect small business but also exploit them. Their refusal to unite with the European Common Market (EEC—which previous Turkish Governments have pledged to do—is only a scheme of the *petty bourgeoisie's* programme of self-preservation. And finally, their fight to establish 'Popular Economic enterprises partly subsidized and protected by the State is no more than an effort to establish a sound environment in which they can invest and try to escape the inevitable fate of proletarianization.

It is interesting to draw attention to the fact that both the NSP and its programme of brotherhood, equality and just competition have emerged at a historical conjuncture of Turkish history when the traditional *petty bourgeoisie* and the small producer is most threatened by the challenge of both the national and multi-national economic corporations.

The NSP which is seen as the epitome of Islamic radicalism, and is surely the only political organ of the traditional social classes, won 11.8 per cent of the national votes in the October 1973 National Elections. Thus it became the third biggest party in the Turkish Parliament with 49 deputies.

A brief biographical inquiry of the NSP's elected members will afford interesting data about their social backgrounds and ideological upbringing. A significant portion of them are professionals, mostly engineers and lawyers. Yet another important group are theologians. They come predominantly from local marginal middle-class families of declining *petty bourgeoisie* in small Anatolian towns. They have been brought up in the classical strict discipline of Islamic values which is the common life-style in this *milieu.* However, most of them have gone to national metropolises and received their education in modern professional/technical schools. This phenomenon closely resembles the evolution of *Ulema* children who were sent by their parents to new secular technical/professional schools founded by Selim

III and Mahmud II in the late 18th and 19th centuries as the power base of the *Ulema* class began to dwindle.

It is this blend of professionalism (this worldliness) and strong religiosity (other worldliness) that makes this Party's members an interesting political group. A scrutiny of two typical NSP members will give a clear indication of the changing character of Turkish Islamic conservatism.

The first one of these members holds a Ph.D. in theology. He has worked as the official *Imam* (spiritual leader) of Turkish workers in Germany, assigned to this position by the Ministry of Labour. The topic of his doctoral dissertation, presented to the University of Koln, is 'Labour Rights in Islamic Jurisprudence.'

The second interesting member of the NSP is a young engineer who has grown up in a central Anatolian village whose population often had to resort to prayer for rain in dry seasons. On his return from Europe, where he went for his internship following his graduation from Istanbul Technical University, he once again attended one of these mass rain prayers. But this time he brought a rain-bomb which he had purchased in Germany.

This list can be extended further to cover other professional bureaucratic members of the NSP including its leader—now Assistant Premier — Prof. Necmettin Erbakan. Dr. Erbakan has left his chair of mechanical engineering in Istanbul Technical University to become the president of the Turkish Chamber of Commerce. In this position he has put up a stubborn fight against the urban monopoly and comprador capitalists in favour of the small-scale national capitalists which are rapidly losing their prominence as the entrepreneural strata of local Turkey.

Presently Turkey is run by a coalition government composed of the left-wing RPP and right-wing NSP. This government seems to be intent on returning to an elaborately planned economy guided by the State, thus checking the increasing power of the monopolist *bourgeoisie* and foreign capital in the most strategic sectors of the national economy.

The new Government also seems determined to create a welfare State to raise the living standards of the impoverished social strata. The NSP has seven ministries in this coalition. Despite its conservative outlook and extreme religious rhetoric, this Party has ratified the controversial General Amnesty Bill for the release of over a thousand left-wing activists who have been suffering in the prisons while all other so-called liberal-democratic parties vehemently opposed this move.

These events show that when the banner of social struggle is raised by the so-called conservative social classes which are increasingly gaining political consciousness and organizational sophistication, two historical processes emerge :

(i) The declining traditional classes wage a struggle for survival which parallels that of the emergent and exploited working classes against the dominant oligarchies and established social institutions that sustain them.

> (However) of all the classes, that stand face to face with the *bourgeoisie* today, the proletariat alone is a really revolutionary class. The other classes decay and finally disappear in the face of Modern Industry; the proletariat is its special and essential product.
>
> The lower middle-class, the small manufacturer, the shopkeeper, the artisan, the peasant, all these fight against the *bourgeoisie*, to save from extinction their existence as fractions of the middle-class. They are therefore not revolutionary, but conservative. Nay, more, they are reactionary, for they try to roll back the wheel of history. If by chance they are revolutionary, they are so only in view of their impending transfer into the proletariat, they thus defend not their present, but their future interests, they desert their own standpoint to place themselves at that of the proletariat.

(ii) Religion starts gaining its rightful place as a belief / value system of the spiritual domain rather than a political ideology of a stagnant and unchanging society that serves the interests of privileged classes.

We witness the emergence and evolution of these processes in Turkey, specially in the course of the 1960's. During this period the working class began to organize along the lines of labour unions and left-wing organizations like the Turkish Labour Party. The traditional social classes, resentful of both the socialist trend in national politics and the state of capitalism which was increasingly encroaching on their life-space, at first chose to reclaim their declining position through religiously oriented semi-political and professional organizations / associations.

Evidence provided by Dr. Yucekok suggests that organizational activities of the traditional strata gained an incredible momentum in the 1950's and 1960's, when the process of rapid capitalization in Turkish economy started to bring about far-reaching changes in the Turkish social structure. While there was one religious organization / association for every 20,868 individuals in the 1950's, this ratio reached 1/2338 in the course of the 1960's.

However, the futility of this disunited and anachronistic struggle, lacking a viable economic programme, forced the Turkish petty *bourgeoisie* to organize around the NSP and draw up a sound economic doctrine rather than basing their action no mere religious sentimentalism. The economic programme of the NSP no longer appears to be a recipe to return to a past 'golden age,' but a well-designed plan that will raise the threatened *petty bourgeoisie* to the ranks of the great *bourgeoisie* through State aid.

These developments suggest that the fiercer the politico-economic struggle gets, the *less effective* religion becomes as the political ideology of social movements, and consequently retracts to its sacred domain. Then it seems that the unceasing historical struggle between the dominant and the disposed and/or newly emergent social forces, which is ingrained in the obfuscated folk-mind as the struggle between religion and infidel innovations, is approaching a grand finale in Turkey. As the exploited and manipulated classes and the declining social strata of a previous socio-economic order enter into the phase of class struggle, it becomes increasingly clear to them that a more equalitarian and just social order can only be created through their direct participation in its making.

The future of Turkish secularization rests exactly at this fulcrum where religiosity is increasingly disassociated from the preservation of the *status quo* in the mind of the impoverished and proletarianized Turk in search of a more dignified life-style in the workshops of his own and other countries.